A Genre of Her Own

A Genre of Her Own

Life Narratives and Feminist Literary Beginnings in Modern India

Gayathri Prabhu

B L O O M S B U R Y
NEW DELHI • LONDON • OXFORD • NEW YORK • SYDNEY

BLOOMSBURY INDIA
Bloomsbury Publishing India Pvt. Ltd
Second Floor, LSC Building no. 4, DDA Complex, Pocket C – 6 & 7,
Vasant Kunj, New Delhi, 110070

BLOOMSBURY, BLOOMSBURY ACADEMIC INDIA and the Diana logo are trademarks of Bloomsbury Publishing Plc

First published in india 2025
This edition published 2025

Bloomsbury Academic India
An imprint of Bloomsbury Publishing Plc

ISBN: HB: 978-93-56408-22-7; eBook: 978-93-56408-39-5
2 4 6 8 10 9 7 5 3 1

Typeset by Integra Software Services Pvt. Ltd.
Printed and bound in India by Replika Press Pvt. Ltd.

Dedicated with love and admiration to the literary foremothers who have become this book

Contents

Note

The texts studied in this book are a combination of Anglophone texts and texts written in Indic languages. None of the translations included are mine, and due credit is given to the scholar/translator the first time translated texts are cited. Likewise, as this project covers a defined time span—the last quarter of the nineteenth century and the first quarter of the twentieth century—all proper names and spellings are as given in the translation or as in usage at the time—for example, Kolkata is referred to as Calcutta. The first time a text is referred to, it is named as in the original (with Roman script) and the translated title is also given; subsequently, only the translated title in English is used.

The logical flow of argument has necessitated multiple repeat references to the same authors across the Introduction and chapters. An effort has been made to briefly contextualize them at each reference for better readability. It is hoped that the Index will add further clarification when required.

The usage of proper names in referencing authors of primary texts posed to be more challenging. The use of a family name or patronymic surname by women (derived either from father or husband) was infrequent in the nineteenth century. The more conventional practice was for the name to be suffixed with an address of respect, an honorific such as Devi or Bai. Keeping in mind that this study is tracing a woman-centric literary lineage, this study will refer to authors of primary texts by their first names, most of which are already attached to the honorific. The first name will be the main referent even with authors who published with a surname so as to ensure uniformity of usage across the book. It is the conviction of this study that such conscious first-naming in scholarship and creative practice is equally an act of identification with literary predecessors and a mark of feminist affinity.

Introduction

Contravention of Beginnings

It was the most unlikely of beginnings. A woman from a geographical periphery of the colonial enterprise composed a book-length life narrative in modern prose. With barely any formal schooling, and confined to a traditional household in rural Bengal where she had little respite from domestic obligations that included the birth of twelve children, Rashsundari Debi completed her autobiography *Amar Jiban* (My Life) in 1868.[1] It was an astonishing literary event untrammelled by considerations of the literary milieu or style of peers for the author had no access to a library nor had she conferred with other writers. The main textual influence claimed was the devotional narrative *Chaitanya Bhagabat*,[2] and the painful acquisition of reading (described in the above excerpt) had come through her own determined efforts to trace alphabets in the smoky confines of her kitchen.

> Those days, we did not see printed letters, the handwritten letters on the manuscripts were immensely difficult to read. My reading was so painfully acquired! Even with such effort I didn't know how to write. It takes a lot to be able to write—paper, pen, ink, inkpot. I would need to spread them all around me and then sit down to write. I was a woman, and on top of that, a married one. They are not meant to read and write. The authorities have decreed that this is a cardinal sin for women. How could I have tried to write in that situation? I was so scared of rebukes. So I killed my desire for writing and I would only read, and that, too, in secret.[3]

This 'daring departure'[4] by the twenty-five-year-old writer thereby produces multiple resonances: it is a skill and craft that requires precious material tools ('paper, pen, ink, inkpot'—the very listing of which implies how rare and precious they are in her daily life); it is an intention that requires space and leisure ('to spread all around me and then sit down to write'); it is a desire that both entices and overwhelms, so much that it must be 'killed'; but most importantly, on account of being 'a cardinal sin' for a woman in her social situation, it can only be accessed through secrecy and waiting for an opportune moment. In every way, her inked letters come to represent a staggering epistemic trespassing. The foundational quest is literacy, for without literacy there is no access to *literature*, and having gained access to the act and pleasure of reading, the production and recording of a new literary text becomes its longed-for consummation.

Three decades later, at the age of eighty-eight, Rashsundari published another edition of her autobiography with an introduction by a reputed figure of Bengali letters, Jyotirindranath Tagore.[5] While Tagore took care to compliment the religiosity of the writer, the sincerity and 'simple sweetness' of her writing, his introduction began with the inevitable annotation: 'This book is written by a woman.'[6] The pronouncement transmits fact and wonderment, the writing of a book by a woman so sporadic an occurrence in nineteenth-century India that it merits a public announcement. And yet Rashsundari Debi's singular literary output had been preceded, accompanied and followed by similar outliers: women who wrote novels and autobiographies alongside more compact literary forms such as essays, letters, poetry, speeches and pamphlets that made recurrent spirited appearances to sculpt a full-fledged feminist aesthetic in conversation with a normatively male literary milieu.

The emergence of literary innovations in modern prose from the middle of the nineteenth century in India has been recorded by several scholars—however, this has been with limited attention to gender performativity in the public sphere.[7] The depiction of the participation of women tends to be either demonstrative of the reformist and nationalist movement or presented as literary milestones (for instance, first novel or autobiography in the language). The present study argues for an additional approach that prioritizes deliberative formalistic instantiations by the writers through their ingenious adaptation of genre conventions, starting from the last quarter of the nineteenth century and extending into the early decades of the twentieth century. Traversing theme, genre and languages (primarily in Marathi, Bengali, Urdu, English), the texts analysed in this book include Tarabai Shinde's polemical booklet *Stri-Purush Tulana* (1882), Anadibai Joshee's published letters to her husband (1883–4), the essay 'Reply' (1887) by Rukhmabai,[8] Rashsundari Debi's revised edition of *Amar Jiban* (1897), Binodini Dasi's autobiography *Amar Katha* (1912), the novels *Kahake* (1898) by Swarnakumari Debi Ghosal and *Saguna* (1887–8) by Krupabai Satthianadhan, Atiya Fyzee's despatches to a journal (1906–7) published as *Zamana-i-tahsil* (1921) and Dosebai Cowasjee Jessawalla's *The Story of My Life* (1911). While questions of region, language and precise historical milieu certainly illuminate, they do not exhaust all the questions and affects outlined above, and the ambition of this book will be to cut across these conventional axes to create new synergies. For example, the fragile, nascent (and yet central) notion of authorship or individuated creativity or the tenuousness of worldly experience (literary and otherwise) is as key to Binodini Dasi in Calcutta as to Tarabai Shinde in Pune, as to Krupabai Satthianadhan in Madras, their domestic and artistic labour all partaking of the same semantic, representational episteme. The writers overtly engage with the centrality of writing, the dangers and secrecy involved, the precise larger spheres and global horizons—of marriage, motherhood, domestic labour and caretaking, romance and sexuality, public service and intellectual prowess, illness and ageing, ritual and religious quests, scrambles for livelihood, and an everyday effervescence of humour and desire. Above all, there is a search for the uniqueness of a woman's literary voice and positioning—for these writers do not have foremothers in modern prose in their social milieu—and this study attempts to probe the creative gears of their aesthetic and public intent. In doing so, the hope is that the 'map of nation' will be substantively re-configured to allow one to claim that women didn't just also achieve or contribute to what men have already claimed to have achieved—rather, the stakes and contours of their literary and political achievement are differently autonomous, perhaps even more incisive, impactful, imaginative, prescient, and unmistakably fundamental even in the constitution of the everyday popular rhetoric.

The epistemic shift that occurred in the middle of the nineteenth century when a 'whole new world became available to educated Indians [...] through their study of English literature'[9] and the subsequent 'invention of private life'[10] elicited multimodal literary forms. These reinventions were also seen in literatures in Indian languages through institutional changes in education, technology, jobs and other social factors.[11] It has been argued that the history of individuation in late-nineteenth-century India was intrinsically an individuation that pivoted on gender, and across complacent binaries of tradition/modernity or passive/active.[12] Women responded to this new public realm in a distinct way—even as they furthered pre-given forms (such as the novel, or poetry), they equally sought to expand the idea of the literary by strongly and consistently recasting their own lived experiences. Since many of these women disrupted social norms to make unconventional choices (as travellers, litigants, divorcees, doctors, lawyers), their life narratives continuously interrogated everyday familial and lived realities, thus simultaneously pushing the boundaries of their social positioning and literary form into uncharted pathways that carried resonances into much of the twentieth century.

The contention of this book is that these women authored a feminist genealogy that arguably resonates unto the present; the authoring is therefore an act of creative and intellectual assertion of authority. Such repeated textual demonstration of a prismatic aesthetic can thus be seen in the disassembling, morphing and layering of textual sensibilities in mottled, often unanticipated modes: drives of ambition, the mesh of filial ties, deep communion with the natural world, witty caricature and scathing sarcasm, the unrest and thrill of wanderlust, the unearthing of love and compassion in strangers, solitude and grieving, aches of an ailing body or mind, spiritual strife and surrender, abandon of performance and the rebellious ideas of material pleasure for pleasure's sake. The choices involved in the style of the writing, be it in narrative voice or the choice of genre, thereby become amenable to any mode that is able to contain and deliver the themes at hand. What is then the desideratum is a new evolving literary identity, bi-focal in nature, non-hierarchical in spirit, with one eye gazing (and metabolizing/absorbing) at the self, the other gazing at and metabolizing the world.

Writerliness and the first-person stance

> *If an unskilled potter makes a lovely pot of his imagination, and if it becomes crooked while drying or heating in the kiln, he still puts it for sale in the market. Similarly, I have written this book to the best of my insufficient ability and placed it before you.*[13]

In this foreword to her first novel, Kashibai Kanitkar (1861–1948) dons the unassuming persona of 'an unskilled potter' to highlight two interconnected challenges—the toil of turning the manuscript into a book, and the trial of new authorship. The novel, *Rangarao*, began to appear in instalments in the Marathi magazine *Manoranjan ani Nibandha-chandrika* in 1886 and stayed incomplete when the magazine closed down. Kanitkar managed to complete the novel over a decade later in 1898, but would not be able to publish it till 1903. The author explains the delay: 'Both the author and the owners of the printing press have suffered severe domestic problems, which is why the book is being placed before readers in this form. I am sorry about this but am unable to make amends.'[14] Kashibai Kanitkar laces her apology about the unexplained domestic troubles with humour, submitting that any reader who takes upon the task of criticizing her book or finding errors would find themselves with 'errata that would make a book of 800 pages, while the original [Kanitkar's novel] has only 400'.[15] Unlike Rashsundari Debi, whose literary proclivity was represented by a single collection of autobiographical compositions, Kashibai Kanitkar actively worked towards building a body of work that included a posthumous biography of a contemporary,[16] a collection of short stories, several essays as well as translations. In other words, we have a literary enterprise: an *oeuvre* that represents one author's strivings and vision but also extends a claim to a collective output—other writers, other women. At hand is thus a literary-historical moment of authors who are not isolated voices but remain interconnected in their reflexivity, in their measure and (uneven) participatory engagement with each other, as well as their purported audience—predominantly female—both within the diegetic space of the text and beyond.

The growing presence and consistent influence of print culture in India induced a significant output of printed texts in English and native Indian languages in the nineteenth century.[17] The proliferation of printers and printed material took place in simultaneous engagement with a growing literate audience, and the corpus of printed material continued to be predominantly religious or polemical in nature (driven by social reform motivations, such as pamphlets propagating widow remarriage). This ensured the centrality of print for public debates around the 'women's question'[18] even as literary texts by women began to receive increasing public attention and appreciation from the mid-nineteenth century.[19] Around the 1980s, a noticeable acceleration and close succession of publications by women can be said to form distinctive literary constellations.[20] Over the next four decades, a combination of factors contributed to a growing literary tradition, 'a feminist inheritance more powerful and complex, but at the same time more troubling, than narratives of suppression and release might allow us to suspect'.[21] In fact, an elucidation could be offered for the inauguration of a distinct clustering of literary creativity, with its most delineated enunciation in the autobiographical frame—the 'I' that speaks to/of its literariness (of voice, structure, device, subtext) and demonstrates its confidence in the immediacy and reliability of the life narrative.

The writers and texts studied in this book attempt varied formulations of the experiential first-person voice, either through shorter compositions (essays, letters, speeches), biographical studies, book-length autobiographies or even autobiographical fiction. The disparate backgrounds and inclinations of these writers defy easy classifications, offering instead a tapestry of revelations: an ardent student of both biomedicine and English literature (Krupabai Satthianadhan), a woman in her seventies who sets off to travel the world (Dosebai Cowasjee Jessawalla), the daughter of a social reformer who becomes a princess (Sunity Devee), a celebrated stage actress in Calcutta (Binodini Dasi), the first woman from India to complete her law education in England (Cornelia Sorabjee), a writer who strives for literary visibility in a celebrated family of writers (Swarnakumari Debi Ghosal), a young woman whose travelogues carry an unsaid tale of passion and failure (Atiya Fyzee), an educator of unprecedented social insurgency whose also seeks reform in poetry (Savitribai Phule) and so on. Several of these writers are self-taught, while others benefitted from structured institutional education, but the shared commitment was to the written and the *published* word. Publishing meant the inevitability of public response, though this was more likely to invite censure rather than celebration for the author. The texts selected for study here offer two explicit assertions about narrative voice: firstly, a claim to writing as an act and an identity, and secondly, the gendering of both act and identity by the reflexive references to the author being a woman. For the first time both personae—I am a writer and I am a woman—were being claimed in the Indian public sphere in a manner that was desirable and exciting, in that it had almost no precedence. By virtue of being women who write—the operative emphasis falling on the verb, the writing which is the chosen vocation—a shift can be discerned to the claiming of an affective noun, the identity and sensibility of *being* writers or a quality of 'writerliness'. Thus, from this reinstatement of scribal desires and identities, one may proceed to trace the preliminary contours of prodigious and momentous beginnings in authorship for women.

A prefiguration of this method is discernible in *Beginnings: Intention and Method*, an early work of Edward Said that seeks to distinguish literary beginnings from the more exalted concept of origins: 'the latter divine, mythical and privileged, the former secular, humanly produced, and ceaselessly re-examined'.[22] Said suggests three steps in the making of such a secular, re-examined beginning: first, 'there must be the desire, the will, and the true freedom to reverse oneself and accept thereby the risks of rupture and discontinuity'; second, ' a beginning must be thought possible, it must be taken to be possible, before it can be one'; and thirdly, 'the beginning will emerge reflectively and perhaps unhappily' as it already engages the writer in an awareness of its difficulty.[23] Hence, in beginnings, Said identifies an intention to produce meaning and a method that then carries out that intention. In the writers that appear in this study, these three conditions are repeatedly articulated: the will to change with the acceptance of rupture, the belief that the beginning is possible and the reflection of its difficulties. For the women who took to writing as an act of visible assertiveness, these conditions are already implicit in their deviation from heavily scrutinized and controlled social roles and expectations. This suggests a fourth crucial component that can be identified in the development of a feminist lineage in modern prose in India. Beginnings *must be articulated*—in being spoken of, it is implicitly given to meta-narrativity, a self-conscious awareness of its own ingenuity and innovation.

Additionally, these beginnings are not just intention and method, in line with Said's thinking, but they are vitally invested in *output* that needs to be appreciated as both creative process and printed product. Much scholarship on South Asia has traced the varied axes relevant to publishing in this period—through literary history,[24] nineteenth-century print culture,[25] the rhetoric of interiority,[26] as representing trajectories of reform,[27] as performative selves,[28] the textual lineage of social realism[29] and the critical interactions of gender and caste.[30]

While the aforementioned scholarship has yielded rich dividends on the social, contextual and public aspect of these writings, this project seeks to foreground a different configuration of subjectivation in the narrative strategies that were employed by women who wished to write and publish. Specifically, it seeks to flesh out the textual intonations of context and subtext as the writers negotiate with a self-making in a literary terrain populated mostly by male authors. The book argues that the writers do this by repeatedly drawing a reader's attention to a sense of a material, grounded, psychological self as it evolves and adapts in its bargains with new thematics—pre-eminently the new ontologies of literacy/education/reading.

Writing of his own beginnings with name, language and identity in his memoir *Out of Place* (1999), Edward Said reflects on 'the over-riding sensation [that he had] was always being out of place'.[31] One becomes aware that the assertions/disclaimers of being in/out of place have very close links to the rhetorical and real possibility of beginnings. But it cannot be a contained, linear extraction; rather, we are likely to be faced with a profusion of voices and literary activities in predictable as well as unlikely locations. A similar approach and structure have informed this Introduction that deliberately entwines its primary arguments through forewords, prefaces and meta-references from texts by women during the given period. What can be discerned in these textual beginnings (say, in forewords) vis-à-vis the beginnings of a literary tradition are plural vivid notes of pride, despair, wit, lament, nostalgia, hope and anticipation.

Writing the new order for the new woman

> *In the following pages I shall in my own way try to present a faithful picture of the experiences and thoughts of a simple Indian girl, whose life has been highly influenced by a new order of things—an order of things which at the present time is spreading its influence to a greater or less extent over the whole of her native land.*[32]

An unassuming literary subterfuge opens the autobiographical novel *Saguna: A Story of Native Christian Life* by Krupabai Satthianadhan. Serialized in the *Madras Christian College Magazine* in 1887–8 and published posthumously as a book in 1895 (soon after the author's death at the age of thirty-two), *Saguna* is said to be the first (autobiographical) novel in English by an Indian woman, a debut that received the notice of the monarch of the British Empire.[33] Krupabai, the daughter of a Brahmin couple who had converted to Christianity, was training to be a medical doctor when her education has to be abandoned on account of poor health (an emotional breakdown is implied in *Saguna*). In her fiction, Krupabai gives primacy to that which can be closely examined, 'the psychological and the interiorized, as well as the public spaces, of young upper-caste Indian women's lives'.[34] The intermediates of genre that Krupabai's writing traverses (between autobiography and fiction) are engrossing—the tonalities of what is dramatized in re-creation (such as the early married life of her parents) and what is reflected or exhumed from her lived experience reveals an astute layering of the memoiric intent. There is a tension and malleability that enliven the narrative, and the opening lines of *Saguna* prime the reader. The 'new order of things' is an overt reference to Christianity[35] but the ramifications of the phrase stretch much further: similar to the author Krupabai, the protagonist Saguna is passionate about her education, loves to read George Eliot, starts to train to be a medical doctor and feels both the excitement and the weight of being perceived as an aberrant in her social world. Despite the self-effacing opening disclaimer of her identity as 'a simple Indian girl', the rest of the novel illustrates a protagonist who is anything but simple, one who is gifted with an intuitive defiance of the conventional. Saguna is spirited and temperamental in a way that asserts difference and individuality, voracious in her pursuit of education, passionate about poetry and free speech.[36] To survive the experience of both isolation and the pressure to assimilate is to find language only in the undulations of her most withdrawn self: Saguna writes of her humiliation at social ostracism, her affinity for landscape and foliage, the chafing of her spirit at injustice and the vicissitudes of lingering illness. The narrative voice has a quality of appearing to address readers/audience, but it is in the tenor of an internal monologue or private reminiscence. It gestures to the tantalizing confessional, and yet dwells within a sentience of narrative propriety. In this submerged psychic vista, unseen to even the narrator's closest companions, the reader glimpses a tumultuous in-between-ness that can only be addressed through a life trajectory in the external world (in the manner of the female *bildungsroman*), a history that is being made because of the subject's acute sense of her own centrality to that sociocultural space and to the causal connections of the telling. Such 'oblique pulsations of history in the timbre of the first-person voice'[37] are thus invariably steeped in the questions of literary selfhood.

To return to the opening gambit of Krupabai's text, the suggestion of the 'new order' at the overt level (as with the spread of Christianity in India) necessitates and facilitates parallel transgressions (in a more secular vein) that are indicative of the affective and stylistic refractions proposed by this study. The novel ends with the protagonist yielding to personal turmoil ('a great giddiness came over me') that follows 'a great whirl of thought' finally leading to her feet being 'firmly planted on the Rock of Ages. There was no fear now, no losing one's way'.[38] The narrator attributes this certainty to her submergence in Christ and faith, offering a circularity of resolution to the entire book, but the telling does not end there. For just then the companion/suitor of the protagonist grasps and kisses her hand; sanitized as a 'holy kiss',[39] it remains a bodily and romantic counterpoint to the abstract ecstasy described. When the narrator reciprocates with the meeting of hands, the religious sentiment is swiftly overlaid with companionate and romantic love, composing the last line of the novel, its final phantasmagoric note simultaneously real and dream-like.

The values that this woman of the new order attaches to herself—the vivid experiences, insights, cautions encoded in her decision to cast herself as the protagonist of an artistic quest—is best teased out from within the text's own aesthetic anchoring. Irrespective of the external influences that might have actualized the vocation of writing for a woman—colonial education, reformist groups, traditionalist tenets, modernity—to labour at the written word was to resist being compacted as metaphor.[40] The explication of women as sites for 'complex and competing struggles' in Hindu society[41] or through the 'substantial [female] embodiment of national territory' mapped as Mother India[42] has been impactful in studies of gender in colonial India. This historical approach emerged from overlapping and concurrent vectors of social reform and nationalist sentiments, many of which focused intensely on the question of women's rights highlighted by three crucial legalistic deliberations and public debates: the Bengal Sati Regulation (1829), the Widow Remarriage Act (1856) and the Age of Consent Act (1891). Sudhir Chandra writes of the imperialist discourse regarding law that took place around the third quarter of the nineteenth century, wherein 'justice, forming with equity and good conscience an irresistible trinity, harmonized with high imperialism'.[43] Such negotiations made evident 'the dialectical relation of "feminisms" and patriarchies, both in the inventions of the colonial state and in the politics of the anti-colonial movements'.[44] In her study of Malayalee society from the late nineteenth to the early twentieth century, J. Devika makes a case for 'the order of gender' which implicitly emerged from the repeated iteration of segregated social ordering in which gender is the primary 'unsurpassable social division'.[45] Whether talking to/of state, clan, family or selfhood, men and women were presented as two immovable categories, each laden with their own set of acceptable moral prescriptivism, and it is against this milieu that this study attempts to locate the enterprise of women in print.

Geraldine Forbes identifies three kinds of redefining for women in the nineteenth century: modifications in the appropriate activities at different stages of female life, an expansion in the appropriate arena for female action and finally the new and growing need of individualism.[46] The rise of such assertions and indeed the entire progression of women's rights during this period were embroiled in a paradox: while on the one hand, there was a rhetorical current that turned away from traditional customs and into the public, on the other hand, this greater assertiveness was most concretely sought after in the primary (controlled) location of the home, natal or married. Rosalind O'Hanlon attributes this predicament to the intention of Indian politicians and reformers to establish a realm of custom and family beyond the reach of the state, which eventually resulted in women's behaviour being subject to intensifying public scrutiny even as they were being excluded from public domains.[47] These boundaries between public and private spheres, Meera Kosambi argues, remained porous and contested,[48] with literature clearly outlining the range of genres as well as the ideological spectrum.[49]

It is important to recognize that such disquiets and transformations within the autobiographical texts or the first-person voice (in fiction or polemical tracts) studied in this book transpire from women's repeated claims upon the rhetoric of individual rights and to a public identity as writer. The 'parallel discourse' was necessitated since 'the reform discourse was constructed as a male project and women were consciously denied a space in it'.[50] Padma Anagol makes a case for 'a conception of female agency that comes on uncovering the intensions and experiences of Indian women as they asserted their rights, addressed social inequalities and rejected or adapted tradition in an engagement with the world around them in what amounted to Indian feminism'.[51] One might argue that as with feminist movements elsewhere, the first volley of arguments in India were consolidated in printed tracts, initially in essayistic or autobiographical mode, and soon after in other compounded and more extended genres such as novels.

This resultant visibility—the publication and circulation of material crafted, edited and printed for self/public edification—offers the rationale for feminist literary beginnings in the 1880s. Beginnings, however, imply something follows, growth perhaps, and equally they extend, change, maturate, recast for further beginnings. The decades following the 1880s support this genesis, and the shifts in historical and literary sensibility see its strongest disruption or redirection in the 1920s with several attributions: the end of the First World War and the post-1917 emergence of socialistic ideas;[52] the polarization of the right and left ideologies, for RSS and Communist Party are both formed in 1925 as the Khilafat movement begins to lay bare the limitations of Hindu-Muslim unity;[53] the growing influence of MK Gandhi in the nationalist movement, particularly his opinion on the role of women in the public sphere;[54] the rise of caste-identity groups[55] and the Self-Respect Movement in Southern India;[56] and the consolidation of women's rights discourse through the establishment and activities of key women's organizations.[57] These changes start to get reflected in the literary output of the 1920s and 1930s onwards and tend to be removed from the thematic and stylistic concerns of the beginnings indicated earlier. Hence, this book locates itself largely between the 1880s and 1920s, allowing for some margin for ideas that may have been seeded a little earlier (as with Rashsundari Debi) or those that linger a little after (as with the memoirs of Haimabati Sen that capture these same decades but were published later). Despite variances caused by personal or publication histories, the texts studied here need to be seen as held together by an amalgam of historical placement, temperament and direction.

While all the texts studied from this time period are by authors who emphasize their first-hand experiences of writing as women, they are consciously not tethered together as any self-evident notion of 'women's writing'—a categorization that brings up several ambivalences of gendered taxonomies and segregations. Rather, this study has attempted to think about ways in which to approach differentiations of creativity and aesthetics even when they share thematic common grounds (such as narratives of girlhood or forbidden education). Susie Tharu and K. Lalita, who pioneered the ambitious project of anthologizing women writers in India (from 600 BC to their contemporaries), identify an intrinsic attribute in the theory and practice of feminist criticism in India. To formulate an aesthetic of writings by women was to 'undo the strict distinctions between the literary and social text [...] and redesign itself to orchestrate contradictions and cherish that agnostic forms of insurgency and resistance'.[58] The agnosticism of an insurgent literary positioning may be seen as germane not only in immediate sociocultural environs but in conversation with the cultural currencies of World Literatures.

A world big enough for the self

> *In the language of the Zenana, there are two twilights [...] Yes, the manner of its loitering is varied, but always, always is it an hour of enchantment, this hour Between the Twilights: and it is my very own [...] The half is not yet told: much would not bear telling—I had no business taking strangers into the walled garden of our intimacy—and some things were too elusive for speech [...]*[59]

An elusive knowledge, the claim to ambivalent time and the breach of intimate spaces all come together in the imagery of twilight in the Preface to Cornelia Sorabji's aptly titled book *Between the Twilights: Being Studies of Indian Women by One of Themselves* (1908). This accent on temporal thresholds and on belonging by virtue of being Indian and woman is also accompanied by the author's personal experiences that fall on both sides of the cultural threshold. Her parents were Parsis who had converted to Christianity and she had studied law in England. For Cornelia, who was equally at home in two continents, the diffusion of light and vision in twilight hours seems pressing and crucial as she seeks to represent the life narratives of elite Indian women in tradition-bound segregations. This imagery and site of the *zenana* (women's quarters) additionally support the 'deliberate concealments'[60] of the author's life and writings.

During the writing and publication of *Between the Twilights*, Cornelia Sorabji had been grieving for a romantic partner, an older married man who died in her arms. In addition, she was adjusting to a recently secured job (after long intense lobbying) with the colonial government as 'the first Indian woman to be salaried as a native informant for the Government of India'.[61] The strains of her inner world emerge in her writing as fleeting turns of thought or sentiment, and may bear further literary ferreting. Cornelia's nephew and biographer Richard Sorabji confirms the significant avoidances and conscious variations of her experiences and memories evident across her substantial *oeuvre*: these elisions include scandalous love affairs, public controversies, romantic indiscretions of family members, in the strategic fragmentations of her client-narratives. The biographer chalks the causes to 'a memory slip, to the wish to protect identities, or to tidying up for literary or other effect'.[62] It is this *literary tidying up* through the devices/choices of the narrative arrangements that allows an acute methodology for textual interrogation.

Carolyn Steedman, the historian of nineteenth-century class formations in England, makes a similar case for stringing together history and autobiography since the two 'work in the same way as *narrative* [italics in original]: they use the same linguistic structure, and they are both fictions, in that they present variations and manipulations of current time to the reader'.[63] What is striking here is not the underscoring of fact or evidence that features in public discourses of history and autobiography but rather the gesture to the elasticity of time and fiction, the unassailable appeal of linguistic structuring and telling. Steedman applies this insight with candour and narrative dexterity to two working-class childhoods—her mother's in the 1920s and then her own childhood in the 1950s.[64] The point about the past, she clarifies early in her memoir, does not stay in the past or in 'the lost time at which they happened' but that 'the only point lies in interpretation' and with 'what people know of a social world and their place within it'.[65] This knowledge of the social world and one's place is a contiguity to the textual experience. The approach accentuates a strategic blurring of the categories of history/fiction/genre and self-narration. Udaya Kumar examines the qualities of autobiographical practice in terms of the 'conditions under which one occupies the position of the subject in relation to self-narration'.[66] Autobiographies by men published in the late nineteenth and early twentieth centuries, for instance, rarely spoke of 'private interiorities' and the distinctiveness in the author's life tended to be 'a pretext to reveal something more typical or larger'.[67] In some contrast, the present study will seek to interpret narratives by their female contemporaries as indicating an increasingly self-confident individuation, and thus a consequent adumbration of interiority and ethical action.

An indicative moment can be located in 'An Explanation', which forms a brief framing note to a collection of short prose compositions in Bengali, *Motichur* (Crushed Pearl, 1904). The author, Rokeya Sakhawat Hossain (1880–1932), lauded by scholars as a pioneering and courageous Bengali Muslim feminist and educationist,[68] had made her literary presence felt through Bengali periodicals—many of these essays and stories became part of the collection *Motichur*. The occasion of the writings reappearing in book form, the author's first such venture, foregrounds her preoccupation with accusations of plagiarism:

> Some of the readers of *Motichur* have expressed in their criticism, the thought that according to them the language and the subject of the book has been taken from the writings of other well-known writers. Such thoughts are not unnatural when they find similarities between this book and some others [...] Why does this happen? How is it that the same subject and sentiments well up from places as diverse as Bengal, Punjab, Deccan, Bombay, and England? The answer perhaps lies in the spiritual unity among the women of the British Empire.[69]

The author's only defence here is to speak of authorial integrity and 'originality' while reiterating that her ideas are free from influences of literary stalwarts. Rokeya is quick to clarify that she does not 'have either the daring or the expertise to misappropriate the subject and the style of others'.[70] For a reader who is unfamiliar with such ongoing controversies and charges, the author gives us more details—the 'similarities' are said to be with the writings of popular contemporary male writers (in Bengali) like Kaliprasanna Sinha (1841–70) and Bankimchandra Chattopadhyay (1838–94), and also the bestselling British novelist Marie Corelli (1855–1924). While Rokeya stoutly denies having read the sources that she is accused of copying, it is her agreeing with the likelihood of resemblances that holds the reader's attention. Quickly getting past the male writers, she mulls on the possibility of similitudes between her writing and that of the novel by an Englishwoman (Corelli) that she has not read. The attribution to 'the spiritual unity' among women across geographies and cultures that are linked by the colonial enterprise suggests identification with the gendering of writing and of the aesthetic scaffolding that travels with colonial education. Even as kinships are traced, there is equally a claiming of resolute standalone authorial presence. Rokeya's stance would be well-aligned with more recent critical approaches to World Literatures that proposes 'literary narratives were not only products of colonial encounter, but themselves produced colonial encounters through their formal explorations of narrative'.[71] It is thus critical to understand these writers to be engaged as citizens in a sphere not easily demarcated as centre or periphery—rather, there is a confident and even exuberant sense of participation in a cosmopolitan and even global register.

Indeed, the novel *Kahake* ('To Whom?' would be the literary translation) directly opens up this question of address and a trans-continental literary affinity. Published in 1898 by Swarnakumari Debi Ghosal, the novel features a conversation in the drawing room of an affluent Bengali family during a social visit of a potential suitor (a medical doctor and a reader of literature). The doctor is reading George Eliot's *Middlemarch* (1871–2) and confesses to be a great admirer:

> Whatever chapter, whatever page I may read, I feel my heart touched by a living sympathy. I am then aware of myself only as a spark in an ocean of consciousness, and am happy in drowning my individuality in the great sea of existence [...] She [George Eliot] had a truly grand intellect combined with the sympathetic heart

> and subtle instinct of a true woman. Has any writer of the stronger sex been able to equal her in that?[72]

A debate ensues when the host insists that Shakespeare is the greater 'creative genius'. The doctor continues to stand by his preference for Eliot, and the conversation ends with genial disagreement. The family and guest loudly cheer both these writers, one from the canon—even as the canon is in the process of being consolidated in the colony[73]—and the other being a more immediate predecessor (Eliot had died in 1880). The female protagonist of *Kahake*, who has thus far been a witness to the discussion on writers and greatness, speaks up: 'Are there no cheers for our own writers?'[74] Her sister agrees and cheers the most popular contemporary Bengali writer—'Honour to Bankim Chandra first of all!'[75]—and the conversation ends with rounds of cheers to India, its women and men. 'The double movement from local to global, particular to universal, and back again'[76]—described by John Rignall as characteristic of George Eliot's craftsmanship as well as the imaginative engagement she seeks from her readers—is evident in this fictional drawing room in Bengal. Swarnakumari's perspective of this hospitable space as a salon that included crisscrossing women's voices can be seen as participating in what the literary historian Rosinka Chaudhuri posits as 'an aesthetic style and a cultural ambience'.[77] The drawing room's different reading and conversational terrains are implicated in a fluid aesthetic, a historical *now*.

Nancy Armstrong has made a compelling case for a political history of the novel wherein fiction functions 'both as the document and the agency of cultural history'.[78] The central trajectory of her work is devoted to women in England who began to write in the eighteenth century, continued their ascent to prominence in the nineteenth century and finally came to achieve the status of artists. For Armstrong, 'the modern individual [as a sexual, economic and psychological reality] was first and foremost a female'.[79] This book is sympathetic to all these key elements of Armstrong's argument—fiction is agential, not merely documentary or reflective; that the continual presence of women writers cannot be just additive, but has been central to the formation, status and evaluation of literary culture. Thus, the Indian woman offering her writing to the gaze of a nineteenth-century reader contends with the givenness of print culture, with the excitement of many newer, exuberant literary forms and with public presentation now available not only from developments in India[80] but also from personal and literary models from Europe. For example, the emergence of the figure of the world-traveller Dosebai Cowasjee Jessawalla is only possible due to women having already actively imagined such an agential/entrepreneurial role. Dosebai, who claimed to have the 'privilege of being the first Indian girl to receive the benefits of English education',[81] attributed her motivation to write to 'the cause of History' and because 'that which is historical within us is higher, nobler, greater and stronger than ourselves, and I have spoken because the voice of Truth within me has bidden me speak. Even now I may be misunderstood, misinterpreted and misrepresented, as I have been in the past'.[82] The anticipation of the reception of the writing as possibly and deliberately or repeatedly hostile cannot be a deterrent for the woman who must write and publish. She must draw from universalist discourses of education and historicity, because history, truth and the conviction to write the personal comprise the narrative engine that pushes the frontiers of a more uninhibited emancipating world.

Narrative architectures for gender and genre

> *All I have done is to waste so much paper and ink. I have realised that the anguish of the heart can only be comprehended within oneself; there is no means of expressing it without. And so I say, what need for a preface or a foreword to that which was never realised.*[83]

The play of meanings in the two iterations of the word 'realised' in this translation of the Preface to Binodini Dasi's autobiography (*Amar*

Katha, 1912) brings into sharp relief the vagaries of life and craft. Despite the seeming self-deprecatory and defeatist tenor, the insight or realization for the writer is that her ambition must/will indeed be realized or fulfilled, not just in the text of the life narrative that follows soon after this preface but via yet another autobiographical account published a decade later as *Amar Abhinetri Jiban* (My Life as an Actress, 1924–5). Authorship as an identity is very much in the doing, the writing, even when the act is deliberately effaced in a rhetorical flourish, to become a self-conscious performance, and subsequently a vital consolidation of writing and identity.

In the process of reading explicitly stated chronicles of private-public lives by Binodini Dasi and her contemporaries, scholarship has to first contend with some entrenched biases and limitations. Well into the twenty-first century, the presentation of the genesis and flourishing of modern prose in India, especially around genres such as the novel or autobiography, continue to implicitly assume the writer as a linguistically/stylistically attuned male artist, with women as focal points of desire and representation.[84] The studies that directly address contributions of writing women have self-marginalized their work by not pushing towards themes hitherto reserved for the normative (male) public figure of a writer—thus, crucial questions of self-fashioning or formal inventiveness or public participation are rarely studied in an integrated, inclusive manner in order to elicit commonalities and differences. A strong, recurring presence of the autobiographical voice or the representation of lived experiences offers some strategies to address such 'traditional maps of genre and periodization'[85] through a genealogy that Leigh Gilmore terms 'autobiographics'—such an approach would encompass the spectrum of women's self-representation across genres to study their assertion as agents of language and experience. The length or professed literariness of the text becomes secondary considerations—for instance, letters or essays as well as shorter genre-within-genre (say, a dream narrative in an autobiography) need also be seen as forming valuable fragments of an intentional intellectual enterprise.

A Genre of Her Own is an attempt to explore these kaleidoscopic patterns in ideas, aesthetics and affective registers within texts authored by women in Britain-governed India. It is organized into chapters of approximate chronology and stylistic reverberation, thus presenting a broad cohesiveness nuanced by questions of genre as well as region/language/hierarchy. There emerge a fairly stable set of questions—selfhood, creativity, artefact of writing and performance, gender debates, genre/self-reflexive tone, negotiating the strictures of family vis-à-vis the public, education as reform, modes of pleasure and so on—that would be mutually intelligible to all these writers even if each writer may not address all issues. Broadly, the method in this book is that of an attentive reading, looking beyond the plainly stated facts to the many veiled, suggestive sub-texts and shifting tones of meaning that capture a literary effervescence not always reducible to filial or social or public context and personae.

While all the primary texts in the book are being read in English or in translation (to English), the analysis attempts to retain an awareness of the linguistic and historical terrains involved—the first chapter studies texts written in Marathi and the second chapter focuses on texts written in Bengali. The third chapter includes two texts composed in English and a third translated from Urdu—what is prioritized here is the strong sense of an encounter with Anglophone Europe as a literary and social field. The chapters should be read as interlacing, interrogating and compounding each other. The lacunae of the study would include the sparseness of representation of several geographic regions and language traditions, and while some of this has been caused by the absence of translations, the argument is that the methodology employed could be extended to other texts in future scholarship.

The architecture of the book is anchored in the long tradition of reading literature by prioritizing questions of genre, especially in relation to form and voice. Current open-ended genre-centric approach scholarship has envisaged genre as 'the enabling device, the vehicle for the acquisition of competence'.[86] A central preoccupation of the book is that of the writing woman who seeks publication in a world where her positioning is markedly off-centre—genre can function not only as the facilitative instrument of successful articulation but is affixed to the very identity and agency thereby claimed.

The three genre-allied identities in Chapter 1 are presented under the title 'The Pamphleteer, the Letter-Writer and the Essayist' and the texts selected were originally composed in Marathi in the 1880s. The pamphleteer is Tarabai Shinde, who published only one work that demonstrates the multifaceted and productive vitality of the affect of anger as seen in her deft wielding of critique, reasoning, mockery and vexation. The letter-writer is Anandibai Joshee, whose determination to become the first Indian woman to train abroad as a medical doctor is fructified largely through her ability to carve strong personal and professional bonds, as demonstrated by personal letters that appeared in public forums—it is precisely the indeterminacy of the personal and professional that mark her voice as distinct. The essayist is Rukhmabai, who argues eloquently and meticulously against a document circulated in the public domain to discredit her position (on restitution of conjugal rights) in an essay whose rhetorical framework is as legal as it is moral, thereby expanding the terrains of public knowledge that women were allowed to attain.

Chapter 2 represents writers that emerged in the fecund literary ferment of nineteenth-century Bengal as 'The Memoirist, the Dramatist and the Novelist'. The memoirist is Rashsundari Debi, who identifies the single greatest accomplishment of her life as the acquisition of literacy and the subsequent demanding road to authorship. The dramatist is an actor and celebrity who composed her sophisticated inner life in intense operatic accentuations—Binodini Dasi's autobiography thus mimics the form and sensibility of modern drama. The novelist is Swarnakumari Debi Ghosal, born in a family of famous writers (her younger brother, Rabindranath Tagore, became a Nobel laureate), creating a culturally hybrid novelistic family for a modern woman invested in a new idiom of courtship and romance.

The third chapter of this book presents 'The Elegist, the Diaryist and the Traveloguer' through three texts that are invested in the ambition of global travel, whether in terms of geographical navigations or cultural ideation. The elegist is Krupabai Satthianadhan, whose autofiction can be read as a meditative defiance of death and illness through the tropes of nature as a mournful, untamed wilderness. The diaryist is Atiya Fyzee, whose despatches of her first-hand experience of Europe are dutifully and sprightly communicated to a sisterhood that includes her biological sisters as well as the readers of a journal for women (addressed as 'newspaper sisters'). Dosebai Cowasjee Jessawalla is the traveloguer who fulfils her ambition to be the first Indian woman to effectively circumnavigate the globe—her autobiography is also a travel diary that showcases her curiosity, industriousness and ingenuity with social networks that finally culminates (for the narrative structure as well as her personal ambition) in a meeting with the King of England.

Whether in the realm of fiction or non-fiction, it becomes evident that these genres do not separate the writers but bridge distinct yet similar aesthetics of personhood, thereby also manifesting a choric presence and identity. To re-examine this premise, the Conclusion of the book—'The Poet and the Chorus'—turns to the social activist and author Savitribai Phule, whose debut collection is one of the earliest of its kind in India. The juxtaposition of two poems by Savitribai that reflect and argue on the ideal purpose and attribute of poetry and poet reinforce the conviction that the excellence of genre is ensured only when mirrored in or through the composer of that genre. This vein of reading genre and writer can be said to be fundamental to appreciating and contributing to a feminist archive. One hopes for more studies not only on the writers featured in the chapters of this book but also on those who feature more briefly such as Parvatibai Athavale, Haimabati Sen, Sunity Devee, Kashibai Kanitkar, Rokeya Sakhawat Hossain, Pandita Ramabai and Cornelia Sorabji.

Moulding a genre to the shape of lived experiences that are unequivocally gendered is an insurgence that cannot be entirely reduced to biographical factors or the socio-historical contexts of authorship. Rather, it needs also to be located in/through the pitch and tenor of the multivalent text itself, paying special attention to its voice and internal narrative strategies. In this scenario, while to write is to act, it is equally intent, context, subtext outcome, meaning. And to write about any conception of womanhood (one's own or others) at a time when public self-articulation was not easily facilitated and was indeed actively dissuaded, when the very conditions that underpin publication (education, travel, publishing industry) were fraught and tenuous, was to become an act imbued with novelty and distinctness—an assemblage of sensibility and identity, akin to interlinked islands in the larger flowing stream of the ideas and ambitions. The paradigm thus established serves as a robust and anticipatory template for gendered modern expressivities of aesthetics and sociality in the later twentieth century and onwards.

1

The Pamphleteer, the Letter-Writer and the Essayist

In one of the earliest examples of a woman critic reviewing a woman author—Kashibai Kanitkar responded in print in 1889 to her contemporary Pandita Ramabai's travels to the United States—the evaluative spotlight falls less on the particulars of the book and more on the low status of women as writers. Both the accomplishments of the unusual traveller (Pandita Ramabai was a widow with a young child travelling abroad without a male escort) and her contemporary reviewer (a practicing Marathi novelist from the same social background) are additional focal points of this text. In unknotting their respective subject positions, the reviewer expands the aesthetic and moral mandate of the essay to include ruminations on gender rights (or the absence thereof) in two countries and the rebellious nature of writing itself. For incarceration 'within the prison walls of social pressure, bolting and locking doors'[1] are both a core reality and a literary trope wherein writing and reading form the escape hatch. As Kanitkar notes:

> If a woman picks up a paper, our elders feel offended—as though she has done something very shameful. If she receives a letter from her relatives, the whole family feels dishonoured. If a woman's name appears in a newspaper, if her essay is published, if she stammers out a few words at a women's gathering, she is certain to be slapped with the gigantic charge of having tarnished the family's honour. If a woman visits a school or a club, people spin exaggerated tales about her.[2]

The repetition of the conditional clause ('if') forms a rhythmic interlude and hook to underline the repercussions faced by women on account of being engaged in intellectual forays and seeking authorship. The repetition also reinforces that such transgressions of reading and writing must be carried out nonetheless and are likely frequent enough to merit the corresponding social outrage. By implication, this becomes the 'good problem to have' for any robust society—a clear harbinger of positive, and even necessary, change.

A seismic shift had occurred: from the middle of the nineteenth century when literate/literary women in Maharashtra (as elsewhere in India) had been almost miniscule, to the 1880s and 1890s when the writing and receiving of letters or publishing an essay or speaking at a gathering had become far more frequent. Bylines by women appeared in Marathi and English periodicals and made a significant impact upon public discourse. It was 'an emergent feminism inevitably born of their experiential world' which involved forging various compromises between conformity and convention.[3] Although such opportunities were accessible to a select few (determined by class/ caste mobilities), the nonconformity or novelty of the reading-writing woman had also started to gain acceptance, and facilitated a growing articulate and assertive community of writers. With colonialism came 'decisive shifts in the structure of cultural production, as well as in the norms for articulating the possibilities of contestation and containment'.[4] The colonial world also offered a generative prompt via which the women 'ingeniously adapted and modernized many of the institutions of the private sphere'.[5] As the historian Prachi Deshpande reiterates, 'the making of Maratha historical memory involves a consideration of […] political, social and intellectual contexts of colonial modernity'.[6] Among the earliest public contestations were access to structured education, as also the fate of pre-teen girls who were married and impregnated, and the indignities heaped on widows. The poet and social reformer Savitribai Phule inaugurated literary careers for women in the Marathi modern print culture with her two poetry collections and essays (see Conclusion of this book).[7] However, more than poetry, which continued to appear in journals, prose featured as the genre of choice, and several writers turned intuitively to representing lived experiences. The memoir-voice proved most malleable and enduring as the lives of women writers came to be featured in essays or autobiographical fiction. Among celebrated/controversial book-length autobiographies were Pandita Ramabai's *A Testimony of our Inexhaustible Treasure*[8] in 1907 and Ramabai Ranade's *Amachya Ayushyatil Kahi Athavani*[9] in 1910. Several women wrote of their childhood or early adulthood several decades later, often through dictation to close relatives. These texts tonally emerge as reflections of women who lived to see the modernity of the twentieth century, as exemplified by Parvatibai Athavale's *Majhi Kahani* in 1928,[10] Lakshmibai Tilak's four-volume *Smritichitre* in 1934–6,[11] Anandibai Karve's *Mazhe Puran* in 1944[12] and Yashodabai Joshi's *Amcha Jivan-pravas* in 1965.[13] Occasionally a writer like Kashibai Kanitkar would produce work in multiple genres, including one of the earliest novels in Marathi.[14] Some of their contemporary novelists from the region, Krupabai Satthianadhan and Shevantibai Nikambe, opted to write in English.[15] Demonstrating 'a strong business sense' and 'awareness of what the market wanted [as well as] the value of the work they were producing',[16] many of the writers held copyrights to their own works. Their literary innovations encompassed prevalent formats such as the public letter, the pamphlet and the essay—these are pivotal to the present chapter. The resultant rhetoric can be seen as symptomatic, catalytic and consolidative of several socio-historic factors, as well as testifying to the sophistication and variety of literary output that women were already generating by the last decades of the nineteenth century.

This chapter features a selection of writings by three authors that will be examined through specific affective strands, stylistic devices and rhetorical resonances: the spectrum of wit and rage that Tarabai Shinde exhibits in her comparison between men and women, unseen strains between intimate correspondence and public gaze in Anandibai Joshee's letters to her husband, and Rukhmabai's employment of legal parlance and argumentative structure for fierce self-defence to a mass audience. The personal stakes for these authors are so high that it can be said that far from the oft-debated binaries of private-public,[17] nothing remains private, and by the very act of speaking aloud, speaking against or recording it, the writings are already entirely publicly charged. The narratives studied below were all composed in the same decade of the 1880s and these authors can be seen as incubating collective gendered resistances among/through their contemporaries in western India.

The vitality of just anger: Tarabai Shinde's *Stri-Purush Tulana* (1882)

> *These phoney reform societies of yours have been around for thirty, thirty-five years. What's the use of them? You're all there patting yourselves on the back, but if we look closely, they're about as much use as a spare tit on a goat.*[18]

Any strategy of comparison in a rhetorical debate invariably works through depth and textures of contrasts and similarities, but when the comparison is driven by the affect of anger and delivered through the mode of wit and irony, we are looking at a literary *coup d'etat* that is Tarabai Shinde's *Stri-Purush Tulana* (1882). Published in Marathi as a fifty-two-paged booklet, the literal translation of the title *A Comparison between Women and Men*[19] is followed by a particularly contoured subtitle that deepens the question of comparison. Rosalind O'Hanlon opts for a broader meaning and context in her translation of the subtitle as 'An essay that clearly shows who's really wicked and immoral, women or men?'[20] Here the phrase 'wicked and immoral' stands for a single Marathi word—*sahasi*—to significantly tilt the tone of the interrogative sentence and thereby the implied answer (of the text) is 'men'. However, there is enough in the language to warrant the more assertive and straightforward translation of *sahasi* as courageous (alternatively, strong, brave, audacious) and to include another adjective that O'Hanlon overlooks in her translation—*spasht* (which suggests clarity). It may be that Tarabai Shinde's moral compass points to men as more wicked and immoral but it is equally important that we register where the anvil of courage is attributed, for it is on this anvil of argument that the solution must be hammered out towards the desired end—to resist and protest the unfair treatment of women in the author's life and society. Thus, the subtitle of this singular text[21] could be reframed as 'An essay to clearly demonstrate who is more courageous between women and men'. One is no longer faced with an oratorical question with an implied answer but has an undiffused assertion to a social experiment to categorical establish the superiority of the author's chosen community: women.

The literary sphere of Maharashtra was relatively enriched by 'a wealth of women's articulations'—which include the genres of autobiographies, journals, diaries, letters, journalistic pieces, biographies, essays—and a scholar must contend not with the paucity of material 'but their retrieval and incorporation as source materials of social history'.[22] One would like to extend this proposition to also include the less-frequently addressed question of the literariness and the range of tonalities within the texts, as well as the aesthetic leanings of the authors. In this mostly unmapped terrain of creativity and critique, Tarabai's work demands extra-analytic dexterity from a scholar who wishes to peer further than the obvious polemical stance and undertake a more discerning reading of Tarabai's rhetorical choices.

Tarabai Shinde was in her early twenties when she made a bold foray into print with *A Comparison between Women and Men* and nearly every paragraph demonstrates the author's self-knowledge of the righteous tides of her 'passionate anger'.[23] She announces—'I've written this small book to defend the honour of all my sister countrywomen'[24]—and indicates an anticipation of stubborn denial and outcry from the other side (a largely male readership). The impact of this pointed, accusatory rage in print was such that the author would face immediate condemnation and never publish again. This section examines such a modulation of anger through the literary devices of sarcasm and dark humour that in turn become the argumentative bait to uphold elementary norms of gender justice.

Biographical records available on Tarabai Shinde remain sparse. The only daughter among five children of a Maratha family in Buldhana, Tarabai was provided access to education (mainly in Marathi, and a little in English and Sanskrit) by her reform-minded father.[25] She was married to a man who moved in with her natal family (as a *gharjavai* or a husband who stays at the residence of his in-laws); they did not have children and there is enough evidence that she outlived him and did not remarry. Of the two recollections of Tarabai recovered from contemporaries, one paints a formidable image of a 'cruel-looking [woman with] a very fiery temper'[26] which O'Hanlon rightly suggests as coloured by the social disapproval of the writer, and proposes an alternate interpretation of 'a hardy, independent and somewhat pugnacious woman, whose shortage of proper feminine qualities was probably due to too much reading.'[27] This emphasis on female literacy and their participation in the collective reasoning for individuated aspirations was foundational to the reformist movement that gathered momentum in the nineteenth century in colonial India. 'With the exception, perhaps, of the issue of caste and untouchability, all major questions of the reform of Hindu society taken up at this period concerned women: sati, female infanticide, child marriage, the remarriage of widows, the seclusion and education of women, prostitutions, brideprice and dowry.'[28] Tarabai's unequivocal castigations and denunciation of patriarchy might not have been the desired result for the reformist leaders (nearly all men), but their rhetoric of progress and public debate had no doubt opened a crucial textual window for her voice to be heard.

One may briefly consider another illustrious debut in the same year as Tarabai, and on a similar topic, albeit in a completely different mode of address and explication of gender relations in Marathi society. In 1882, Pandita Ramabai published *Stri Dharma Niti* (with the English title *Morals for Women*), 'offering advice to women about the duties of good wives, housewives and mothers' in which she 'adopted the speaking position of a surrogate male reformer'.[29] As the years progressed, Pandita Ramabai's extraordinary career as a public intellectual and writer would take on more subversive, outlier trajectories, but in this early effort at writing a book, she is fairly conventional in directing the didacticism towards the self-improvement of women. Understandably, unlike *A Comparison* which was castigated and prematurely ended Tarabai's writing career, the first edition of *Stri Dharma Niti* was sold out and helped fund Ramabai's travel to England.[30] By addressing men instead of women, and by openly accusing and denigrating their commonly held beliefs and practices, Tarabai launched a different voyage of the mind for her contemporaries.

Scholars have hailed and studied Tarabai's essayistic booklet for its feminist affinities and as 'an anguished diatribe against men's double standards of morality and the consequent discrimination against women'.[31] Equally, the argument is read as endorsing humane and impassioned ideals. However, the text is richer than a simple liberal call to greater equality. To write with the haunting self-consciousness of being a woman in a specific social order in nineteenth-century India would not only entail the 'anxiety of authorship' suggested by Gilbert and Gubar in their influential study of women writers in the same period[32] but also necessitate an amplification of an emergent, volatile authorial persona. There is thus an argument to be made that the documentation of life narratives in India, as seen in a text such as *A Comparison*, cannot be satisfactorily accommodated as merely individual expression or 'representation' of collective interests or a reaction to the canon or an act of resistance to being shut out of literary production. To do so would be to allow our approaches to the text and author to be over-determined by socio-historical or biographical frameworks, to allow for an unreliable and uncontested one-to-one mapping between historical fact and literary imagination. Instead one must consider a new mode of self-recognition, an identification as much with the act of writing as with the result printed on a page.

For this self-identification, more than an *anxiety* of authorship, there is a self-conscious *autonomy* in the act of creation. One need look no further than the brief Introduction to *A Comparison* for the inventive resourcefulness and quicksilver wit that seeks to establish its motive and approach without apologia.

> Of course, I am just a poor woman without any real intelligence who's been kept locked up and confined in the proper old Maratha manner. This is my very first effort, so the book has passages that are disconnected and fragmentary, and it's written in the rough and harsh language of the Marathas of old. But every day now we have to look at some new and more horrible example of men who are really wicked and their shameless lying tricks. And not a single person says anything about it. Instead people go about pinning the blame on women all the time, as if everything bad was their fault! When I saw this, my whole mind just began churning and shaking out of feelings for the honour of womankind. So I lost all my fear. I just couldn't stop myself writing about it in this very biting language.[33]

The language that bites is also one that protects and delivers the writer's literary sensibility, particularly in the nuanced gradations of tone. Being aggrieved by the many injustices heaped on women, the author has to present a sustained anger (the injustice has deep roots and long antecedents) that must be modulated in the semantics of justice. The full impact is only possible in a *just* anger that must be read in the allied meanings of justice and justified. The third import of 'just' as something meagre or dismissible—the perception of a dominant oppressive group (men) who are expected by the author to belittle her call for justice—would also be relevant here. Such anger must then take on the veneer of sarcasm, scorn, irony, dark humour or scathing critique in developing an argument that speaks directly, fearlessly, to a reader in its unwavering conviction that wrongs must be set right. The dynamics between speaker-writer and listener-reader in *A Comparison* is as delineated as the two sexes pitted against each other in the essay's title. On the one hand is the sole speaker of the tract, referring to herself as 'poor woman' lacking 'real intelligence' who is bound to write prose in a 'clumsy way' that is 'disconnected and fragmentary' but at the same time communicating that her 'rough and harsh language' of droll sarcasm has been enabled by her outrage. On the other hand is the addressee, a mass audience repeatedly referred to as 'you men' from the stringent opening pages of the book till its plaintive conclusion. The text carries imprints of a precise blend of intense emotions and sharp rationalization. 'Don't just ignore this book'[34] is Tarabai's caution, for such justified anger being ignored is probably the only thing worse than denial or retaliation.

An immediate focal point for Tarabai's ire is the newspaper coverage of a court trial—Vijayalakshmi, a twenty-four-year-old widow, was accused of killing her new-born child to avoid public shaming (Brahmin widows were strictly required to remain celibate). Vijayalakshmi was initially sentenced to death by hanging and the sentence was later revised to transportation. The essay opens with: 'These days the newspapers are always writing about poor helpless women and the wicked things they do.'[35] The ethical mores of the print culture and the moral judgements on the women being hounded are in the same breath linked with a clear second-person address in the question that follows—'Why won't any of you come forward and put a stop to these great calamities?'[36] It is made known that the ones who will exploit are no different than the ones who will witness (and thus permit) the exploitation.

This initial proposition and its subsequent channelling into an intelligent/universal and altruistic sarcasm can be examined through three approaches in the overall narrative: (a) the clarification around two traditional social values that sought to control women's conduct and sexuality, that is, *stridharma* (what has been proposed by tradition as women's moral conduct) and *pativrata* (homilies on the ideal conduct of a married woman); (b) the hypocrisy and corruption in the social behaviour of men; here, the charges made by men against women are methodically shown to be more applicable to men than to women; these charges are women as evil incarnate, as whimsical, as debauched, as ignorant, as receptacles of guilt, as deceitful, as the source of wickedness; and (c) the author's awareness and consternation about the wide-ranging impact of the print culture of her times and their validating or perpetrating several shades of misogyny in the reading public.

The constellation of observations was as distinct to Tarabai as was the tenor of her delivery and is better understood in the context of her predecessors and peers. This is especially important considering that in the early decades of the literature of social reform (1820s–1830s), women's voices were 'consigned to the domain of silence' and could only be 'guessed from indirect evidence'.[37] However, by the mid-nineteenth century and in Tarabai's lifetime, an accumulating awareness and acceptance of the transformative possibilities of social reform had become well embedded in the literary output.[38] Women were getting more bylines in articles and essays on gender rights—for instance, against the practice of Sati or child-marriage, or in support of education for the girl child.[39] The manner of presentation of these tracts showcased a decorum and even tempo that could be said to be in the tradition of Mary Wollstonecraft's celebrated doctrine of 1792 which began with an address to a (male) bishop to reconsider his regressive views on the rights and duties of women, and then argued for women and men being given equal access to education and occupation.[40] In such writings, although charged with personal conviction, the case being presented was underlined by the knowledge that the audience for the writing would be predominantly other-than-women[41] and cannot be aggrieved. Very often the target was society at large, whether a particular regional/caste collective or India as a whole, for 'the root thereof lies in our evil-laden social mores'[42]—this diagnosis by Kailashbasini Devi in 1863 was not much different from Pandita Ramabai in 1882, who berated 'the sloth and lack of diligence among the native people'[43] in a manner that deflected blame from any gender to an irresponsible society. Irrespective of accountability, it became commonplace that one who endured the experiences had access to its representation and thus gradually the memoirist's position and voice gained sanctity and force. Radhabai Inamdar, a young widow studying in the fifth or sixth grade in Poona, wrote an essay in 1910 on the experience of widowhood in which she quoted the Marathi poet Tukaram: 'How a fish can sleep under water can only be learnt by being born a fish.'[44] The historian Uma Chakravarti underlines a crucial distinction between the knowledge of oppressive widowhood (as was the case with male reformist discourse) and the feelings or first-hand experiences of the women themselves.[45] For Tarabai, this reality of birth and experience was being offered to women in a world distorted by unequal power to such a degree that it veered on the absurd. For women whom she considers to be shut 'endlessly in the prison of the home',[46] enslaved to the whims of men and continually humiliated, the oppression was too great with almost no autonomy in sight.

Within a page or two of the tract, Tarabai's reasoning for parity quickly amplifies into a pantomime of anger where men are provocatively lampooned (among others as idiots, asses, cunning jackals, great thugs[47]) and the world of the divine is not allowed to fare any better. In her characteristic tongue-in-cheek anecdotal storytelling, Tarabai scans popular narratives from Hindu mythology to point out unacceptable and unfair behaviour by the male Gods against their womankind, and to any umbrage a devout reader might take, nonchalantly writes:

> Anyway, I just have to point out things like these, when they're true and there right in front of me. I'll say my prayers to the gods and ask them to excuse me if I've thrown a bit of blame on two or three of them there. They may forgive me, they may not; they'll go on being gods in any case.[48]

It is such truth-telling on her side, and the hypocrisy on the other, that forms the keystone and leitmotif of the text. Tarabai chafes at the many moral injunctions offered to women, especially around purity of behaviour, as much by the traditionalists as by the men of reform who by virtue of their colonial education (and newly acquired 'foreign' habits) are to her 'half white and half black, like a piebald horse!'[49] Every law imposed on women, whether by the *shastras* (religious texts) or by the injunctions of male family members, is to Tarabai an abominable invention made up by men for the comfort of men.[50] Several paragraphs are devoted to dismantling one specific example of such double-standards, that is, in the treatment of widows who are inhumanely locked away like murderers while men who have lost their spouses, no matter their age ('the old corpse' she calls a potential groom), acquire underage brides as if he were buying goats.[51] As the mockery continues, hypocrisy is shown to be wickedness that clings to men, that starts with them and them alone.[52] But what likely appears to be an outburst or a rant (by the author) cannot be taken to be merely that: the absoluteness of the delivery and distinct repetitive patterns throughout the text make apparent that it is a writing strategy that aims at the highest impact and strongest consolidation against moral apathy.

A narrative detail worth a closer look in *A Comparison* is the sprinkling of references to writing and writers. The nomenclature of 'writer' (apart from the first person narrator) is given to either men who have authored regressive religious doctrines or men who thanks to their 'English education' are needlessly proud of doing nothing more than 'pushing pens'.[53] Tarabai writes about the spread of education and printing presses under the colonial government that has the undesirable outcome of the publication of several books that in the guise of entertainment or storytelling are in effect regressive cautionary tales by male authors written for the edification (and control) of women. She mocks a selection of these dubious narratives that are far from reality and wonders, 'What's the point of writing all these stories?'[54] As she dismantles plot and character absurdities in tale after tale, she directly addresses a personified imagination behind such falsities: 'So what I want to say to you, Mr. Author, is—don't even dream of pretending that the story will frighten men and women so much they'll never do it again […] And even when women do wicked things they're still better than you.'[55] It is this curious dynamic that reveals the indomitable ingenuity of the text: for Tarabai Shinde, the antidote to the oppressive arrogance of writing (by Mr. Author) necessarily lies in her own (remedial) arrogance of writing. It is only just.

Letters for an eavesdropping public ear: Anandibai Joshee's letters (1883 – 1884)

> *You might wonder at this long introduction: it is the prologue to a play. Act I of the play has already appeared in your* Subodh Patrika. *Act II is still to be published, and may take some time. This is Act III and its prologue. This act will not end for another seven to eight years, by my conjecture.*[56]

The above excerpt about prologues and acts is neither about theatre nor about a play. Rather, it belongs to the opening page of a long letter written at the end of May 1883 from St Mary's Home in Berkshire, England. The letter is addressed to 'Dear Brethren'[57] (*bandhav* in Marathi) by Pandita Ramabai who is remembered for being 'articulate, learned, confident and forceful—a woman who got considerable media attention when she first burst upon the public arena in the 1870s'.[58] Ramabai had set sail from India with a two-year-old daughter and a female companion (who would commit suicide not long after the writing of this letter) with the intention of studying for a medical degree that was eventually denied to her due to a hearing difficulty. The excerpt draws attention to the choice of trope: the reference to the three acts of a play is meant to map three phases of her life as autobiographized by the young writer. A narrative of the first part of her life had been published in the addressee's journal, while the second was yet to be consigned to writing/publishing, but the reader's privilege is being privy to the third phase that is being written both as it unfolds and also in anticipation of the life that is yet to be lived. Seemingly, the author's plans (an education in England, for instance) are expected to hold stability and pattern for seven or eight years to come.

These disclosures of ongoing experiences, the reference to a life narrative that had already been published by the addressee and the three-act structure of playwriting (conventionally employed to build, complicate and resolve dramatic tension) were being offered as much to a contemporary patron/publisher as to future readers. One could argue that what Gauri Viswanathan calls Ramabai's 'outsider position'[59] helped her present an unexpressed but implied desire (as can be gathered from the hints dropped in these lines), that the letter (with her current life experiences) be published and shared with a curious public.[60] It was unsurprisingly made accessible to a readership that was already a moralistic panopticon.[61] The letter thus travelled to an eavesdropping ear, one that belonged to the Marathi literary sphere.

In their study of the literary networks created by women writers in the Romantic period, Winckles and Rehbein make a case for 'reading the letter as literature—rather than as ancillary material whose primary purpose is to contextualize [...] Letters were not only the primary means through which literary networks formed and were sustained, they provided a discourse structure which women could and did adapt when they made the move to print.'[62] Equally, as Maire Cross and Caroline Bland point out, the letter as a genre 'contains the seeds of its own potential for creativity or destruction'[63] because of the telling gaps between immediate responses of contemporaries and strategic posthumous readings. One of the most celebrated examples of this in modern India would be the Gandhi-Tagore correspondence that began in 1914—this time-period was a little after Tagore won the Nobel Prize for literature and a little before Gandhi returned from South Africa to take on an increasingly influential role in the nationalist movement.[64] Their letters to each other would continue over twenty-five years, and some of these letters also functioned as public debate. Both writers commented earnestly and doggedly on public issues and vital aspects of national policy—they took distinct stances. These exchanges of unfailing mutual respect and affection were dutifully shared in publications such as Modern

Review and Young India, and were faithfully followed by the rest of the nation. Equally, during the 1930s, are the influential letters (in the Hindi literary domain) between authors Premchand and Jainendra, where too the exchanges of ideas respectfully intermixed personal, literary and public disagreement.[65] Such socially attuned dialogues by well-known male public intellectuals had already been employed and developed in different ways in the late decades of the nineteenth century by women in their life narratives. They had grasped the simple clear kernel that to be heard, to convince (a judgmental public) and to be relatable, one had to speak from/of personal experience and one had to be aware of how such private confidences could gather sympathies/antipathies in print. Thereby for the women of this generation, their letters become 'idiosyncratic documents'[66] towards private-public edification (in Marathi and English) and offer an opportunity for kaleidoscopic representations.

The 'epistolary dialogues'[67] between Anandibai Joshee and Theodocia Carpenter, her host in the United States, offer glimpses of an intense personal camaraderie being woven across wide cultural difference.[68] At a time when access to publication or publicity was neither structured nor accessible to women in traditional folds, the form of the letter offered a way to address the intimate terrain for/through public support. Some letters were directly composed for journalistic forums: for instance, Rukhmabai's letter on child-marriage customs to the editor of *The Times*[69] or Pandita Rambai's letter from the Government Plague Hospital published in the *Guardian*.[70] But mostly the letters were exchanged in familiar modes, addressed to family members, even if at times they were published almost immediately in newspapers with or without the writer's full consent. This transgression of privacy was seen as justified due to the high public curiosity about unconventional women, as with Anandibai's letters to her husband about her medical education in the United States. Similarly, the letters that Atiya Fyzee wrote to her sisters (about her stay and studies in England, addressed in detail in Chapter 3) were published both in contemporary journals as well as collated later in book form.[71] The immediate family unit thereby functioned as a proxy for a wider (linguistic/regional/national) readership as the writers explored intricately nested self-representations. While a study devoted exclusively to the rhetorical flourishes of letter writing (as argument, as persuasion, as confession) by this generation of writers is not available, the rest of the chapter attempts to tease out some possibilities through a sharply focused case study of two marriages which contained pen-wielding wives (Anandibai Joshee and Rukhmabai) whose writings tug at the seams of those marriages.

Born a year or so apart from each other in mid-1860s and married as children (as was the norm) to men who deliberately or inadvertently pushed them into the public limelight, Anandibai and Rukhmabai endured scathing public deprecation for their unconventional life choices. Anandibai belonged to the Chitpavan Brahmin community, and Rukhmabai to the caste of *suthars* (carpenters). Anandibai was pushed towards a medical degree abroad by an ambitious and by all accounts cantankerous husband who likely 'hastened her death'.[72] Around the same time, Rukhmabai openly declared her preference to be sent to prison rather than cohabit with an undeserving husband, leading to a lengthy and highly publicized public trial, where her decisions were subject to the scrutiny of a court of law as well as public opinion. The former begot a son who died in infancy and the latter refused to consummate her marriage. In time they both trained to be medical doctors, though Anandibai would die of tuberculosis a month short of twenty-two, and Rukhmabai died in independent India at the advanced age of ninety. They read extensively and wrote several letters documenting their life experiences, some of which gained public scrutiny and notoriety by 'exposing' the hitherto intimate space of marriage. What follows is an analysis of key letters from Anandibai sent to her husband, which he channelled in part or full to popular publications in order to bolster public support for her cause and polish his own self-image.

Anandibai Joshee had been married at the age of nine to a twenty-six-year-old widower, a man with 'vicarious ambitions'[73] who often treated her with verbal and physical violence. At the age of twelve, she gave birth to her only child who died ten days after birth, and the pregnancy at that tender age likely affected her ability to conceive again.[74] Her husband, Gopalrao Joshee, was prone to vacillating (in his views) between the orthodox and reformist camps, which made for deep-rooted insecurity and anxiety.[75] Nonetheless, his overt and keen motivation was to be celebrated as a social reformer. Towards establishing such credentials, he began a 'Pygmalion-like process'[76] of educating his wife and pushing her to become the first Indian woman to gain a medical degree, often under circumstances of extreme duress to her.[77] Anandibai in turn expressed keenness to expand her learning and to be of service to the women of her country, especially to support their reproductive health by training as a physician. She addressed a large public gathering in Serampore in 1883 where she responded to the many questions regarding her unpopular desire to cross the oceans to study in America. At a time when women of her upper-caste community rarely left home without escorts nor mingled with strangers from other communities, Anandibai wrote to Mrs. Carpenter, her American patron, that no matter the obstacles in her path (which included social ostracism, physical or financial hardships and public protests), 'I will see America, the dream of my life, and I will stand or fall as I deserve'.[78] She achieved this goal in 1883, at the age of eighteen, when she enrolled at the Woman's Medical College of Pennsylvania.

To be a doctor in the nineteenth century, as Narin Hassan points out, a woman 'had to negotiate her identity as simultaneously objective, scientific and familial—she had to be able to compete in the masculine world of medicine *and* bring comfort to domestic realms [italics in the original]'.[79] In addition, as a solo traveller who was breaking several ironclad social conventions, Anandibai was under great pressure—as much from her own internalized value systems as from a wary public—to maintain her traditional costume and vegetarian diet. This became more acute after Pandita Ramabai, who had travelled to England at around the same time, converted to Christianity. Anandibai was held up as the perfect foil[80] to Ramabai's 'betrayal' of caste and nation. The two women were said to be related and had been in correspondence—Ramabai was invited from England to the United States to attend Anandibai's graduation and used the opportunity to promote her own projects through varied forums.

Being thus tracked and scrutinized (in newspapers back in India) while she navigated a foreign culture meant that Anandibai had to constantly establish her cultural authenticity in her letters (regarding choice of food, clothes, language). Her letters contained observations akin to an anthropologist's field notes about the host (American) culture and charted her ascent through a gruelling three-year medical training while managing the loneliness, longing and aggravations of a (temporarily) long-distance marriage. In these writings she sought to nurture personal connections with specific recipients rather than formulate documents for a newspaper readership. The earnestness of these documentations about everyday living and the inward gaze of her struggle to retain poise under duress suggest a strong inclination to privacy. Anandibai's biographer, Meera Kosambi, notes that it had not been possible to verify the language in which many of the letters were originally written (Marathi or English) since Kosambi had to translate them (into English) from a Marathi biography written by Kashibai Kanitkar, one of Anandibai's contemporaries.[81] One surmises that Kanitkar also had to translate some of these texts from English to Marathi in the first place. Irrespective of what might have been lost or gained in these back-and-forth translations, the voice of the letter writer comes through as attentive to sensory details, self-conscious about her embodied presence in different spaces, attuned to social perceptions and appropriateness, and inclined to a positive outlook in the overall self-representation of her life. One might argue that the letter writer is deftly employing a deliberated, measured and impactful *language of distances* to traverse the many geographical and affective force fields ensconcing her. Irrespective of the context or the addressee or even the length of the letter, the cadence and clarity of Anandibai's sentences make her a distinct stylist of the personal epistle.

Anandibai's first long letter to her husband was written on 25 June 1883, a little after her first arrival to the United States, and was publicized by him in the *Indian Mirror* and then reproduced by the *Theosophist*.[82] He was clearly seeking to reinforce his new celebrity status in reform circles. The letter was composed in English and lead Kosambi to surmise that it was presumably the choice of language for all the couples' subsequent correspondence.[83] There are no indications that Gopalrao had his wife's permission to publish. Equally disconcerting are some lines in the middle of this specific letter (soon after her fifty-nine-day voyage) that change tone and content, and do so noticeably (to describe 'the physiognomy of the negro' or 'the characteristic of the Arab Egyptians') which leads Kosambi to understandably wonder whether those sections had been inserted by Gopalrao.[84] Such detailing about racial differences was a common occurrence in the travel narratives of scientific expeditions in the time, but do not feature in other letters by Anandibai and hence become suspect. Irrespective of this violation of textual integrity (Gopalrao possibly rewriting his wife's letter for publication without consent), the letter was suffused with a distinct authorial persona that the young student was claiming for herself. She wrote fluently of her voyage: the absence of joy, the plentitude of trouble, the near starvation (due to her dietary restrictions as a Brahmin woman), the severe dental pain (new wisdom teeth), the racial discrimination and mockery by fellow-passengers and above all the acutest of loneliness.[85] The clear vision of the writer noted several tribulations with crisp economy and without demurring. And she was not beyond claiming resilience: 'God has given me a strong, nay, hard heart which stood, and I hope will continue to stand, any trial or difficulty in the world.'[86]

While Anandibai was working hard at medical school in Pennsylvania, her husband was embroiled in several controversies in India, especially with his superiors at work, and often wrote 'tactless letters' to her about his grievances to which she counselled patience and wisdom.[87] She was also preoccupied in facilitating his visit to the United States and sent her plans and travel advice to him in great detail. One of her suggestions was to travel with tea supplies ('The people here are quite addicted to Chinese tea') and to even explore the possibility of setting up a business exporting tea from India to America ('With honesty in business and a well-founded plan, victory and wealth will be ours').[88] On 6 July 1884, the *Mahratta* credited her with the ingenious idea of the tea business while reporting on the Amsterdam Exhibition of 1883.[89] One may thus discern how for the journalistic public, domestic financial concerns seamlessly flow into designs and hopes for an internationally networked economy. Gopalrao himself does not take up the suggestion of the business but continued to send complaints. In letter after letter, Anandibai patiently identified these resentments to take a position of self-defence or sagely pacify him with the suggestion of a healthier attitude. She was able to be as blunt as she was persuasive and diplomatic—'There is absolutely no consistency in your letters'[90]—and yet reminding him that he was a source of happiness and pride for her. The word 'love' made regular appearances in her letters to Gopalrao.[91] The safety of epistolary distances probably allowed for rhetorical contradictions—she refused to condone his prejudices even as she continued to express love and gratitude for the pathways to knowledge and professional identity that he facilitated for her. The marital waters are thus muddied with conflicting emotions, for the former child bride appeared to be talking to partner, rival, abuser and father-figure all at once. Considering what she knew of him, she could not be sure of the extent of his trust-worthiness and was explicit about her desire for privacy as well as her distrust of his attention-seeking instincts. She addressed this in one of her letters to him:

> In the letter which came last week, you have written about your intention of publishing in book form a collection of all my letters and all the newspaper accounts about me. I know that your motives are pure, but I do not think it would be proper. It will look quite ridiculous. There are those who speak well of me, but there are just as many, or more, who speak ill of me. Moreover, whatever we do is not for show. Nobody would stop us from showing off, but what purpose would it serve? Those who think it right may certainly do so; but not we. We have not made ourselves ridiculous so far. […] If you find my letters difficult to read, I have no objection to your copying them in a notebook. But I request you not to publish them.[92]

The request to refrain from publishing would be ignored, and while there is no verification of Anandibai's knowledge of several long extracts that Gopal had already fed to newspapers, the letter itself, the positioning and delivery of the request, suggested that Anandibai might have had some inkling. She was anyways receiving letters and updates from other relatives who would likely have informed her. In any case, the possibility of such a 'leak' being real is evident in the above excerpt, as also her efforts to protect her autonomy. Different aspects of her life in the United States would find their way to public forums, such as *Kesari* and *Mahratta* in Pune, the *Theosophist* of Calcutta and Madras, as well as in American newspapers, ensuring Gopalrao visibility and publicity.[93] When Anandibai shared with him a handwriting analysis that she had undergone in the United States, the details predictably appeared in an Indian newspaper editorial. However, the newspapers (and their readers) had no access to Gopalrao's bitter letters to his wife, which remained in the realm of marital intimacy. Similarly, to read some of Anandibai's letter that he did not share with the public is to witness the unfolding of entirely different, grim tale.

A letter written in early 1884, during the first year of Anandibai's medical education (which she would complete in three years), is extraordinary for the range and intensity of emotions that are tucked in the crevices of sentences. Word after word bears testimony against injustice and attempts fearless resistance to bullying of such magnitude that her stance is likely to have few parallels in the archives. There were several references to a letter she had just received from her husband and all her resultant turmoil that must be unpacked one by one. The stakes were high: 'I know only too well that the fault will be mine, if I do anything to incur public censure.'[94] She notes the 'heavy sarcasm' and 'severe criticism' evinced by Gopalrao regarding a recent photograph of hers that she had sent him—the blouse as not right, the fabric as not adequately covering one shoulder and the drape as not Maharashtrian.[95] She defended the charge of obscenity with apologies for not obtaining his consent in advance for her changed clothing, but just as quickly and methodically pointed out that there was no time to do so. The circumstances were such: the weather was harsh and she was protecting her health, the fabric had slipped inadvertently and without her awareness, and the Gujarati dress was equally a part of her national heritage. Refuting any flippancy or vanity, she stood by the decisions she had to take in unfamiliar and unfavourable circumstances.

The offending photograph itself offers evidence: a mid-waist portrait features a seated teenager who does not meet the camera eye but fixedly gazes a few inches to the left of frame—her hair neatly combed into a knot, her lips unsmiling but relaxed, her neck taut and her expression determined. She is covered from neck downwards in a dark blouse and sari, not an inch of skin to be seen apart from her face. The unfairness of Gopalrao's accusations of indelicacy is not lost on the modern viewer, as it must have also registered with Anandibai. She seized the moment to return to sites of psychic trauma—the early years of her marriage—and wrote down the brutality endured in those early years. On the screen of her letter, Gopalrao was pinned, made to revisit his past actions against her when she was just a child of ten or twelve or fourteen—hitting her with chairs and books, threatening abandonment, 'inflicting other strange punishments' (probably sexual, since it is left cryptic unlike the other assaults), till she would beg him to kill her. 'In our society, for centuries there has been no legal restraint between husbands and wives; and if it exists, it works against women!' Having registered her protest, the next paragraph seemed to withdraw from the site of marriage to a quieter introspection. As if anticipating the wonderment of some unseen reader, Anandibai reflected on why she is wont to express love for her abuser and traced further back to memories of being severely beaten by her mother with stones, sticks and live charcoal. As with many abused children, she had trained herself to cope with guilt and self-blame by professing love of some kind for her abusers—it was a problem she now claimed to understand and to never repeat with any children she might have. Even as the accusation of marital abuse was fringed by words of gratitude and supplication to her husband for his compassion and understanding, this intensely private letter was probably the most public of outrages for it refused silence and pushed to make the unspeakable visible in ink.

Anandibai graduated with her medical degree in 1886 (ranked eighth in a class of forty-two) and while still in the United States accepted a job offer at a hospital in Kolhapur in Maharashtra. However, three months after her return to India, following a diagnosis of tuberculosis and deteriorating health, she died in February 1887. According to Caroline Healey Dall, the earliest biographer of Anandibai, her last audible words were, 'I have done all that I could.'[96] These words are not attributed or recorded; they may even be imagined keeping in line with the romanticized approach to Anandibai's life narrative, but it is a testament nonetheless to a reputation of grit and ambition that would endure.

Assertions, contradictions and speaking of law: Rukhmabai's "Reply" (1887)

The same year that saw the end of Anandibai's promising life and career was equally notable in the history of women's rights in Maharashtra for a libel case that was fuelled by public debates around Age of Consent (legal marriageable age for a girl child) and conjugal rights.[97] On 29 June 1887, Rukhmabai, a resident of Bombay, composed a 'Reply' in response to a pamphlet circulated by her estranged husband that was titled 'An Exposition of Some of the Facts of the Case of *Dadajee vs. Rukhmabai*'.[98] Rukhmabai's 'Reply' was published in *The Times of India* and the *Bombay Gazette* and merits being read as a blended genre that is essay, letter, memoir and tract. The historian Sudhir Chandra's detailed presentation of deliberations from the courthouses, on public forums and within kinship circles offer multiple insights on this landmark case for restitution of conjugal rights and of the stance taken by Rukhmabai.[99] In light of this context, the 'Reply' needs to be read as a composition of dissent, particularly in the mode of the public essay, and as a feminist response to the available jurisprudence. One may further interrogate the tonal palette of Rukhmabai's essay as displaying a virtuosic range—from sarcasm and mockery, to argument and defiance—and featuring several registers of address, including the colonial government, legal system, social circles and belligerent relatives. The legal arguments in this instance were nearly continuous with the familial and conjugal disagreements, and the writer had to defend the right to public dissent with the knowledge that there would be repercussions for the writing (dissenting) woman.

The document in its opening paragraphs featured a table with two columns: the one on the left was titled 'Assertion', below which were stacked nine details from the pamphlet ('Exposition') circulated by her husband and his supporters. Rukhmabai prefaced these claims to be in actuality 'fictions, pure and simple',[100] which must be refuted. Thus the column on the right titled 'Contradiction', which sought to undo the 'fictions' with nine corresponding clarifications or truths that she wished to protect and present. Nowhere was this starker than on the ninth and last 'Assertion' by Dadajee and 'Contradiction' by Rukhmabai, which was presented thus:[101]

	Assertion	Contradiction
9.	I have never quarreled with Rukhmabai, nor have I given her occasion to dislike me.	There is some truth in the first assertion, the other is untrue.

Rukhmabai's stance vis-à-vis her husband's declaration about conflict and agreeableness was as pithy as it is absolute. She disliked him and he had given enough cause. The rest of the essay expands, illustrates and weighs in on all nine claims and counter-claims, towards a singular intent—resisting the forced wifedom and exposing falsehoods of those who want to browbeat her into submission. She noted her husband's behaviour as such that her 'aversion for him was firmly settled' and she had made up her mind 'to wash my hands of him for ever'.[102] Such sentiments and situations were not uncommon especially when child marriages were the norm and women were compelled to adjust to inhumane demands on their body and labour. But it was the first time in India that a woman had written frankly to a mass readership about her repugnance of a marital arrangement and had endured a long humiliating legal battle to be free of the said offending husband. The document being studied in this section demonstrates a proficient co-opting of the language of law and legality, in particular its argumentative structure and delivery—a unique strategy for an unequalled situation.

On the printed page, the two columns (Assertion and Contradiction) of the essay visually form an unbridgeable divide, as had been the situation between husband and wife. The writing equally draws from and reinforces the courtroom positional binaries of plaintiff and defendant, of evidence and alibi, of testimony and cross-examination, of charge and verdict. In other words, not only was Rukhmabai fighting for the right to permanently sever from her husband, both in the court of law and through intense lobbying in multiple newspapers, she was unabashedly and skilfully borrowing the rhetorical strategies from the legal system in constructing her essays.

Apart from the 'Reply', Rukhmabai had authored two other public documents: both essays in the form of letters to editors that appeared under a pseudonym ('A Hindu woman') with sufficient details to reveal her identity. Of these, the 'Reply' made the most audacious move (and perhaps a desperate one, in the given circumstances) of explicitly naming people and incidents. As a result, a case of libel was filed against Rukhmabai, separate from and in addition to the long ongoing litigation (1884–8) to be free of her conjugal connections. To orient to these multiple legal troubles that necessitated and preserved her essayistic voice, one would have to turn to Rukmabai's childhood and upbringing.

Having lost her biological father at the age of two and a half, Rukhmabai was raised by her stepfather—'an eminent medical man known for his reformist predisposition.'[103] Unlike the Chitpavan Brahmin[104] community previously discussed (to which Anandibai Joshee and Pandita Ramabai belonged), Rukhmabai's Suthar community permitted widow remarriage.[105] Not only did Rukhmabai receive ownership of her deceased father's property, her stepfather Dr Sakharam Arjun ensured that she had access to colonial education and kept delaying the ritual consummation of her marriage that is traditionally allowed when the wife attains puberty. Rukhmabai was eleven years old when her marriage had been solemnized to the nineteen-year-old Dadajee Bhikajee, with the understanding that the groom would live with his in-laws to receive an education and train for a profession. Despite the family's best intentions to groom him into a suitable partner for Rukhmabai, Dadajee turned out to be slovenly in his studies, began to keep poor company, displayed indolent behavior, lived on the largesse of other people, and was hence considered an irresponsible adult. As he turned thirty, he was instigated by an uncle with questionable morals to lay claims to his conjugal rights and to Rukhmabai's property. Meanwhile, Rukhmabai was making rapid progress in an education conducted at home and proved to be an avid and intelligent learner. She lamented being deprived access to conventional schooling in the 'only confessional moment' in her long letter on child marriage published in the *Times of India*: 'This wicked practice [child marriage] has destroyed the happiness of my life. It comes between me and the thing which I prize above all others—study and mental cultivation.'[106] It is evident that her distaste for marriage was as much with the inherent prejudices of the institution itself as much as with the man who had been selected for her. With Rukhmabai firmly refusing to accept married life with Dadajee, and with his growing desperation to have access to her property, Dadajee's well-wishers and other traditionalists supported him to file for legal action for 'restitution of conjugal rights' or rather to compel Rukhmabai to cohabit and consummate their marriage. At the time of this notice, Dadajee was residing at the house of his uncle. Rukhmabai refused to comply and hired solicitors who helped frame her argument against her husband—he did not have a means of livelihood to provide for her, or a house of his own, and his health (after contracting tuberculosis) was such that she could not live safely with him. To read the charges exchanged on both sides is to quickly discern that if Rukhmabai were to compromise on any point, she would have to forfeit her entire ethical stance and lose considerable control of her well-being—the battle thus was as much for reputation as it was for financial power or intellectual freedom or the crucial matter of consent in cohabitation and sexual obligations. As the case unfolded, the public came to be strongly divided into camps: 'Some turned her into an icon; a martyr to suffering sisterhood. Other saw personified in her their worst fears about "modernized" women subverting family and society.'[107] Sudhir Chandra, the historian and biographer of Rukhmabai, thus examines the legal situation involving Rukhmabai and Dadajee to be shifting patterns between internal variations and contradictions of three separate discourses: the orthodox/reactionary, the imperialist and the reformist.

A crucial landmark in the judicial history of colonial India, the case involving Rukhmabai and Dadajee brought to the fore 'unresolved tensions between justice and law' and became an 'illustration of the inescapability of injustice as law took precedence over justice'.[108] In other words, the question of what was just/moral/ethical could be completely misaligned with what was legal—and the price for this would be paid by people such as Rukhmabai. During the course of the litigation, Rukhmabai lost her stepfather (in 1885) but continued to represent her views on the injustices born by Indian women due to early marriage in two letters published in the newspapers.[109] At a time when a girl's legal age for conjugal relations was ten, with the Hindu orthodoxy loath to move it up by even a year, Rukhmabai's letter boldly proposed fifteen years for girls and twenty for boys, speaking repeatedly of a 'longed-for freedom' for 'millions of daughters of India'.[110] The publications were seen by many as a strategic move to influence the outcome of her trial.

During the deliberations, Judge Pinhey was sympathetic to the moral weight of Rukhmabai's argument[111] and his comments in court demonstrated his conviction in the dignity and freedom of choice for Indian women. He rejected Dadajee's appeal and 'immediately aroused diametrically opposed reactions [...] No longer two anonymous litigants, the wife and husband now emblematized two opposing socio-cultural positions which their private dispute had helped sharpen'.[112] Several stakeholders (the liberals, the orthodoxy and women's rights advocates in India and in Britain) simultaneously pressured the colonial government to either support or penalize Rukhmabai's stance,[113] and turned the case into 'something of an ideological football'.[114] The metropolitan press in Britain brandished the case as evidence of the necessity of imperial rule in India just as an Indian nationalism was itself emerging.[115] For the Hindu orthodoxy in particular, the judgment had overstepped its legal mandate into matters of religious beliefs and traditional practices and the colonial government was cautious towards these charges of interference in indigenous laws and usages which had been sought to be minimal after 1857.[116] The commentaries on the case in the Marathi newspapers, particularly from the key nationalist figures such as Balagangadhar Tilak (1856–1920), were persistently and powerfully on the offensive towards Rukhmabai, such that she 'became a folk devil, a sign of evil "westernised" modernity, for a wide spectrum of Hindus all over India'.[117] Far from being passive in this discursive melee replete with vicious personal attacks, Rukhmabai had to strive to ensure that her voice was heard through publications sympathetic to her.

In response, Dadajee was advised by vested interests to file for an appeal in 1886 and the case was heard by two of the most senior judges of the Bombay High Court who in turn upheld Dadajee's appeal. Then followed an unexpected and extraordinary response from Rukhmabai. She rejected the court directive to live with Dadajee and opted to face the repercussions—six months in jail or attachment of property or both—and thus offered an impressive case of passive resistance before it 'had captured either political theory or popular imagination'.[118] In any case, it was a clear moral victory for Rukhmabai.

It can be argued that even more than her two public letters on the injustices borne by Indian women, or the two landmark court cases (the first verdict supporting her and the second in favour of her husband), it is this essay ('Reply') that offers uninterrupted vistas to the churn of emotions that had become Rukhmabai's lot. Although it was just as deftly structured as the argument of the public letters, the pace of the 'Reply' had an immediacy that was unafraid to be too deeply indignant, even reckless. Her affective responses were given primacy over what her readers might consider propriety. Yet, the legal entanglements having come to define her marriage in the public debates, Rukhmabai tilts the opening pitch of the document fully into the judicial mode. First, the charge(s) that had necessitated this defense in the court of public opinion get addressed. This charge in the 'Exposition' she mentions as having been circulated with 'the signature of Mr. Dadajee'—the mention of the attribution (signature) rather than authorship—was to quickly establish that Rukhmabai was responding not to her husband's words but to a ghostwriter who wished to present Dadajee as a defender of Hindu religion.[119] She writes of her certainty: 'Mr Dadajee cannot write or well understand

English'[120] and the many cultural references made under his name would also be unknown to him—she herself was in 'an exceptionally delicate position'[121] as she was exposing herself to further abuse in her own name and with her own words. There are multiple references in the essay to 'the person who writes for Mr. Dadajee' or 'Mr. Dadajee's writer', and the sustained repetition of this nomenclature ensured the reader remembered that the other side does not even speak for itself but is a proxy, while her integrity and her words are her own.

Thus are presented the nine points (mentioned earlier) that get split into the two columns of 'Assertion' and 'Contradiction'—the latter is tonally a counter-assertion (not just refuting but reinforcing the other side of the story).[122] While all the nine points are around 'facts' that need verifying or correcting, the nature of these facts bear all the varying shades of interpretation that might come up in a courtroom cross-examination. When Dadajee's assertion was that Rukhmabai was thirteen years at the time of marriage and that the marriage was sought by the bride's family, the counter-assertion was that the bride was actually eleven and the marriage had been the initiative of the groom's mother. At times the counter-argument turned threadbare and highly subjective: to Dadajee's claim that his health had been and continued to be 'sound' (Assertion No 4), Rukhmabai offered only two words in response: 'Quite untrue.' The reader registers this and is being prepared for a longer explanation on this matter later in the document. But the verification of the claims starts to get more muddled around the question of her property and his financial status (Assertions No. 5, 6 and 7): Rukhmabai insisted her property was worth not even half of what he claimed, nor was it in the charge of her mother and grandfather. As for Dadajee's circumstances, 'his family house was broken and he went to live with persons of objectionable surroundings'. The words (and domestic image) of 'family house' features a second time in the immediately succeeding 'Contradiction' (Rukhmabai's stance) but not in Dadajee's testimony—this eighth assertion by him (as selected by Rukhmabai) is a one-lined sentiment: 'I asked for the removal of my wife to my family house.' This sentence, unlike all the other assertions, offered nothing to refute. On the contrary it had been a truth that everyone familiar with the case would unequivocally concede since Mr. Dadajee had gone to court precisely to insist on cohabitation with Rukhmabai. But it is here that the author's lawyerly inclinations shine and the writing gets an apt touch of nimble wit and wry humour: 'This is a misnomer. Mr Dadajee had no family house. As he correctly puts it, in his plaint, what he should say is the "house he resided in."' It was not a matter that merited repeating (this lack of a family or house), and yet her words pushed for it, elevating the rhetorical quality of the document from fact-checking to a linguistic and moral triumph—here is irony and derision reminiscent of Tarabai Shinde.

The document's main provocation (for the libel case) was Rukhmabai's disclosure of the rot in another marriage in the family—the uncle (who was supporting Dadajee) had a mistress who was living in the same house for fourteen years and the uncle's behaviour had once caused his wife to jump into a well. Rukhmabai declared that she did not wish to live in the same house as the companion of this uncle's mistress. The people who were judging and harassing Rukhmabai for rejecting an oppressive marriage were demonstrated to be morally bankrupt, their own marriages in shambles. Similarly Dadajee, who believed in them, had been just as unreliable, for he neither earned as much as he said he did, nor was he honest in his court statements. The credibility and credentials of the accusers were thus swiftly dismantled. Aware of standing apart from her peers and yet being unluckier than them, Rukhmabai asked, 'Had there not been scores of cases in our caste, where wives had to refuse to live with their husbands? But those husbands had not, like Mr. Dadajee, prosecuted their wives, served them with solicitors' notices, and dragged them to Court.'[123] During those four years of litigation, Rukhmabai and Dadajee had to confront each other as irreconcilable individuals but also as representing and safeguarding interests of their respective genders within a shared social institution. And towards this, one must return yet again to the question of authorship for Rukhmbai herself does so in her 'Reply'.

Both Dadajee's 'Exposition' and Rukhmabai's 'Reply' are documents that bear the imprints of other (sympathetically aligned) writers. The historian Sudhir Chandra notes that while there are 'marks of external revision' on Rukhmabai's writing, 'it bore the stamp of her conviction, courage, and pain, whereas neither the reasoning nor the sedulous flourish of the "Exposition" belonged to Dadajee'.[124] After elaborating on all the nine 'Contradictions' that she offered in the initial tabular form to Dadajee's 'Assertions', Rukhmabai introduced a new objection—about insinuations around her ability to comprehend and employ language or writing—that appeared to annoy and offend her, a noticeably different consternation than the accusation of abandoning wifely duties. The writer of Dadajee's 'Exposition' declares that Rukhmabai did not understand her own statement because it was in English and she had signed it in Marathi, without mentioning that it had been the protocol followed by the authorities of the day. It is hard to say what riles her more—the devaluation of her comprehension skills or her language skills (and thereby education) being compared with Dadajee whose abandonment of education she had repeatedly disparaged. Dadajee's text had taunted, 'all I contend is that Rukhmabai is by no means my intellectual superior' and that his notes were composed by himself in English although 'revised by a male friend'.[125] In response, Rukhmabai had to provide several examples of the factual inaccuracies in Dadajee's statements under oath in court in comparison with those made in the 'Exposition'. She had to then defend her authorship as 'A Hindu lady' of the much-discussed letters to the *Times of India* because the 'Exposition' doubts the veracity of its voice. This is personal in a new way, as we can see from the equally personal address and accusation: 'I wonder if Mr. Dadajee understands the words he uses. Has Mr. Dadajee read my letters?'[126] Under no circumstances, she claimed, did she avail the services of a proxy writer nor did she plagiarize—her language and her ideas, she wanted it to be known, are very much her own. She noted that she had clearly acknowledged (at the start of the first letter) that she was accepting 'literary help' and 'correction' where necessary from a kindly friend who cared for the cause of women, and that she had been writing on the subject in vernacular newspaper long before they came into prominence in English publications.

The 'Reply' ended with a postscript that returned to the ethics of authorship, not of the author's text, but of the 'Exposition'—Rukhmabai had guessed the identity of the writer. It being similar in 'style of thought and writing' to another contemporaneous text, she noted 'a certain young Hindu doctor' who had been dependent on the goodwill of her stepfather in the past. Rukhmabai had decided to hold nothing back in defending her righteous stance in the 'Reply' but the libel case was just as degrading as the 'Exposition'. The proceedings and the strategies of Dadajee's legal team to put the twenty-five-year-old woman in a 'prurient male gaze'[127] as frequently as possible caused her intense harassment.[128] Fortunately for her, in the judgment on 24 September 1887, the magistrate found no evidence of either legal or actual malice in the libel case over her 'Reply' and acquitted Rukhmabai.[129] This was a vital but minor reprieve because the main court case (regarding Dadajee's marital claims to her personhood and property) was yet to be resolved and came to a boil when the court sided with Dadajee—one must recall that she had decided to risk being put in prison rather than live with him. The (in)famous legal battle resulted in a compromise brokered at the end of July 1888, ending 'the way it had begun—as a private marital dispute—leaving unresolved the momentous issues it had raised'[130] regarding women's rights in marriages. And yet, the extensive media coverage in Britain, the involvement of Queen Victoria (who issued a royal decree preventing Rukhmabai's imprisonment), and public outcry in India 'made it imperative at last to rewrite the narrative of love and pleasure in the language of force'.[131] By insisting on the non-negotiability of her rejection of a marriage and a partner that she found repugnant, Rukhmabai had forced open 'the sexual double standard'[132] of Hindu conjugality and she deserves credit for positively impacting the campaign to revise the minimum age of marriage for girls from ten years to twelve years, leading to the modified Age of Consent Act of 1891.

Rukhmabai did not have to go to prison, for Dadajee agreed to drop his charges in exchange for two thousand rupees towards his legal costs. Exhausted and humiliated with the public spectacle she had become during this hard-fought legal freedom, Rukhmabai decided to leave for England (in the following year) to study medicine, while Dadajee married another woman. There is cause to wonder how strongly she associated her authorial persona with her courtroom battles, for while she continued to serve the public as a practicing physician (after returning to India on the successful completion of her medical studies in 1893), there are few records of her life in her own words made available to readers even though she lived to see independent India. It is only right that both speech and silence are acknowledged as powerful choices and well-earned entitlements of her long legacy of public service in letters, law and medicine. As the remaining chapters of the book demonstrate, attention must be paid to the sheer variety of ways in which women articulated their freedoms over the course of the anti-colonial movement. It is to some of these other dimensions of this enunciation (life-writing, performance, romance) that the following chapter will address.

2

The Memoirist, the Dramatist and the Novelist

In an essay titled 'The Better Half' published in 1904, Rokeya Sakhawat Hossain, a noteworthy writer from Bengal, mocked any idealization of marriage, especially in comparison with the Victorian rhetoric of partnership.[1] She invited readers to imagine themselves as having two halves—the right half as male and the left as female—and to then gaze at their full-figure reflection in a large mirror. The writer's mockery of such a body (and reflection)—the male side with high shoulders, long arms, large foot and 'elephant ears', while the female side with slim arms, low shoulders, small feet and ears 'like that of an ass'—established that there can be no 'better half' or an integrated whole in a marriage—she cited this as analogous to India's difficulties on the path of development.[2] Not long after this essay, Rokeya published *Sultana's Dream* (1905), a long story/novella in English, to imagine a utopian feminist country where women reap the benefits of education (under the stewardship of a wise Queen) to establish progressive governance, while men in the kingdom are secluded and relegated to mundane chores. The audacious capsizal and reversal of gender roles in fiction in a manner that is unattainable in society has resonances with a similar imagination of a Utopian kingdom in a Marathi novel that came to public attention around the same time—Kashibai Kanitkar's *Palkhincha Gonda* (The Palanquin Tassel) was published serially between 1889 and 1928. This advent of feminist utopian fiction as a mode of social critique by writers of the same generation, albeit in opposite geographic and linguistic regions of the country, is significant. Such Utopian imaginings that often represent a quest for community 'come to reflect discussions about the progressive or regressive aspects of historical development in a microcosm'.[3] The claiming of equality—of imagination if not of social status—in fiction conjuring utopic societies, therefore, suggests the anxieties of social atrophy inherent in gender debates from which no aesthetic can emerge untouched.

The 'persuasive rhetoric of British liberalism' saw women's education as a necessity for social transformation[4] and had been debated (hence reinforced as cardinal in the public mind) parallel to three momentous legal campaigns in Bengal, each laced with the rhetoric of gender justice—the Bengal Sati Regulation Act of 1829, the Hindu Widows' Remarriage Act of 1856 and the Age of Consent Act of 1891. All three campaigns, accompanied by several headwinds and tailwinds of public deliberations around propriety and native pride, spanned the length of the nineteenth century—the preoccupations mainly with challenges faced by children forced into sexual intimacy with adult husbands and their fate when widowed—the institution of marriage (implicitly of upper caste Hindus) as the unmistakable discursive keystone. Scholars such as Lata Mani, Geraldine Forbes and Tanika Sarkar have extensively studied the contentious nexuses drawn between marriage and law, or marriage and education, and the present study further extends to enunciations around marriage and women's literary and artistic output. This would include situations when marriage (depicted at times as social imprisonment and at other times as companionate relationship) is rendered invisible or cloaked in proxy terms, as with the theatre artist and author Binodini Dasi, who wrote as a single woman about relationships outside the marital fold. While Rashsundari and Binodini choose to claim experiences through personal testimonials (the word *amar* or 'my/mine' featuring in the titles of both their autobiographies), the entanglements between a woman's artistic leanings and the seeming inevitability of marriage are both idealized and bemoaned. These two autobiographical texts, alongside a more explicitly formulated fictionalized mode by another contemporary, Swarnakumari Debi Ghosal, constitute the chief elements of this chapter. One might further notice that in all these cases, marriage/singlehood is often a smoke screen to sexuality—the authors task language with making intensely private longings visible to a public eye, a risk that they both take and mitigate through textual artifice.

The childhood of nearly every girl born in nineteenth-century Bengal was oriented towards a marriage arranged by the family before the onset of puberty, and equally prevalent was the superstition that a girl seeking literacy would cause her husband's death or create familial unhappiness.[5] At a time when widowhood was 'rendered intolerable in every possible way',[6] and widow remarriage was strictly forbidden for the upper castes and most of the middle-ranking castes,[7] the efforts of some women to pursue knowledge 'was tantamount to suicide'.[8] The choice to read or not to read was indeed presented to the girl child as a matter of life and death. And yet, what appeared to be a social annihilation was also the space for the aspirational self, unafraid to court 'an illicit passion'[9] carved by language. This relationship with a forbidden pleasure that suggested dangerous outcomes (scathing social judgement, alongside the looming threats of widowhood) may be seen as an inevitable outcome of a determined striving: first for literacy, and subsequently for artistic expression and publication. Apart from the popular genre of poetry, the *Bengal Literary Catalogue of Books* records publications (by women in Bengal between 1850 and 1900) under categories of art, biography, drama, fiction, history, language, miscellaneous, philosophy religion, science and travel—likely encouraged by the development of the vernacular prose structure that eschewed the formal syntax and grammar of the classical tradition.[10] This chapter argues for a closer look at how the writer conceives genre, as well as the nesting of literary styles that construct the primary genre and feature reflections on her style. For instance, the thematic and stylistic contours of the dream-narrative by Rashsundari Debi can be read as a sub-genre within the canopy-genre of the autobiography—the author presents an (other) worldly experience through a stylized, selective recollection (via sleep, via death) that establishes an 'ordinary life' as actually distinct and deserving of a memoir status. Similarly, Binodini Das writes an autobiography in the idiom of theatre and operatic intensity—a retrospective, reflective, yet assertive recounting of a high-visibility profession (acting) in which she had attained unprecedented repute. Finally, Swanakumari Debi Ghosal recasts the novel of courtship to imagine what might have felt like the unimaginable in her milieu—an educated young woman who speaks of singlehood past the culturally prescribed age for marriage. This narrator is an active participant in encounters with more than one suitor, even as the readers understand these suitors to be incidental, the spotlight of the telling falling upon her investment in the experience of love itself. The divergent lives and creative styles of these three writers who entered a highly competitive (and male) artistic sphere can be seen manifesting into equally adventurous models of imaginative language and literary form.

The interlocutor of dreams: Rashsundari Debi's *Amar Jiban* (1897)

> *It was as if my mind had sprouted six arms. Two of them served the whole household, so that none should be unhappy. Two others were clutching my sons close to my heart. But the other two thrust themselves up to reach out to the moon. Really, my own mind amazes me!*[11]

This dexterous mind with its figurative arms reaching for the moon belonged to Rashsundari Debi (the author of *Amar Jiban*, studied later in this chapter) and the amazement of such an audacious reaching for education—as luring and as dauntingly distant as the moon—is a matter with considerable import. Despite the lack of access to formal schooling, Rashsundari had taught herself to read and write within the confines of a busy household, and composed an autobiography that became the first of its kind in modern prose in India. In order to tell a story that has not been told before—that is, Rashsundari's own individuated experience as well as that of a woman in her social position as an upper-caste, married woman—a textual architecture needs to be configured that overlaps genres, and is chiefly composed of small vignettes. Most of the fifteen short narrative fragments that meld verse and prose in the form of 'compositions' rather than chapters start with a verse invocation to the divine followed by crisp distilled remembrances of the author's life in prose. The strong position of a subject in the opening sentence—'I was born …'—may have the gesture of a Victorian novel (say, *David Copperfield*)[12] and certainly it is a commitment to enunciate a lived experience, but it is soon clear that the motivation of the telling is a courtship of two pursuits that hold immense value to the author—the grace of the divine, and the ability to read and write. Both these pursuits align in the narrative arc of *My Life*, for Rashsundari Debi claimed to seek literacy in order to read books that praise God, and expressed gratitude to God's benevolence for helping her to both attain and then maintain her prized literacy. She thus offered an emphatic provenance of her text, a writing self she could offer to a reading eye. This section spotlights the autobiographic impulse betwixt two dream-narratives—the first dream early in the narrative offered as inspiration towards her literacy, and the second towards the end as a clairvoyant anticipation of grief. Towards the end of the text, Rashsundari directly addresses the nature of dreams and dreaming:

> Truly, people dream of the strangest things. When they wake up, however, all is gone. Likewise, all that you had in this world vanishes before your very eyes, so that, later, it feels as if it all had been a dream. There are two kinds of dreams: one that you see when you are awake, and one that you see in your sleep.[13]

In a swift shift of address and perspective from the third-person to the second-person voice, these lines from Rashsundari Debi's *Amar Jiban* (My Life) pose a literary riddle around the tenuous links between representations of sleep and wakefulness and the gestation of desires in narratives of recollection. Here the gains of hard-fought life battles are envisaged as given to dissolution, similar to a dream outside the realm of sleep—one must consider why the agentiality of aspiration merits a rhetorical entanglement with the strange involuntariness of dreams. The circumstances of Rashsundari's life could be seen as largely 'uneventful, unremarkable'[14] except for the creation of a book-length autobiography—the first in the Bengali language and it would be more than two decades before the next (by an eminent male litterateur) would be published.[15] Rashsundari accomplished this in 1868, her fifty-ninth year and noticeably also the year of her widowhood. This first edition has been elusive to scholars and the more popular revised edition of 1897, with its important introduction by Jyotirindranath Tagore, is the text studied here.[16]

Mostly a linear record of Rashsundari's experiences, the resultant self-portrait in *My Life* included mentions of social roles (daughter, wife, mother) but primarily foregrounded the supplication of a devotee driven by the vision of a persuasive scribe. The better-known version of the text, published in 1897 when the author was eighty-eight years old, comprised of two parts—this present analysis focuses on the first part which has mostly been translated in full.[17] The historian and translator of the autobiography, Tanika Sarkar, provides an exemplary detailed reconstruction of the different contexts, both historical and literary, in the genesis of the text, while arguing for Rashsundari's 'compulsive yet hesitant move towards self-disclosure and self-creation [as] a profoundly modern possibility'.[18] One is inclined to agree on Rashsundari's compulsions, self-creation and steps to modernity, but the quality of hesitation might require a more detailed examination. As a pioneer of a genre and with no comparable peers, Rashsundari speaks the language of hesitation, but in her literary treatment of her life, especially through a repeated engagement with (un)certainty, the writer's tenacity is on display. In fact, with her self-awareness of being a woman who first became a reader and then a writer with minimal access to education or books, Rashsundari presented her life as singular and yet commonplace at the same time, just as she repeatedly projected herself as both an extremely fearful person but also proudly heroic. Such extremities of affect and outcome encourage pertinent questions of literary form: Why did Rashsundari choose to cast the dream-narrative simultaneously as metaphoric, factual and narrative? Why the insistence on two categories of dreams (one seen within sleep and another during waking) all the while evoking the affect of loss? Could it be that the entirety of Rashsundari's autobiography was a sustained scribal dream-narrative that chips away at a reader's assumption about reality being more concrete than dreams even as the latter was asserted as being more potent, especially in its drive and transformation to writing? Additionally, the fragmentation inherent in dreams recollected upon waking gets mirrored in the design of the text that is highly selective about the memories it shares or omits or dims. For instance, the husband of several decades is barely a shadow presence in domestic events narrated. The diegetic discernment makes Rashsundari a proto-memoirist, moving away from the older conventions of the autobiography as a structured representation of a lifetime, towards the stylistic intonations and selectiveness of the literary modernists of the twentieth century—in this she is clearly extraordinarily ahead of her time.

A curious parallel worth a quick addendum is the earliest known autobiography in the English language—*The Book of Margery Kemp* (1436) records the experiences of an unlettered pilgrim, a woman who repeatedly seeks to detach herself (in her presentation of her life) from her domestic fetters and instead proactively seeks divine benediction.[19] While Margery Kempe began her life narrative *media res* from an episode of sickness following the birth of a child in her early twenties (suggestive of post-partum depression), Rashsundari's text opened with a modulated retrospective voice—'I recount whatever little comes back to me.'[20] The 'lone, heroic'[21] recounting voice led directly to an unsteady childhood of many terrors and silences, bolstered only by the love of her mother. Rashsundari wrote of having a lisp, of being beaten up secretly by other children and of living in constant terror, of bursting into tears in the presence of any loud voice. She insisted, 'Really there was no child as nervous as I'[22] and her dread was oppressive—it involved endless brooding, the loss of all joy in living and 'a nameless pain' that did not give respite for even a moment.[23] The occasion of her upcoming marriage (at the age of twelve) was the immediate cause of distress for the fatherless child who would be separated from her mother as well as the comfort and familiarity of her childhood home. In the midst of these multiple closely packed references to fears and tears, Rashsundari turned to the memory of time spent around a 'memsahib' who taught at the vernacular school in the precincts of the family house, giving the child a chance to hear and absorb the recitation of alphabets. The first composition of *My Life* thus gets constructed with a childhood of debilitating anxieties as the central point and with elementary education as its emancipatory counterpoint. The overall design of the text works through a potent leitmotif—of prison (bondage) and animals in captivity—that functions as links between fearful silences and the breaching of such silences. As recounted in the fourth composition, 'I gradually became tamed. I was their pet bird. Memories of my childhood are but a heap of rubbish. However, I have gone and set them down.'[24] One must consider that this anchoring of the visceral suffering in the prison of her daily reality was also a preparation for the release and freedom of the dream-narrative that would be presented in the sixth composition.

The memoirist voice traverses twenty-five years between the first composition that introduced Rashsundari's early years with her mother to the sixth composition when she became 'possessed by a single wish: I will learn to read.'[25] Alongside her childhood fears, the narrator bemoans her first experiences of wedlock and the unfamiliar environs of her marital home, as the writing gets increasingly punctuated by metaphors of animals in captivity—the sacrificial goat at the altar,[26] the bird in a cage,[27] the fish in a net,[28] the bullock yoked to the oil press. The last of these was also a direct reference to the veil that she was compelled to wear and that reached down to her chest: 'My eyes were covered, like the eyes of the oil presser's bullock.

I had to look down, all I could see were my own toes. This was how young married women were supposed to work. And I worked that way too.'[29] Thus single-handedly managing a household of around twenty-five people, cooking for them through the day, birthing and raising twelve children, caregiving for a blind mother-in-law, Rashsundari depicted the unpaid, unappreciated 'life of labour'[30] that at times had deprived her of food and at other times would not allow her to visit her dying mother. The last line preceding the sixth composition is heartbreakingly stark—'I was shut up in a cage'[31]—and primes the reader for the opening of the cage, albeit through literacy, and through a dream that Rashsundari credits with leading her to the first (religious) manuscript that she desired to read.[32] The dream itself comprised a single act—reading—and was reported in a single sentence. The rest of the dream was about its residue upon the dreamer's waking—the 'unearthly joy' and divine grace promised by the dream:

> Then I had a dream: I was reading the manuscript of *Chaitanya Bhagabat*. When I woke up, an unearthly joy possessed my body and heart. I kept closing my eyes even when I was fully awake. I kept going back to the memory of the dream. It was as if I had been given a priceless jewel. [...] I had never seen this book before, I wouldn't even recognize it. Yet I was reading it in my dreams, I can read nothing at all, let along something like this, it is impossible. Even then, I am blessed that I was at least able to read it in my dream. Since I am always praying to God to teach me to read, he has allowed me to do so in my dream, for he never actually did teach me.[33]

The impossible was written as a dream whose visceral quality spilt over into waking hours and carried for the dreamer the approval of divinity. In her version of events, God approved but did not teach, because it was important to Rashsundari to reiterate that she was self-taught. The progression of this self-teaching gets explained in careful detail—she hid a page of the manuscript in the kitchen to glance at while cooking; she also hid one of the palm leaves on which her son was practicing his letters; she then matched letters on the palm leaves to the sounds of the letters she remembered from her childhood schoolroom; she also matched words with what she would hear during the day to her hidden manuscript page. It was an excruciatingly slow and difficult path to literacy. 'All day, I would try to go through this in my mind. With tremendous care and effort and over a long stretch of time, I learnt somehow to limp and stammer across *Chaitanya Bhagabat*.'[34] Hard-fought desire put the allure of dreams as continuous with the constricting reality of being a householder with innumerable duties. Thus when Rashsundari asked herself and the reader the rhetorical question—'Why cherish an impossible dream?'[35]—it followed that the dream seen in sleep must alchemise from a waking desire to an ambition realized.

Despite this breakthrough with her reading practice, Rashsundari's textual self-representation continued to place the act of courage (self-educating despite social disapproval) in sharp contrast to ongoing fears of rebuke and criticism—'Truly my fears were my worst enemy. I was always afraid. I feared everything.'[36] Reinforcing the severity of her constant nervousness, Rashsundari dedicated considerable space in the seventh composition to demonstrate how she was afraid to be seen even by a horse that belonged to her husband. But the retrospective voice (of the octogenarian memoirist) abandoned the storytelling linearity to reflect on an immediate time (as she is composing the text) when the fears had been replaced by fearlessness: 'Now I fear nothing.'[37] In this eighth composition, Rashsundari credited the materialization of her desires and erasure of her fears to God, but it was not the last note on the matter, for the author's own efforts continued to have primacy—she took the bolder step of reading aloud to other women while they remained watchful of any intruders into their literary pleasures.

Having thus announced her literacy to her immediate peers and having made her way through the few books in the house to her satisfaction, Rashsundari longed for more. She petitioned her sons to send her a specific religious text that she wished to read so keenly that she 'felt quite ill with longing.'[38] This longing resulted in her receiving her first printed book that required to be read with more effort since the small letters were different from the handwritten manuscripts she had handled till then. The gap in the narrative timeline of the text between Rashsundari's encounter with print culture as a reader and her ability to write her own words collapses to barely a page. Rashsundari revealed that while visiting her son's house, she finally had access to writing materials and the leisure to write. The author was thus making her debut, and to ensure the reader fully absorbed this momentousness, the tenth composition that followed contained a quick recapitulation of her life and ended with the death of her husband (he gets referred to in the text only as *Karta* or master, as was the norm). It is worth noting that this loss was described in the mode of 'a social catastrophe, not a personal tragedy'.[39] The scene was set for the text to move towards its own last pages, which seemed to offer more than one conclusion.

The last and fifteenth composition of *My Life*—a 'self-consciously formal obituary report'[40] of her husband—was prefaced by an apologia for not sparing words for him in her autobiography. This reserved conclusion suggests that the previous (fourteenth) composition was most likely the conclusion that Rashsundari would have preferred, and there are several clues to support this inference, especially the finality of the framing: 'Anyway, I have written about what I have seen. This is a partial account of the sixty years of my life.'[41] The writing was not only underscored with veracity (the chronicler who bore witness to first-hand experiences) but was an edited version of a long life. Rashsundari was also inclined to balance the pride in her authorship with a note of modesty. The name given to her in childhood, she wrote, had been subsumed into the generic name of 'mother', not just of her children but also to everybody around her—her age and gender giving her a community status just as authorship had individuated her. It was followed by a final oblique and muted reference to writing and identity in the last lines of the composition: 'This is the account of my life upto this point. Another account will be written at the time of my death.'[42] The meta-repetition of the text being a discerning 'account' demonstrated the self-conscious and self-aware positioning of her authorship. Tanika Sarkar in her notes to the translation surmises that this other account for Rashsundari might be the idea of death as the last landmark to the story of her life.[43] One could also suggest that Rashsundari was perhaps referring to life itself as an ontological narrative (writ by God) and her faith in the many inscriptions of memory and faith that constructed human experience across the lines of life and death. This introspective tone would be better appreciated if one considered the thirteenth and fourteen compositions that testified to the writer's faith in supernatural occurrences or suspended realities.

The structure of *My Life* could be comprehended as two halves—the first resolutely moving from Rashsundari's early years to her quest for self-education and culminating in her rare ability to write in the memoir voice, while the concluding half as episodic with 'unusual' occurrences from her later years. These occurrences include the following—dreams where she spotted danger to her sons, which are then confirmed (and suggest extrasensory perception); an intense account of her own physical demise and resurrection that demonstrated an 'out of body experience' (in modern parlance); and a 'ghost' she saw in the middle of the day that was described as a large dog wearing bangles. Among these, the account of a dream in the thirteenth composition contains some of the most vivid writing in *My Life* and its highly sensory detailing is at odds with previous approaches to the autobiography as being 'astonishingly bare of visual or sensuous content'[44] for Rashsundari wrote the entire dream as a series of striking images, each accompanied by palpable emotion.

Before presenting her dream to the reader, the framing of the thirteenth composition claimed its validation from two dream-narratives in religious texts (the *Chaitanya Bhagabat* and the *Ramayana*) where the dreams of the protagonists come true. Understandably, to Rashsundari, these are not textual dreams but are as real as they might be historical or mythical, and thus created room for her own dream to be both textual and mystical. The dream that

Rashsundari claimed to set down with care was about her twenty-one-year-old son Pyarilal who had been studying in a college in Behrampore. In her dream, a weak and ill Pyarilal died before his mother's eyes and she exploded into lamentations: 'I started shaking convulsively. I flung myself down up on the ground and burst into sobs [...] I was going around the cremation fire, crying. My heart was bursting, I wanted to throw myself into the flames, but I couldn't quite bring myself to do that.'[45] There was no respite from the agony for the dream-protagonist or the reader, for the somatic grieving of loud cries continued from the cremation ground to the backdrop of the river Ganga, where her body streaked with mud and 'crying like a madwoman', the mother saw the dead son come towards her in a boat rowed by another man. The son had only one question for her: Would she like to hear the recitation of a religious text? Overjoyed to see him alive, Rashsundari walked with Pyarilal to a royal palace where he ascended a throne and did not glance back at her even as she stood there crying out to him. This was where the dream ended. Rashsundari then wrote of waking but did not cease referencing her dream and soon enough reached for her pen:

> I woke up from the dream, crying so hard that my clothes and the bedsheets were soaking wet. Even after I woke up, I felt as if I was still dreaming. I kept crying in my sleep. I could hardly speak, my heart was beating hard with dreadful anxiety. However much I tried to comfort myself, I would not be calm. I wrote down the date.[46]

The written date would confirm that her son had indeed died on the same day as her dream. The inscribing of an experience of clairvoyance (with all the implications of 'clear sight' offered by the word) within the narrative folds of a dream may be read as a reinforcement of the writer's faith in composition and imagination as prophetic. Towards the end of the composition, Rashsundari returned to her preoccupation with fear but then attempted to reassure herself and the reader that there was nothing fearful about death, for she too had an experience of dying—of watching people grieve over her own corpse, and then returning to consciousness 'as if I woke up from sleep'.[47] The analogy of sleep and dream thus brought her near-death episode back into the legitimacy of the real and the mundane, which to Rashsundari was synonymous with the truthful. The insistence on truth-telling became repetitive—she had been embarrassed to confide of this to other people for fear of being disbelieved. Rather, the reader of the memoir gets positioned as the trusted confidant, since the event ('what actually happened to me') was submitted to the certainty of print.

If the opening of an autobiography is given to birth and childhood, then the logical conclusion for Rashsundari was contained in the narrative of her own death which she writes as both corpse and witness. And yet, standard perceptions of real-unreal, as also the sequence of telling are splintered by a memoir sensibility—time frames of life must get diffused because time is suspended in the teller's subjectivity. One may recall that this life narrative was composed in the year that the author lost her husband—despite the commonly held belief that her reading and writing would result in widowhood, a dreaded fate to be avoided at any cost, Rashsundari Debi had courageously pursued both activities for her own edification. But the public was made the audience for her life without hesitation or delay when she was finally a widow—death became a literary progenitor, an end required for new beginnings. By collapsing death and sleep into each other, as also the renditions of dreams and visceral life struggles, the dream-narratives of *My Life* represent strong provocations—thus, the text may be said to be more than representation, but indeed the inauguration of a genre of self-fashioning whose affective and formal innovations reach far into the following century.

A literary staging of operatic interiorities: Binodini Dasi's *Amar Katha* (1912)

Mahashoy says that I have pleased the audience. But did the members of the audience ever see my inner self? When I had the opportunity to pronounce Krishna's name, with what absolute

> *yearning had I called out to Him; was the viewer ever able to perceive this? Then why did my only lamp of hope flicker away? As to repentance! My entire life has been wasted in repentance. [...] But has repentance borne anything?*[48]

The mélange of narrative practice and retrospective voice forged by Rashsundari Debi from within her nondescript domestic location would find an equally superlative textual echo by her younger contemporary, Binodini Dasi, who emerged in contrast against the backstage intrigues of Calcutta's famed public theatre.[49] The monikers Debi and Dasi respectively attached to the writers, Rashsundari and Binodini, are indicative of their marital and social status (class and caste) as well as perceptual moral binaries—wife and mistress, goddess and servant, householder and professional. Binodini (1863–1941) had an unrivalled trajectory as a professional actor for a dozen years—between the ages of eleven to twenty-three (1874 to 1886). It was during these years subsequent to her stage career that she composed the first account of her life *Amar Katha* (My Story) in 1912, following it up with another incomplete account titled *Amar Abhinetri Jiban* (My Life as an Actress) in 1924/5. The life-narratives have been noted to be 'among the earliest first-person records we have of a woman who remained single and worked for a living'.[50] The nature of the author's work adversely impacted the reputation of her texts—any literary output from the world of theatre was treated as inferior by middle-class intelligentsia.[51] Binodini Dasi was popularly known as Nati Binodini—*nati* translates to actress, and was considered synonymous with *patita* or 'fallen woman' (in contrast with *sati* or the chaste woman) and often led to the acting profession for women being equated with prostitution in public eyes.[52] This social taint had antecedents in the practice of female impersonators playing women characters in early Indian theatrical productions—a practice 'writ with anxiety of homo-eroticism'.[53] As the *sadharon rangalay* or the public theatre began to recruit women to act, they were often from professional entertaining communities[54] and/or drawn from singers and dancers living in the city's brothels.[55] Rimli Bhattacharya examines the process by which the *nati* 'became the ultimate pariah'—untouched by the zeal and resources of the social reform movement (around education or marital status) as well as her visible dependence 'on male mentors and patrons for almost every aspect of professional life'.[56] Binodini in her autobiography is assertive and non-apologetic about having a paying career—'I had always worked for money'[57]—and the confidence has some resonances with the social mobility that the public theatre was facilitating for middle-class men as well, no longer in the grasp of upper-class patronage.[58] Working as professional artists gave women access to fame, money and recognition, thereby establishing what Partha Chatterjee considers 'a new, entire urban occupational category'.[59] Tanika Sarkar writes of yet another innovation: the reserving of space in the theatre for middle-class female viewership and advertising campaigns aimed at adding 'respectable women' to the audience, thus bringing 'the well-born woman and the prostitute face to face [due to which] complicated circuits of desire began to flow'.[60] Being among the first women to be paid to perform in theatre[61] and the recipient of community adulation (a celebrity in modern terms) would thereby provide Binodini the wherewithal for a literary self-fashioning of her intense personal pain as being inseparable from her stagecraft.

At first encounter, the autobiography highpoints unremitting, self-deprecating laments about the actor's misfortunes or 'lowly status' (as woman/actor/writer), but also powerful self-assertions of pride—this affective chiaroscuro invites a consideration of the techniques and tenor of melodrama that was drawn from a dominant tradition of operatic theatre and applied to the literary enterprise of the autobiography. This section would therefore argue for Binodini as a dramatist-autobiographer applying her theatrical skills to the crafting of life narratives and for reading *My Story* through the semantic and affective connotations of melodrama. The adoption and composition of melodrama here need to be understood not as disingenuous but as emphatically resistant of platitudes and moral constrictions. To study life experiences narrated in the melodramatic mode does not imply that the telling is a performance or make-believe but makes a case for the text being propelled by the energies and insights of performativity. For Binodini, if the life telling were to have credibility and garner empathy from an audience accustomed to heightened registers of emotions on stage, then any overstatement had to be accepted as the prerequisite literary stance.

The scholar and translator of Binodini's autobiography, Rimli Bhattacharya, in her nuanced background and orientation to the text, draws attention to its palimpsest quality—sections written, revised and published in discontinuous instalments by the author.[62] As the first woman to speak of the 'inner story' of the public world of theatre in Calcutta, 'writing afforded Binodini Dasi a substitute for acting, or rather she used prose in order to translate the expression of bhava manifested in acting into its expression in words [and the primary challenge is] the move from performance on stage to expression in print'.[63] A brief examination of an older aesthetic and formalist tradition of melodrama is helpful to understand how performance as relegated to stage and articulation in print is telescoped by Binodini to simultaneously suggest articulation on stage and performance in print. The multiple opening frames to the autobiography offer a strong dramatic prelude in support of this observation, but first one must consider how to accommodate a reading of melodrama in this context, especially since the form has been 'a target of critical ridicule and derision' for most of the two centuries in which it has been identified as a dramatic category.[64] English theatre had a presence in Calcutta since the eighteenth century,[65] and in the nineteenth century it 'overlapped and interanimated' Bengali theatre.[66] The far-reaching influences of Anglo-European theatrical traditions thereby offer a reasonable point of comparison, as also the integration of colonial models with the aesthetics of classical Sanskrit theatre and other performative arts—the result being a fertile cultural amalgam.[67] Among the new genres that would play an impactful role was the mythological, 'adapted for the proscenium stage from the devotional *yatra* performance of Bengal's traditional Vaishnava sectarian culture'[68]—this will be discussed later in this section in the context of Binodini's role in the play *Chaitanya-Lila*.

Binodini writes of being anxious to see the performance of any famous British actor or actress visiting Calcutta—the proprietors of the theatre would arrange for her to see English plays following which her mentor would quiz her on her comprehension of these works. The proximity (of aesthetics) with world literature/theatre is palpable: Binodini reels off names of famed performers—Mrs Siddons, Ellen Terry, Bandmann[69]—and the influence of English writers (William Shakespeare, Walter Scott, Edward Bulwer-Lytton) on her self-gained theatrical education. She learns by listening to her mentor and his friends discuss numerous works by authors in English, Greek, French and German: 'I did not merely listen to these stories, but absorbed from them whatever I could of their bhava and then constantly meditated on it.'[70] It could be inferred that Binodini's adaptations of 'bhava', which in Sanskrit poetics indicates emotions or feeling, was finding intersections with the genre of melodrama, which was fairly integral to European drama and opera of her times.

The etymological implications of melodrama (*melos* or song combined with *drama* or act) are mirrored in its emergence as 'a welter of hybridization that includes musical, spectacular, theatrical and dramatic genres'.[71] It also manifested from its inception as an 'actor's category' that could mix 'media and practices of representation in new ways [that] readily migrated into other domains'.[72] For Binodini, such an artistic migration would lead from stage to the domain of print and life narrative, the years given to her writing nearly three times that of her time under the stage lights.[73] The film studies scholar Ben Singer makes a case for understanding melodrama as a dramatic mode rather than a genre.[74] The most common assumption or element associated with this mode is *excess* or an exaggerated quality. Singer suggests a 'cluster concept' that would include at least two of the following features: pathos, overwrought emotion, moral polarization, nonclassical narrative structure (given to amplified digressions, coincidences) and sensationalism.[75] One may notice and argue for all these five affective modes being featured at different moments in *My Story*. Binodini references her own writing as a *bedona-gatha* or a narrative of pain and from the outset calls herself a *janmadukhini* or a woman born in sorrow—subsuming her telling in pathos.[76] Bhattacharya notes the framing to the narrative to also be in the tradition of a *shok-gatha* (or elegy, which in this instance is for a departed beloved). *My Story* is largely composed in the epistolary mode with dated letters addressed to 'Mahashoy' (gentleman)—indicated as her mentor Girishchandra Ghosh. The text also features a multipart opening framework with four short essayist components in the following order: (a) a prefatory note titled 'And Why a Preface to my Story of Pain?'; (b) a dedication called 'A Gift' that offers 'the burden of these mad black scrawls' to a partner whose death has left behind 'only burning memories, bound with life and death and drenched with tears'; (c) a second dedication to the same partner with comparatively more romantic overtones as intimated by the title 'What is the gift? A blossom of love!'; (d) and finally another note of gratitude called 'An Unworthy Woman's Dedication' addressed to Girishchandra Ghosh. This last note of gratitude to the professional mentor is unusual for focusing on a quibble—Ghosh had composed a preface for the autobiography but the mentee-author had found the draft inadequate and evasive of important facts. Binodini did not publish the preface in the first edition, although she relented after his death and published it in the second edition of *My Story.* What was Ghosh's specific position in this preface and what was Binodini's expectation?

Ghosh was candid about his discomfort with the actor's 'bitter critique of society',[77] and the brandishment of her intimate relationships and emotions in 'such a harsh manner'[78]—instead, he encouraged her to write about her performances and the contemporary history of the theatre. The response contained a suggestion to his audience (and to Binodini) that her inscribed pain be accepted as a narrative of redemption.[79] Whether intentional or not, his effusively generous praise of her talents as an actor emerged against an inadvertent containment of her autonomy and personhood, as though she mattered only because of her prowess on the stage, her personal life bracketed for obliteration—this interpretation is supported by Binodini's response. Without naming Ghosh, she repeated the platitudes she frequently received (to be at peace with herself or avoid fretting), and wrote her response to the hollow consolations: 'I feel they do not understand my condition [...] one does not understand such a condition unless one has personally encountered it.'[80] In stating it thus, different rhetorical values were allotted to experience, identification, interpretation and empathy in the writing and reading of life narratives. Both prefaces—Binodini's and Ghosh's—mentioned her insistence that he revise his preface (even during his painful illness), and to her great consternation, Ghosh died before he kept his promise. By her initial rejection of Ghosh's preface, and by writing blatantly of her 'wounded pride', Binodini asserted her moral right as an author to be heard above the voice of a mentor/critic, thereby managing the reception of her autobiographical persona on her own textual terms.

The four short introductory fragments of *My Story* construct a rhythmic and tantalizing build-up to the self-disclosure or dramatic reveal of a behind-the-scenes life of a feted public figure. The sections overlap in their affective intent—marinating pain, expressing gratitude, or mourning death—and act as storytelling backdrops or setting for the first-person *sutradhar* (a narrator in classical Indian theatre who often addresses the audience and is the observing conduit to an unfolding story). In *My Story*, this provided Binodini the vantage of being both an emotionally involved narrator and an agential character, pacing and preparing the reader/audience for a tale of woe and gritty endurance. In the first Preface, effectively the opening note for a reader, one would do well to be attentive to closely packed phrases and images that evoke the atmosphere of melodrama, such as references to her 'everlasting despair' and 'a sinner [with] no kit or kin, no society, no friend', 'a despicable prostitute', 'uneducated, ignorant, lowly woman [who] has not been able to achieve anything'.[81] The shadows of death and dying elongate with every subsequent preface/dedication because both her mentor and her partner who assuaged her hurt and protected her honour[82] are no longer alive. Death, arguably the most potent and pervasive operatic trope, was thus setting the stage for complex interiorities to be played out.

The autobiography itself opens with a series of letters (the chapter title being 'The Seed')—all letters are addressed sans any accompanying salutation to 'Mahashoy!'. This is quickly understood by the reader to be the same mentor as the dedicatee of the previous page. Girishchandra Ghosh was a 'confidante as well as a kind of oppositional figure'[83] for Binodini and the concluding chapter of *Amar Katha* records that Ghosh was also the initiator, first-reader and editor of the autobiography. Binodini was quick to clarify that despite his close involvement during the writing process, he did not write a single line—rather, she insisted on independent authorship characterized by simple and unadorned language that delighted her mentor.[84] The entire autobiography shifts between the second-person address to Ghosh and writing of him by name (as a third person) even within a letter purportedly addressed to him. Significantly, the reader also feels addressed. The second-person voice adroitly postulated a double audience for the autobiography—the mentor on the page acted as the screen on which Binodini could seamlessly (and early in the pages) project her grief over the devastation of two lost childhoods: the first being the death of her young daughter and the second being her own childhood that ended with an early employment in theatre. The voice of the mentor was heard in direct quotes that attributed his professional opinion and private advice to her, and acted as a form of ventriloquism that animated the immediacy of the text. By the third letter, the autobiography shifted from a conventional preoccupation with the past that has been lived to shift focus on a bleak present and future:

> Whatever may have been the earlier situation, of what use am I in my present condition? I am sick and feeble, lacking all hope in the

> future. Unchangingly, the days follow the nights: I lack all enthusiasm for life. Facing the bitter blows of sickness and grief, engulfed in a listless torpor, I am caught in the flow of an unchanging current. Food, sleep and my cares: the image of one day is to be found in any other—nothing change from this day to the next. The only difference is in the intensity of the pain which sometimes increases while uneasiness remains a constant companion.[85]

The present self as the suffering self that speaks of its unease or dis-ease is the main driver of the narrative. Binodini had called herself 'a luckless woman' on multiple occasions in the manuscript, and the dirge for her dead daughter was a heightened presence from its opening pages: 'It is painful to speak of her; yet, it is only in speaking of her that I find my happiness. There is no other happiness in the heart of one who has lost a child.'[86] The words held a fledgling rationale for the writing of her life's trajectories wherein bittersweet pathos provided causality as well as galvanizing affect. The writer pre-empted any explanation of her life's tragedies as the will of God or as the process of being prepared for what providence has intended from her. She counteracted the platitudes with her absence of faith or unbelief:

> You say that if you heard the entire story of my life you would be able to explain to me how I have been created for the Lord's work. [...] If you kindly listen, you will realise how my unbelief has only deepened and how impossible it would be to uproot it. The root of peace is faith; this I might, perhaps be able to understand, but where is that faith? [...] As you listen, should you begin to feel irritation, then tear to pieces my letter. Will you listen?[87]

The conditional—'If'—was attached to the quality of listening and it was accepted to be present and continuous ('as you listen') but the crux of the matter lay in the choice of listening. The question was so entirely audience-facing that it presented as an exposition for a crucial dramatic arc, and one may argue that Binodini's creative treatment of the autobiographical material was perspicaciously cast in the aesthetics of the stage. At times, entire episodes were presented in the manner of 'scenes' or 'acts' with strong visual cues and dramatic action, even pantomime. Binodini's instinct for audience-engagement, and her wielding of dry wit and narrative tension, was exhibited in a 'life-and-death-scene' with a former lover when he discovered that she had chosen a new patron—the jealous and jilted young man stormed into her room in military gear with a sword at his side. When she refused his offer for money (in lieu of abandoning theatre and new patron), he unsheathed his sword, announced his resolve to cut her into pieces and brought the sword down. The description of the sequence of events demonstrated impeccable comic timing, and hovered between the macabre and the ludicrous.

> Just as he had raised it to strike me I sat down by the side of a table-harmonium. The sword struck the cover of the harmonium and went several inches into it. In a moment he had prised it out and had struck again. But I was not fated to die and that blow too fell on the stool on which I had kept some music. I got up immediately and caught hold of his upraised arm.[88]

The frenzied young man was finally resisted by her own hand and speech about not being 'burdened with sin' on account of murdering 'a despicable prostitute'.[89] The lover departed from the scene, a foolish and chastised figure of the narrative, while Binodini returned to a larger tale of valour, perhaps the one that most represented her literary motive and selfhood.

After many years of being in service to various theatre entrepreneurs, professionals and patrons, Binodini decided on a courageous economic and artistic choice—to participate in a new venture for a dramatic company would carry her name (or rather the more suggestive pithy gesture to her identity—'B Theatre'). Towards this dream, she boldly staked her intellectual capital, professional time, social currency, artistic legacy and even physical labour (carrying basket-loads of earth during the construction). Most importantly, it required her to become the mistress of the promoter and financer of the project, which after much agonizing (for she was in love with another man), she decided to accept for the cause of theatre.[90] The commitment she had towards the stage was explicitly talked of as a connection of love, an undying romance for which she would endure indignities from others.

If one were to think of a classic playwriting structure in terms of rising action, climax and denouement, it could be argued that this episode of the autobiography, where Binodini strove to become the first female artist in the country to have a theatre dedicated to her name (as well as hold part-ownership), is the climactic episode. Binodini spared no words or feelings to assert how much hinged on the fulfilment of her ambition and quest 'to legitimize her professional as also her social identity through a building in the metropolis'.[91] However, when the theatre was built and registered, with the opening event just a few weeks away, Binodini found out that she has been betrayed. The new theatre had been named 'The Star'. Devastated and cornered, Binodini struggled between being vociferous about the injustice and being reflexive about her own failings. When the promoter suggested giving her 50 per cent of the shares, a solicitous Ghosh thwarted it—the episode was reported with uncharacteristic restraint by Binodini in the autobiography without accompanying commentary. She quoted Ghosh as saying to her mother, 'Binod's Ma, you needn't bother yourself with these matters. You are women, you will never be able to bear such trouble.'[92] This recollected speech was tucked away in a long chapter that had been crafted entirely around the theme of her dedication, hard work and efficiency in taking care of her financial and other responsibilities. Binodini recollected Ghosh reiterating his loyalty to his mentee, calling her indispensable for the company, but as with his contested preface to her autobiography, his inclination was to make Binodini a shining example of artistic integrity rather than accept her very tangible material ambitions or personal despair. If Binodini felt any resentment about Ghosh's stance or her family's conceding to him out of respect, thereby excluding her deserved ownership in a theatrical venture marketed with her name, she was careful not to voice it. Instead, she dwelt on her *abhiman*, which could mean self-respect or pride, but also 'encapsulates what have been called "outlaw emotions" such as rage, obstinacy and protest'.[93] The reader is left in no doubt about these emotions of resistance as subtexts to the recollection.

The full catastrophe of being deprived of what Binodini considered rightfully hers can only be fully appreciated if one takes into account the childhood of abject deprivation that had led Binodini to the stage career in the first place. The heart-wrenching helplessness of a child in the midst of poverty and death and compelled to work to feed her family (a familiar Dickensian trope) was narrated in affective amplifications but at the same time the writing made room for the child-Binodini to step out of being an actor in the play of her life to an observer and chronicler. One must also note that the structure and content of the childhood narrative had strong replication in Binodini's prolific career later on in her life, especially in the affective cycles of struggle and triumph.

Raised in great poverty by her mother and grandmother, Binodini's life took an early bleak turn when the lack of resources for medical treatment resulted in the death of her young brother in a charity hospital. Soon after, her mother descended into grief-drenched madness. Having no other means of survival, the family decided to apprentice the girl to the stage. There were many hardships in store for the young breadwinner. Binodini wrote of herself as attentive to the art of acting, applying her intelligence and knowledge to adapt to each role she played, or what she considered her 'trance-like involvement'.[94] The trance or submergence into the psychic terrain to draw out the resources for a worldly engagement (through art, livelihood) was addressed by Binodini in an event that would come to define her public reputation—playing the role of the Chaitanya, the sixteenth-century founder of Bengali Vaishnavism. In fact, Chaitanya provided a curious textual parallel and connection between the two autobiographies studied in this chapter—by Rashsundari Debi and Binodini Dasi—the former claiming to turn literate to read

Chaitanya's biography and the latter receiving her highest artistic accolades and spiritual endorsement by playing Chaitanya on stage. In a gender reversal and foregrounding 'the androgynous aspect of the saintly figure'[95] Binodini prepared to act the part of Chaitanya in the play *Chaitanya-Lila* through rituals and intense prayers alongside her theatre practice. During the first performance, she wrote of a feeling akin to a powerful light suffusing her heart. 'My body thrilled and all of me filled with a blossoming. Everything around me appeared obscured by a mist [. . .] I felt that there was someone in my heart who sang these words. I was no one. There was no consciousness of the "I" within me.'[96] With subsequent performances, Binodini described her involvement in her performance as being possessed, often leading to fainting spells on stage in the middle of the play. In a fascinating collapse of the secular (entertainment) world and the religious community, Binodini recorded the many spiritual teachers who came to watch her intense performance of Chaitanya, the most noted being the religious leader Ramakrishna Paramahamsa—known for his own charisma and talent for mimicry[97]—and his chief disciple, Swami Vivekananda. The recording of such interactions that involved shared singing and generous blessings made porous the proscenium theatre with its neat divide of cast and audience, as also the world of performance and lived religiosity, the body of the actor acting as a bridge: 'My body that was dedicated to the theatre had truly been blessed.'[98] The mind of the actor was equally strained, wrote Binodini, for the role required a performance of 'madness' or the delirium of a person lost in Godhood. The precariousness of such passions evoked the convention of opera: 'The movement from a low to a high, and then finally to the highest pitch of cerebral excitement made me feel as though I was on the brink of something and would come crashing down any moment.[99] The pressures, however, were only too real for the performer. These spiritually charged performances into which the audience had come to expect her to dissolve into states of abstraction took a toll on Binodini's health and wrought a deep change in her personality in the ensuing months. While the audience and mentor might have been interested in her acting as a morally redemptive journey, her own inclination was towards a self that prioritized solitariness over the solidarities of the stage—this would lead her to ultimately reject the performance arena.

Towards the end of *My Story*, the leave-taking from stage (due to problems and betrayals) lingered over several episodes and revealed a consolidation of the multiple strands of dramatic tensions in the genre of the autobiography, more specifically in the act of writing. Sheetala Bhat argues for Binodini's writing-self and actress-self as being in a continuum, wherein writing 'records and solidifies' her experiences in an artistic realm that is otherwise known for its transience.[100] Binodini thus must return to the lingering question from the opening frame of the text—why write?—and alongside her own edification, she factored in the possibility that it might help some other 'unfortunate woman' who like her 'has stumbled on to the path to hell'.[101] Her life as polluted by psychic pain and the filth of the world was made analogous to the darkening of ink on a white page during the act of writing: 'Like my own tainted and polluted heart, I have tainted these pure white pages with writing. But else could I do! A polluted being can do nothing other than pollute!'[102] As Bhattacharya points out, Binodini adopted the strategy of speckling her writing with the disparagement anticipated from her readership both at the start and end of the autobiography.[103] Similarly, the heightened emotive declaration signals a contrarian stance—the seeming self-dismissal ('a heap of nonsense called *Amar Katha*'[104]) intends to draw attention to the beating heart of the autobiography—Binodini's innate pride in her stage career, her artistic resilience as well as her entrepreneurial instincts that include writing. Like Rashsundari, Binodini was wont to think of an end to her narrative—if childhood was the literal and conceptual start, then death must be given the final lines. Binodini lingered longer on the theme of death—it was no more a dour fact but an entire melodramatic spectacle. The suggestion of an end was suspended, for the narrator was said to have no end or beginning, because even the cremated body created ashes: 'There will never be a final death. Never. Never. I listen now to the lament of the ashes while I endure in little slivers the pain of death [...] See now, how the ash moves further away, lamenting all the while.'[105] The mesmeric quality of such lamentations is in its covert celebration of the covenant of speech, even when it speaks of pain or of multiple magnificent ends that can only lead to more beginnings.

The novelty of romancing in prose: Swarnakumari Debi Ghosal's *Kahake* (1898)

> *When I retrace the history of my life, as far back as memory carries me, I see that I have always loved, love and life have been so blended that they became one. And were this love ever taken from me, life would be worthless, a mere blank, my individuality lost.*[106]

This paean to love sets the opening tone to Swarnakumari Debi Ghosal's novel *An Unfinished Song*, first published in Bengali as *Kahake* in 1898 and translated by the author into English in 1913. The thematic orientation of the plot marks it as a 'courtship novel' where the female protagonist's choice of suitor is centred on love and the narrative showcases her 'significant, though modest, prerogatives of choice and action'.[107] The literal translation of the Bengali title ('To Whom?') underscores the deep directionality of love—from self to other—and simultaneously presents coupling as demonstrating radical individuality. This novel of less than a hundred pages carries an epigraph from Lord Byron's *Don Juan*: 'Man's love is of man's life a thing apart / 'Tis woman's whole existence.' Neither poet nor text is named, but the lines are attributed to 'a great man' in a manner that suggests that its readers would immediately recognize and relate to both poet and sentiment from within a shared cultural cache. The first-person narrator, her tales of love and the reader are thus spontaneously assumed to be placed in a continuum of text, literacy and literariness within the 'English tradition'. It also aligns the author and novel as participants in world literature, 'a mode of circulation and of reading' which the scholar David Damrosch demonstrates to be a double process of being read as literature and circulating 'beyond [the text's] linguistic and cultural point of origin.'[108] Thus, despite being clearly of a rich Bengali and South Asian literary milieu, the novel also partakes of a more global semantic circuit—it was published in London and is replete with narrative allusions, conversational sequences, and tributes to literary stalwarts (William Shakespeare and George Eliot feature in a narrative centrepiece; Shelley's poetry facilitates flirtation) even as plot-twists and character preoccupations are explicated.

As a member of one of India's foremost cultural families—the Tagores of Jorasanko—Swarnakumari was witness to several literary initiatives spearhead by her siblings, many of whom were keenly invested in a global reorientation of aesthetic and religious sensibility. Swarnakumari's father Debendranath Tagore helped establish the influential Brahmo Samaj, which was one of the most profound (and well-funded) engagements of Indic thought as it negotiated both secular modernity and Anglican Protestantism, and thus their outlook equally straddled London and Calcutta, commerce and religion, even as it grounded the poetic and novelistic accomplishment of Swarnakumari's generation, as also of her illustrious younger brother, Rabindranath Tagore.

It is this sensitivity for poetry and song which motivates and guides the narrator of *An Unfinished Song* and creates a plot structure that stacks many motifs of a romantic adventure—'love, separation, longing, misunderstanding, coincidences, contrivances, mistaken identity, delightful unexpected discovery, reunion and fulfillment'.[109] This in itself would not seem unusual, for the novels familiar to Swarnakumari's generation tended to be crammed with characters, often across families and generations, and lengthy plotting necessitated a background scaffolding of social status, milieu and conventions for the fate of these characters to be played out. However, in lieu of such measured unfolding of a personal/social backdrop, *An Unfinished Song* begins *media res* with the narrator, Mrinalini Mazumdar or

Moni, mulling on love. Within a page or so, Moni confides in her readers about two unusual facts about her life: the first is that she has remained a spinster till the age of nineteen, which would have been unthinkable and 'an unpardonable offence'[110] in a society where pre-pubertal marriages were the norm; the second delivers a more potent confession. 'I, a Hindu maiden, knew love before I entered wedlock. I loved a man without even expecting him to become my husband.'[111] The anticipated incredulity of a reader to the first disclosure is pre-empted by the novel's Preface that claims to be the story of life in a community that has adopted Western customs (namely, the Brahmo Samaj). However, it is the second claim, of having explored and experienced romantic love without the expectation of marriage, that not only marks this book to be a courtship novel but also actively addresses the moral qualms of its readers. Thus the most scandalous information (the heroine's premarital romances) does not unfold as the novel progresses—as in Anne Bronte's *The Tenant of Wildfell Hall*—but is laid bare at the outset, partly as provocative defiance, and partly as beguiling sincerity. The first instance of attraction is located in childhood friendship, and Moni eloquently reconstructs her deep emotional attachment to Chotu, whose unfinished song is saved in her heart. After she moves with her father to a different location, she loses contact with Chotu, but memories of him are rekindled when she hears the same song being sung in her sister's drawing room by a visiting guest, Romanath Roy. Despite being besotted with song and thereby amenable to the singer's wooing, the relationship does not work out when Moni finds the gentleman to be wanting in his moral fibre—he has romanced and betrayed an Englishwoman. Around the same time, a second suitor, Dr Binoy Krishna Chaudhury, enters the story and soon becomes the object of Moni's romantic aspirations. When Moni's father arranges for her marriage with her childhood friend—after announcing that 'I want no more of your English courtships'[112]—Moni is torn between old loyalties and the new vagaries of her heart. The novel quickly moves to its resolution when it is conveniently revealed that her present suitor is the same person as the childhood friend (Chotu being the doctor's nickname). This deft tying up of loose plot ends can be seen as integral to the 'sympathetic values and identifiable conventions' of the romance genre[113] and cannot be presumed to be simplistic or trite. In fact, Swarnakumari employs the predictable to draw attention to the *unfinished* nature of the heart's desire (epitomized as unfinished song) and in the language of love being embraced without qualms or apology by a first-person female voice. The narrator is far from being the object of desire or courtship in the plotline and yet every word or action within the ambit of a romantic gesture is delivered through her reception or interpretation. Despite false suitors and the looming threat of social dishonour, the story of love between two children leads to their marriage being solemnized in adulthood. The concluding scenes fulfil many of the tropes of idealized courtship, including seamless communion of heart and spirit with a handsome doctor under a moonlit sky, brokered by constant banter about serendipity and the triumph of love irrespective of how and when it manifests itself. The most significant aspect of the moonlight culmination remains the continued privacy that is afforded to the pair—the promise of impending nuptials is in the air, but it cannot be allowed to break the spell of courtship itself.

The practice of such romantic encounters in drawing rooms and gardens sans escorts being barely plausible in Calcutta even among the urban educated, the narrative form poses a challenge for its author. How might one write courtship and consensual marriage in a society where child marriages were the norm, and where any intermingling between the sexes tended to be limited to familial circles? *An Unfinished Song* addresses these challenges in ingenious ways: by skilful recasting of narrative convention, by deliberate avoidance or blatant coincidences, and most importantly through creating an unprecedented first-person voice that could deliver a modern female consciousness. Such innovations in craft are artfully linked through the novel's central and explicit preoccupation with romance, whether as an impetus to plot, as affective colourations, or as an aspiration and realization of freedom. The young woman setting out on the great adventure of romance is enabled by her access to comfort and leisure. More importantly, the usual bind of traditional expectations and familial obligations remains suspended in the duration of the courtships. She participates in tennis parties, listens to piano recitals in drawing rooms, quotes poetry from memory, reads novels, gathers flowers in the garden, writes and receives letters and repeatedly reflects on the nature of love in abstraction, as though it were being played on a screen for the self to admire and mull on: 'Love creates love, there is no other power so potent [...] there is always the desire in the female breast to make another happy by self-abnegation, for love is woman's whole nature, its desires and aspirations are her life blood.'[114] The idealizations are occasionally punctuated by an underlying wisdom and meta-narrative about the chasm between language and sentiment. Attempting to reply to a love letter from her suitor, Moni finds herself in a bind:

> I positively found myself perspiring under the strain of this enormous tasks, and became terribly confused in the selection of synonyms and floundered about among adjectives and propositions until I was half mad [...] Once or twice it really seemed as if language and sentiment agreed, but then it occurred to me that *the thing read something like a novel* [emphasis added], and I discarded it again.[115]

The simile that projects the unwieldy fictionality of a novel upon Moni's yet-to-be-written love letter is also a wry authorial comment on life, art and artifice. The paradox for romantic love is that its ardency depends on language to serenade the object of desire; or rather it nestles in a narrative structure of 'the love story' to represent its own intensity and sincerity without lapsing into affectations and clichés. In fact, the novel form is also evoked in a previous episode of Moni's heartbreak when she faints—while nursing Moni back to health, her sister calls the condition 'an attack of hysteria', suggesting that staying up 'late night reading novels' had not helped the situation.[116] The courtship novel thus echoes popular sentiments about its perceived frivolities, and thereby must draw from a parallel genre, such as song and melody, to be the incubator and carrier of Moni's childhood attachment that will ultimately triumph and manifest as romance.

The song features several times in the novel albeit through different singers and varied listening situations: 'It was ever the same song, and that song was the enchantress.'[117] While the encounters between the sexes get orchestrated in the chaste settings of family rooms, often in view of family members, the erotic charge of that encounter is transferred to the song itself. The opening of the fourth chapter is entirely devoted to the hypnotic effect of the song on Moni, the descriptions and rising tempo of the reaction to song mimicking a sexual consummation and release:

> It poured a flood of feeling over me that awoke the dormant emotions of the maiden, and ere the song was ended, it created a vortex in which I felt myself carried into the realm of the ideal, searching for something I knew and yet I knew not. I was lost in an intense longing; it seemed as if a God had taken possession of him who sang. Anon as I listened to the melody it broke the barriers of time until the past and the present were blended and the singer himself became identified with one I had known of old, until I felt as if I were walking in a trance. Nor was the spell broken by his departure; I often remained in a partial stupor during the entire night.[118]

Moni considers her ardent response to the song as a condition that is an enigma even to herself, and the evoking of flood, vortex, trance, stupor, or the breaking of barriers of time suggests the dissolution of self in another. As the novel develops, each return to this passionate reaction to melody signals Moni's bourgeoning sexuality. The plot resolution is not linked to marriage, for Moni frequently questions the imposition of wedlock, not wanting to marry for convenience,[119] and wonders about the option of staying unmarried.[120] Equally, she informs the undeserving suitor that she does not want to marry for convenience. Even when she decides to reject marriage altogether, Moni writes to her father that she would like to 'dedicate my life in service to the Motherland'—an unexpected patriotic sentiment that seems to emerge only to justify singlehood. In actuality, Moni's wilfulness or independence has a thin veneer, for the patriarch swiftly overrides her preferences, insisting on arranging a marriage that he considers suitable for her. Yet, the promise of the courtship novel is met when her father's choice and Moni's choice coincide—the narrative stops with a happy union that has no more impediments to overcome.

Swarnakumari had to reconcile how an Indian woman might enjoy a companionate marriage or a partner of choice when social conventions decreed marriages between children as decided by their families. The devices of narrative serendipities or artistic affinities through other genres, such as song, became crucial for the novel's resolution—the female protagonist finding a way to the 'happy ending'. Fantasy and nostalgia, as much as utopian desires, thereby manifest as reachable and real in narrative terms, even as they retain the chimeric lure and perceived fulfilment of romance.

Several such narrative subtexts and intertextual overtones in *An Unfinished Song* indicate recasting of the female novelistic tradition of England (such as Jane Austen and Charlotte Bronte from the Romantic era or the Victorian novelists George Eliot and Elizabeth Glaskell) wherein the novel's wordy girth (whether in theme or length) gets whittled down to the concentrated preoccupation of romance as manifested in courtship and wedlock. At the same time, Swarnakumari can be seen as participating in her contemporary literary trends where narratives of romance (often in sub-genres such as gothic or historical or social) enjoyed mass readership. In a study of the circulation and consumption (through select Indian libraries) of the British novel in nineteenth-century India, Priya Joshi argues that although books of 'serious standards' had been introduced 'as a means of propagating and legitimizing Englishness in the colony', the literature that was 'discussed, copied, translated, and "adapted" most avidly into Indian languages and eventually into the Indian novel [...] was the work of highly popular British novelists [...]'.[121] This is not to imply that early novels in India were largely a mimetic enterprise, and as Meenakshi Mukherjee points out, it is important to read 'beyond their stated intentions and prise open the operations of other, often subterranean, forces in their formation'.[122] Throughout the second half of the nineteenth century, as the novel form began to make its presence felt in various Indian languages, it was indeed drawing from multiple resources including premodern storytelling traditions and other narrative forms, often innovating and hybridizing with great economy and efficacy. Several of these novels attempted to capture regional distinctness, social obligations and ethical concerns around gender relations, especially the fate of child brides and widows.[123] The social reform novel offered constructs of womanhood that were primarily drawn from the discourse of elite male reformers.[124] Considering these novels carried more moral heft than the novel of humour or pleasure, Swarnakumari's decision to delink marriage from the reform debates and move the plot towards an imaginative and narrative realm of desire is noteworthy.

Moni, the protagonist of *An Unfinished Song*, discloses falling in love more than once and is candid about shifting romantic allegiances. This even occasions a lament from her brother-in-law about the undesirable outcomes of the liberty afforded by education for women that has enabled the rejection of a deserving (in his opinion) suitor. Moni muses how 'the young woman of today must learn to bear her sorrow alone, especially when an affair of the heart is involved'.[125] Just as the independent woman was seen as disgracing her family, the family was also no longer a dependable ally for her.

It is when the situation appears to be most uncertain for Moni that the narrative features a long dinner table conversation on the virtues of the novel form, where her doctor-suitor holds forth on the creative greatness of George Eliot, insisting Eliot to be on par with Shakespeare. The doctor reminds his peers, as perhaps Swarnakumari wishes to remind her readers, that 'the moralist and the novelist are not the same person' and that Eliot 'only expresses life as she finds it and awakens in her reader love and sympathy'.[126] He argues that Dorothea (of *Middlemarch*) and Maggie (of *The Mill on the Floss*) ought to be considered portraits or bearing characteristics of its author and praises Eliot for her 'truly grand intellect combined with the sympathetic heart and subtle instinct of a true woman [...] Has any writer of the stronger sex been able to equal her in that?'[127] Moni is a silent audience to this debate of the greatness of a writer's talents not being limited or defined by their gender. The suitor's question has larger reverberations for the gender debates in the morphing literary landscape of colonial India.

Similar to pioneering women writers elsewhere, Swarnakumari chose to publish her first novel, *Dipnirban* (The Flame Extinguished, 1876), without attaching her name to it. It was the first time a Bengali woman had published a novel. Although Swarnakumari's progressive-minded father had facilitated access to education to his daughters, their intellectual explorations had taken place within the confines of the house under the supervision of an orthodox mother. However, within the Tagore household, the children had constant exposure to musical concerts, theatre performances, visual arts and literary enterprises. Swarnakumari was married at the age of eleven to a government official who was supportive of her continued education, and they had four children while she was a teenager. The anonymity of her literary debut seems to have been not just for the general readership, but also to the family fold. One of her older brothers reviewed the novel while he was in England, unaware that the author was his own sister, and declared it to be 'of unprecedented merit' expressing excitement at finding 'a Bengali woman [...] capable of writing a novel of such artistic merit'.[128] As Swarnakumari continued to publish, her novels were as popular as those of Bankimchandra Chattopadhyay, the most celebrated Bengali author of her time.[129] She wrote twenty-five books in Bengali in multiple genres (fiction, verse, drama) and was the editor of the journal *Bharati* (established in 1878) for more than three decades.[130] Simultaneously, she was an active participant in several social and political forums. In the opening decade of the twentieth century, she began to focus on translating her older novels into English, including *An Unfinished Song*, and published them in London, most likely at her own expense. This was a substantive step that Swarnakumari took towards canvassing for her literary oeuvre to be placed alongside her global contemporaries, and a point of substantial resistance came from within her own family.

Rabindranath Tagore, Swarnakumari's younger brother by about five years,[131] had gained considerable stature as one of India's most promising novelist, dramatist and poet. He became the first Asian to be awarded the Nobel Prize (for Literature) in 1913 following the English translation of his book of Bengali verses, *Geetanjali*, which was dedicated to the reputed British printmaker William Rothenstein. In a letter to Rothenstein in February 1914, Tagore responded to the petty rumours discrediting his award (especially attributions of his work to W.B. Yeats). In the same letter, he wrote of something else that was troubling his mind—his sister and fellow-novelist Swarnakumari. He cautions Rothenstein about her in blunt terms:

> She is one of those unfortunate beings who has more ambition than abilities but just enough talent to keep her mediocrity alive for a short period of time. Her weakness has been taken advantage of by some unscrupulous literary agents in London and she has had her stories translated and published. I have given her no encouragement but I have not been successful in making her see things in their proper light. It is likely that she may go to England and use my name and you may meet her but be merciful to her and never let her harbor in her mind any illusion about her worth and her chance. I am afraid she will be a source of trouble to my friends who I hope will be candid to her for my sake and will not allow her to mistake ordinary politeness for encouragement.[132]

Tagore's thoughts on his older sister's literary ambitions, beyond the obvious churlishness, are critical for revealing his distress about Swarnakumari actively seeking access to a London literary circuit. It could represent an explicit ambition in Tagore to be the prime or sole spokesperson for literary matters from India, and perhaps he would have found his sibling-rival a lot less exasperating if she had sought an obscure publisher in Bengal—in any case, it is her claim to internationalism that provokes him. Current scholarship emphasizes the trans-nationality of literary circuits, and writing as a political imperative of claiming a position in an alternative narrative of the 'world' category.[133] Commenting on the layered literary self-analysis presented in the Preface to this novel of manners, the scholar Barnita Bagchi identifies Swarnakumari as simultaneously protesting against the racism integral to colonialism while presenting it to a cosmopolitan public sphere confidently claiming a literary status.[134] In cognizing Swarnakumari's breadth of literary ambition, one must, however, also factor in enormous constraints of direct access and resources by virtue of being a married woman with young children. It could be surmised that Tagore won this round as Swarnakumari's output did indeed end up relatively obscure, while his reputation—as, ironically, a detached, spiritualist poet—remains largely intact up to the present. Unfortunately, even later editors of Tagore's selected letters accede to his peremptory judgement about his sister. In a footnote to the offending letter, the editors refer to Rothenstein's opinion of *An Unfinished Song* and declare Tagore's evaluation of Swarnakumari's literary prowess (or assumed lack thereof) to seem 'fair enough, if unnecessarily caustic in its phrasing'.[135] Drawing a comparison between this situation and the trope of 'Shakespeare's sister' created later by Virginia Woolf in *A Room of One's Own*, Susan Stanford Friedman points out that this principle (of the male 'genius' who has every means to thrive in art while his equally talented sister would be denied the same opportunities and come to a tragic end) 'played out its subterranean sibling rivalry in their lives and works'[136] between Tagore and his older author-sister. Swarnakumari's explorations of popular, open-minded female courtship and romance were understandably more uncomfortable (to her nationalist-minded literary milieu) than the more familiar, comforting ideal of the male spiritualist poet—and thus set a tone that has lasted over a century.

Unlike the short-form genres (such as booklets, letters, speeches) or even pared-down episodic life narratives or short fiction, which were seen as more amenable to writing by women whose family obligations left little time for intellectual pursuits, the genre of the novel, with its expanded lattice of plot points and characterizations, has created formidable literary personae for several male writers across the Indian languages. The publishing output by women and the public acceptance of the merit of novels by women in various languages can be discerned more in the second half of the twentieth century—often bracketed as 'women's fiction' or for a female readership. Perhaps Swarnakumari's instincts about gaining some competitive edge from the English language (in comparison with the regional/Indian readership) may require further investigation. Several of Swarnakumari's contemporaries composed directly into English, rather than via translation, and expressed their specific preoccupations with personal liberties and social identities through genres such as nature writing and travelogues. As will be examined in the chapter that follows, the genres tend to merge and modify into other formal registers—the novel evokes the elegy, the memoir turns into travel diary, and the personal diary becomes a public screen for coded longings.

3

The Elegist, the Diaryist and the Traveloguer

Early in the twentieth century, a woman who had travelled from India to Oxford to qualify as a lawyer, even as women were yet to be admitted to the British Bar, composed an evocative essay titled 'Social Relations—England and India'. Written as 'problems for consideration at the Pan-Anglican Congress',[1] this essayistic framing of two countries is predicated upon beguiling narrative premises and inroads of gender, geography, language, encounters and enactments:

> 'You have warmed yourself at two fires—the Indian Sun and the English hearth', said once to me a dear friend, long passed beyond the veil. 'Yours is a great privilege and a great responsibility'.
>
> And, if to feel in one's pulses the great axioms of two continents, if to love two worlds as different as East is from West, to vibrate with one set of susceptibilities to the griefs [*sic*] and joys, the folktales or literature of both, be privilege, then indeed am I blessed and privileged among women.[2]

If the 'privilege' for a woman who loves the cultures of both East and West was to vibrate with the cultural heritages of disparate worlds, then the 'responsibility' was to write for 'the furtherance of a better understanding'.[3] The author, Cornelia Sorabji (1866–1954), who later became the first female lawyer with a post in the British Raj, had arguably accumulated the most adaptive credentials to present such schisms and fusings between cultures that could be entirely encapsulated in the colonizer-colonized hegemonic paradigm. Her own beginnings were mired in exceptional complexities of identity and affiliations—her father Sorabji Kharsedji was a convert from Zoroastrianism to Christianity, an act that nearly cost him his life, and her mother, a Hindu raised by Christian Missionaries and adopted by an Anglo-Indian family, was a social worker and educator who founded several schools. Cornelia and her seven siblings were raised in 'English ways' as much as in their Parsee culture in the environs of Poona.[4] The fifth of seven children, Cornelia was the first woman to sit for the Oxford law degree in 1892, although she was denied a scholarship and had to wait for three decades to be awarded the degree on account of her gender.[5] As a practicing lawyer, she specialized in representing the interests of the *purdanashins* (women from wealthy families of India's princely states who followed a widespread social practice of segregation between genders) and represented them in several of her books. Her detailed notes on the lives of the women, as well as her many timely interventions on the behalf of their physical safety, freedom and the safeguarding of their properties, offer a rich archive. The scholar Antoinette Burton argues for a more expanded sense of the home-archive, that is, 'history conceived [...] as a narrative, a practice, and a site of desire'.[6] Burton studies how Cornelia fashions herself as 'the perfect historian-guide'[7] on account of her frequent travels (within India and to England), her anglophilia and her status as professional woman. To speak in the language of definitive and factual record-keeping and to also maintain a novelistic romance of facilitating passageways to veiled spaces, Cornelia developed a distinct writing persona that, both in intensity of voice and quantum of pages, is fairly incomparable.

As her nephew, biographer and the philosopher Richard Sorabji presents it, Cornelia's prodigious output of legal and personal writings emanates 'from the position of being an outsider herself, a woman among males, an Indian among the English, a Christian among Parsees and a Parsee among Hindus and Muslims'.[8] One might argue that the public negotiations with such shifting positions that resist the insider-outsider binary find an ally in both the language of expression and a hospitable attitude to a vast range of Western epistemology. The scholar Ellen Brinks considers the self-locations of the Anglophone women writers of this period (1870–1920) as being 'notoriously pluralistic' and occupying a place of 'cultural and literary betweenness' that comes from adopting Western literary forms to Indian contexts within an ecosystem of publishers and audience that spanned continents.[9] In the case of Cornelia, this is especially evident in the concrete, applied forms of the Western epistemology—such as the legal discourse that she professionally partook in—and her own personal idiosyncrasies that were not without challenges. Cornelia's positions on public matters were often perceived 'anglophilic, antinationalist, and anti-women's suffrage'[10] even as scholars like Suparna Gooptu make a more sympathetic case for Cornelia as having to operate between the strict confines of colonial logic.[11] For the purposes of this present chapter, which precludes a more detailed enquiry of Cornelia's exceptionally large body of work, her essay on 'social relations' offers a conduit to comprehend the mobility (of thought and status) afforded to women via colonial education, even when they may be fraught with stereotypes and collective judgements.

The figure of 'the advanced Indian lady'[12] makes a fleeting but perceptible appearance in 'Social Relations' as someone both admirable in her accomplishments and tedious in her mannerisms and social engagements. In the Preface of a book that she published that same year (*Between the Twilights*, 1908), Cornelia continues the portrayal thus: 'the Anglicized and English-educated Indian, the capable woman who earns her own living, the cultured woman of the world or philanthropist'.[13] While this description would perfectly match Cornelia herself, she emphatically writes of the woman as a mirroring other. The need to identify more with her own 'Englishness' which predicated the 'socially sanctioned means of becoming a citizen [...], albeit an imperial one'[14] is indicated. Nonetheless, Cornelia's perspicacious outlining of the English-educated woman who was making active inroads in the sociocultural urban Indian milieu in the closing decades of the nineteenth century and the opening decades of the twentieth century is the literary prompt for this present chapter that brings together three of her contemporary writers: Krupabai Satthianadhan, Atiya Fyzee and Dosebai Cowasjee Jessawalla. These writers were largely raised within the Anglophone world, and their lives and travels, within and outside of India, have many resonances with Cornelia's experiences, even as they have completely different social and professional outcomes.

Similar to Cornelia, Krupabai was born to parents who were first generation converts to Christianity, and she too had to give up medical education in England. While Cornelia successfully completed her education in law, Krupabai had to abandon her plans to travel to England as well as her medical education in India on account of poor health. Krupabai's debut novel is a compelling autobiographical *bildungsroman* in English that offers an elegiac portrayal of an ailing body, frequently against the backdrop of riotous and evocative landscapes. The protagonist's love of learning and language, especially of the British authors she is reading, is a crucial resource for her to be able to commit to words a tormented psyche that must contend with debilitating depressive episodes, death of loved ones and her own impending finitude. The second section of the chapter studies a travelogue that is quilted from multiple letters of varying lengths written in the mode of diary entries (or perhaps diary entries that were fashioned as letters) intended for publication in a popular Urdu journal edited by a woman and addressing women readers. The repeated reference to 'sisters' or 'newspaper sisters' by the author Atiya Fyzee is tinged with several layers of meanings, not in the least because these letters were being first received (and partially edited or censored) by her biological sisters. Atiya's journey to London that begins with pride and optimism in her plans to train as an educator on a prestigious government scholarship ends with the disappointment of a premature return that is sketchily attributed to reasons of health.

A prodigious letter-writer, akin to Cornelia, Atiya's travel notes are studied here for the linkages between her address to 'sisters' and explicit awareness of the gendered compatriot audience and her vivid observations of her social world, whether clothes, domestic staff, or the wish to partake in the social and intellectual cosmopolitanism that is London. The third and final section of the chapter studies the memoirs of Dosebai Cowasjee Jessawalla who belonged to Bombay's Parsi community and aspired to travel around the world (as well as chronicle those travels) in her seventies. Any perceived disadvantages of gender are portrayed as surmountable, and these include any preconceived notions of the ageing female body. The present study focuses on what Dosebai perceives as the summation or the highest arc of her many unconventional forays in travel and strategic socializing—her efforts to make inroads into the circles closest to the British Crown, culminating her personal encounters with the King and Queen of England. However, *The Story of My Life* at its core is the story of Dosebai's travels and her repeated striving for social legitimacy, prestige as well as knowledge and a sense of exposure to the larger world.

All three writers had an early exposure and grafting in Anglophone social circles and literary traditions, including Atiya, whose writing first appears in Urdu, and the centrality of travel in their writings as well as life experiences becomes their crucial passageway into a more global idea of modernity. Whether between continents or within the Indian peninsula, between cultures or within family folds, between public engagements or within personal relationships, the writers document continuities of family and self-fashioning, as much as they do of disruptions and new beginnings. Dosebai writes of 'that which is historical within us'—this to her indicates the personal choices that create impactful public reputations even if they be 'misunderstood, misinterpreted and misrepresented'.[15] Without such unconventional odysseys, these women would not have been able to create powerful legacies of fruitful literary transnationalism.

Elegiac landscape for the unruly body: Krupabai Satthianadhan's *Saguna* (1888)

> Saguna *was first published serially in the* Madras Christian College Magazine *in 1887–8. It was published posthumously as a book [...] in 1895. The book was presented to and read by Queen Victoria who expressed her interest in it and requested any other work by the author. It was translated into Tamil in 1896. Although it has been inaccessible to the reading public for a century,* Saguna *was popularly read and reviewed when first published, both in India and in England. [...] The original title,* Saguna: A Story of Native Christian Life *has been changed to* Saguna: The First Autobiographical Novel in English by an Indian Woman.[16]

This fact-reciting and contextualizing 'Note on the Text' by the scholar Chandani Lokuge accompanies the novel *Saguna* by Krupabai Satthianadhan (1862–94) over a hundred years after its first publication and subsequent disappearance from the literary marketplace. At the time of writing this present study, the aforementioned edition of *Saguna*, like previous editions, has again disappeared into spectral print-lessness only to exist as stray electronic copies or tucked into older libraries, a baffling, lamentable fate for a path-making text that has every claim to distinction, and displays a profoundly mature novelistic sensibility.

Lokuge's framing of the salient features of the text's inception—first appearing in serial form, a posthumous book version that is translated immediately from English to Tamil, admired by an imperial sovereign and receiving popular reviews in two countries—is also making a crucial intervention, and in the title no less. While Krupabai described her book as 'A story of native Christian life'—identities of region and religion duly foregrounded—the twentieth-century subtitle of *Saguna* as 'the first autobiographical novel in English by an Indian woman' lays stress upon the author's importance in terms of gender, genre and language. Krupabai's bold forays in print, the access to an international readership and also her identification with the novelistic lineage of George Eliot are some common grounds shared with Swarnakumari Debi Ghosal, whose novel of courtship was studied in the previous chapter. Unlike Swarnakumari, who was born and trained in a family of literati seen as integral to the cultural legacy of Calcutta, Krupabai was raised in a family that was fairly isolated in its social choices. Her parents were the first Brahmins to convert to Christianity in the Bombay Presidency and Krupabai was the thirteenth of their fourteen children. After her father's early demise, her older brother, Bhasker, became the most formative influence of her young life, encouraging her curiosity and education till his death at the start of her teenage years. Krupabai registered for a medical education, but discontinued it on account of her health. At the start of her twenties, Krupabai married a man of her choice and began to publish short pieces. Around the time of writing *Saguna*, she gave birth to her only child, who died within months. Even as she continued to struggle with her deteriorating health, she completed the only two novels in her oeuvre—*Kamala* and *Saguna*—and both were published in book form posthumously following her death at the age of thirty-two. While there is no denying the superb novelistic instincts and skills that Krupabai demonstrates in these books, both named after their central protagonists, the subtitles suggest them to be novels of ideas in which the destiny and choices of her feisty heroines need to weigh against and be configured within their social matrix, especially of religion—'native Christian life' in *Saguna* and 'Hindu life' in *Kamala*. The novels are far from prescriptive or pedantic, and the struggles of the protagonist with their social world pale in comparison to their entanglements within their own temperaments and desires.

In *Saguna*, the Christian ethos depicted often demands compliance to prayer and surrender to faith but gets compacted against the high-spiritedness and proud defiance of a girl on the threshold of womanhood. The counterpoint to the staidness, the predictability of the social or the religious, is reconfigured in terms of the unruliness of the natural world. It is the eponymous heroine Saguna's sensitivity to her environs—particularly robust wilderness, her ability to parallel it with her bodily struggles and her quicksilver artistic spirit ('nature' being the operative word between environment and personality)—that resonates through the length of the text. The Sanskrit word *saguna* implies a 'virtuous woman', thus evoking a likely moral tilt to the narrative, and the novel presents itself as a female *bildungsroman*—its first-person narrative plotting episodes from a childhood of curiosity and loneliness to an adulthood of companionship and hard-gained wisdom. Within this frame, and notwithstanding plot resolutions, an argument could be made for the novel's heightened reactivity to the somatic and spatial sublimation of the female narrator as cast in the tonal nuancing of the elegiac form.

The traditional elegy's 'emphasis on silence and absence' tends to shape the poetic form as 'a structure for mourning and consolation that is always on the verge of breaking down and whose efficacy is therefore perpetually in doubt'.[17] Such tenuous narrative transitions from sorrowful reflection to eventual succour gain further complexity when explored in sustained prose, such as the novel-form. John B. Vickery studies the basic triad of the traditional elegy—lamentation (of death), confrontation (with human mortality) and consolation (of death's inevitability)—for how these transform and perform in modern prose. Vickery argues that the interrogations in prose tend to shift away from traditional forms of authority (such as religion) and are more amenable to exploring 'romantic love, marriage, multiple cultures, philosophy, and the self as providing grounds for enduring mortality and all the other loses that human beings face'.[18] Each of these themes is prominent in *Saguna* from the very beginning, and in addition one might argue that the self's imbroglios with mortality and emotions is especially manifested in the narrator's inhabitation of a certain geographical terrain (the Upper Deccan plateau in the present-day state of Maharashtra). This topography of hills and forests, often written as grand, unkempt, awe-inspiring, becomes analogues to Saguna's own physical being. The 'page after evocative page [...] devoted to Romantic word-painting of the natural scene'[19] and the tumult of the body written continuous with the locale were frequently seen in novels of the Romantic Era (such as Emily Bronte's *Wuthering Heights*)—these were likely influences on Satthianadhan, who references her extensive reading in nineteenth-century British fiction.

The ideas and concepts in *Saguna* draw equally from the discourses of medicine and literature—they are both evocative imagery as also inscriptions of intense bodily suffering. As argued by Ardene Hegele in her book *Romantic Autopsy*, in many of the novels of the Romantic Era, 'a set of resonant ideas, metaphors, and terms floated between literature and medicine, producing a rich and flexible nonspecialist register that brought the knowledge of each field into the other's sphere'.[20] It is no coincidence then that the young protagonist, Saguna, sitting alone in the wilderness, reads Spencer's *Faery Queen*, and professes devotion to George Eliot ('forbidden books'[21]) and trains to be a student and practitioner of medicine. The more Saguna is expected to contend with the crisis of mind and body, and with deaths of loved ones, even the possibility of her own early mortality, the first-person voice dips into the reservoir of nature-writing. The distressed body speaks thus through nature with only the unbridled expression of the natural world as fully capable of grieving and enduring. The novel, *Saguna*, that intonates as a sophisticated 'pathography' displays all the features of a 'modern adventure story' with dramatic and terrifying elements of illness and death.[22] The literary form and affect of the elegy, when perceived through the lens of the rich contemporary scholarship on disability studies, actively encourages a reading of the novel as interrogating human suffering (both psychic as well as socio-historical), that nevertheless is able to concretely articulate a durable subjecthood in the world.

This section examines two specific instances in the text—the first being the illness and death of Saguna's brother in the opening half of the novel, and the second towards the end of the novel when her own feeble health disrupts a hard-fought medical education. Both episodes are written with sensitivity and constant affinity to elements of nature. When illness leads to a hallucinatory space of experience that cannot fully be accessed or shared within the consciousness of the first-person narrative voice, the text opens up into long sections with detailed descriptions of hills, streams and skies that are presented as thinking and feeling, often in near-delirious pitch. The prose of the novel thus often turns poetic in its elegiac valence, with illness not relegated to a plot-point, but narrated with visceral immediacy, an experience illumed from within.

By way of brief context of the novel as a whole: as autofiction, *Saguna* recreates many details of Krupabai Satthianadhan's life. The opening chapters introduce a precocious fatherless girl in a large family who displays a deep feeling for knowledge—as much in her embodied exploration of the outdoors as in her hunger for reading books—under the loving guidance of a paternal older brother. Her life takes a darker turn following the illness and death of this brother, and the next setting of her life is within the confines of a school run by European women missionaries where she lives among other girls, the sense of being an outlier more acute than ever. She is constantly questioning and resisting any inequities in her social world, professing nationalist pride, unwilling to succumb to suggestions of romance and marriage, and resolutely pursuing her innate talent for learning. A kindly teacher-mentor begins to train Saguna for a medical education, and soon arrangements are made for her to continue her training in England, but her constitution and other factors lead her to a medical college in a different region of India. One of the few women enrolled in that medical college, Saguna proves her mettle by scoring the highest marks in her first year. However, this is soon followed by poor health leading to a breakdown that is delivered in narrative ellipsis, some details spelt out but most left unsaid. Saguna turns away from education to recuperate her body and mind under the care of her family. The opportunities of the public sphere juxtapose with the inviolate sanctuary of the private domain and appear to be at an impasse till the promise of a romantic alliance emerges towards the end of the novel.

Throughout the novel, and with unfailing recurrence, it is these majestic mountains along with their scenic rivers, trees, sky and sun that provide the affective punctuation for Saguna's reflections on her life's journey. Her childhood is spent largely 'in a picturesque part of the Deccan'[23] that is seamlessly cast in romantic gothic overtones of 'pointed rocks, hidden caves, deep caverns, foaming, rushing torrents, bold, barren, breezy uplands and dark wooden lairs'.[24] The young girl's personhood is quickly conflated with these surroundings: 'My whole being took a great bound, as it were, as the wide expanse of land and sky unfolded itself to my view. I felt the freedom of nature; nothing seemed too great to attempt here; all was on a grand scale. [...] I went bounding everywhere and was filled with new life and spirits.'[25] The vistas written in the language of 'the tropics' can also be seen as borrowing from nineteenth-century colonial interpretation and reduction of India's climactic features—'warm, fecund, luxuriant, paradisiacal and pestilential', as the historian David Arnold elucidates.[26] When understood as a conceptual, and not just a physical space, Arnold points out that 'the tropics' also facilitate an 'otherness'—'a Western way of defining something culturally alien'.[27] Krupabai echoes some of these biases, as when Bhasker compares the wilderness of the Deccan to a traditional society that is 'shadowy, dark, mystic, weird, with superstition and bigotry lurking in every corner, before the light of Christianity comes into a land'.[28] It is again written as Saguna's first-hand experience at the end of the novel, but this time the light is not shining over a pre-Christian bigoted past but over her own body's deteriorations. The nostalgia for the Eden of childhood or the future promise of unsullied heaven is thereby reposed in the same landscape.

In addition to projecting her emotions upon topography, flora and fauna, the narrator also places herself among them as a 'child of nature'—the birds, stream and wind responding to her thoughts, a personification of the spiritual communion she shares with her brother on the mountain top. The emotional load is almost unendurable.

> The tension of feeling was too great for me to bear; I rushed down at the first sign of the dissolution of the magic scene. I could not bear to watch the mist clouds rise like giants from the earth, or be driven hither and thither, a fantastic mass of light and colour. When I reached the valley below I received a broad shining smile and a merry laugh from the stream I knew and loved so well [...] and the wind that thrilled all the leaves and wrapped itself round me so softly seemed to speak to me. I listened for its voice and felt its sad meaning in the low moan that fell on my ear through rocks and trees, and childlike I felt that the winds and the birds were sorry too.[29]

Values of robust health are steadily imparted to this empathizing landscape—its health evident in the solidity of the rocks and giant spreading trees. In contrast, life back in the town with its 'sea of houses' under a 'sickly light' seems dejecting to Saguna.[30] As Bhasker falls ill, Saguna takes it upon herself to nurse her brother. Soon the family goes back to the countryside to help Bhasker's health and Saguna notes his improvement, drawing connections between what she calls his 'high-strung' temperament, his physical suffering and the natural world:

> The sensitive nerves of my brother by suffering rendered more sensitive still, were alive to every impression, and seemed to magnify and brighten the most commonplace delights. The moon rose for him with chastened and sublime glory, and the stars shone more brilliantly than ever before. The wind was alive to him and spoke to his soul in innumerable voices.[31]

But the ecstasy of this closeness with nature, its 'sublime heights' would entail 'corresponding depths' and what Saguna names as 'strange depressions'—her lingering sadness and morbid moods are again placed in the wilderness.[32] In this, Saguna as a young sister is helplessly bearing witness to a terrible suffering, while her older, retrospective narrative voice is ripe with the knowledge that she would contend with a similar suffering in her own adulthood. The landscape of light and air that promises health also suggests melancholia and death. The presence of an old fort with 'eerie, wind-swept windows [...] witching shadows, and mournful, rustling trees'[33] deepens Bhasker's depression but also precipitates a desire to recover. As Bhasker becomes more aware of his impending death, he turns to walks by the river and the groves to protect his time of solitude and reverie, while keeping up a more ebullient persona at home. He speaks about the acceptance of inevitable death as not something to be feared. At the start of the chapter that records Bhasker's death, the first-person voice falls silent. The novel is now driven forward by the gentle entry of a third-person voice that takes on the role of an observant, detail-oriented chronicler of the deathbed scene in this room:

> It was midnight. A soft, subdued light filled the room. The wind moaned and rustled through the creepered window with a strange wail, the only sound that disturbed the calm which prevailed. The moonbeams kissed the twinkling leaves and fitfully glanced into the room. Several figures were seen moving about, but all were hushed and speechless; their eyes seemed to be watching one object, their looks pointed to one thing, and that was to the pale, thin, wasted figure of a young man lying silent and still.[34]

Even as several figures are described gathering around the dying man ('pale, thin, wasted figure') the narrative notes a young girl who 'seemed not to comprehend the situation'.[35] Two pages later, just as discreetly, and in the midst of describing the worth of the dying man's life, the first-person voice returns, but this time to powerful grieving—the touch of the dying brother's hand becoming a mighty force that shakes Saguna, and she loses her consciousness even as he takes his last breath. Overcome by misery and darkness, she describes herself as 'a rudderless boat [that was] driven by every wind'.[36] Saguna's state of mind in the days following her brother's death is written as a gliding into 'a visionary kind of state' that seems to suggest a break with reality, or perhaps as a release into a private comforting irrationality, which is seen by her visiting sister as 'peculiar moods'.[37] She turns again to the nature that had cradled Bhaker and her in health and sickness and must now extend its power over bereavement. Saguna describes it thus: 'I saw him in the stars, in the moon's faint ray. Often I heard him calling to me, and I rushed out in the dusk and sat in an ecstasy of delight, thinking that he was watching and caring for his sister just as he used to do of old.'[38] The night sky and stars are not as frequent in the novel as the scenes lit by sunlight, but they often provide access to more brooding, inward thought processes, especially during the long sleepless night that serves as prequel to a final concluding scene: one of optimism for Saguna, and of the entire novel when cast in a retrospective light. While sunlight inspires towards health and creativity, it is starlight that seems to promise afterlife and restfulness.

Following Bhasker's death, Saguna is sent to live at a boarding school facility for her first extended exposure to structured institutional education—it being already established by now that she is well-read and brighter than others her age. What should have been a nurturing start and excellent exposure for a girl who delights in school, and professes even to strangers that she wants to be clever, leads to an unexpected development—Saguna begins to experience her own bouts of illness, often so indisposed as to be incapacitated and needing to return home on account of it. Saguna confesses that this is also the time when she gets into 'the habit of morbidly reflecting and analyzing [...] In my ill and depressed moments, especially, it became very strong.'[39] She attaches a range of adjectives to her grief, such as mad, intense, rebellious.[40] The depressive spells are featured in different ways for the rest of the novel. In fact, it is curious that Saguna's name stays muted in the narrative till this point when her mother enters her into an institution that promises 'a high-class English education'[41] for native Christian girls. Here, the seed of ambition, to study medicine, starts to grow. One notices Saguna's resolute turning away from her longing for mountains and towards a more social sphere of personal aspiration. The narrative is devoted to showcasing a 'restless untamed spirit'[42] alongside worldly, academic excellence. However, the missionary in charge of arranging her trip to the colder climes of England refuses to support her visit on account of her poor constitution. It is again health and climate that forms a fence between Saguna's inner desires and the world she is forced to inhabit. But Saguna continues to draw solace from solitude and the outdoors: 'I learnt many a thing in the silent darkness, in the midst of which the nature that was so much a mystery lay revealed in all its glory [...] The native ruggedness outside only made the hidden brightness more startling.'[43] Saguna's prayers are of forbearance and optimism (the brightness described as hidden) but the repeated narrative patterns of night and ruggedness signal to the reader a constant return to darker eventualities.

In this concluding ninth chapter of the novel, Saguna describes her journey to a different region of India, the Christian people who become her guardians and her excellent showing at the end of her first year of studies. But the jubilation also brings on 'a feeling of complete prostration'[44] and further fears of a breakdown. Saguna returns home hastily and the journey back in the coasting steamer is described against overcast monsoon skies. The likelihood of Saguna's medical education coming to a premature end entirely on account of unreliable health starts to look more likely against this daunting imagery of an impending storm. Even a return to her beloved mountains is not enough to support her full recovery. 'A great change had come over me. I was not the Saguna who had returned to her family after a year's study, to enjoy rest and change. My health had become enfeebled, and I had gone back instead of advancing.'[45] As she feels and expresses her helplessness, Saguna turns to reading and hopes to be inspired by the 'spirit of the writers'; she finds herself lost again 'in a labyrinth of morbid and unproductive thought'.[46] This ennui and lassitude lasts for five months, till the coming of 'the stranger' with 'large melancholy eyes' who remains unnamed in the novel that is now a mere seven pages away from concluding.

The feelings of sorrow and grace alternate in ever shorter intervals: Saguna sheds tears through a night of 'silent mortification' which is followed by a halcyon period—'a golden haze'—of time with family, books and 'quiet passive enjoyment of the grand scenery around' (158). Saguna equates her illness with being undeserving: 'What right had I to feel this joy?' (158). This is one of the few sections of the book that is bracketed off entirely for pleasure on the protagonist's own terms and not linked to any purpose or person. And yet, the menacing darkness beneath or around is not far. Days begin as idyllic and lush, with glorious sky, cool breezes, moist clouds—imparting 'an exquisite sense of rest and peace' that also puts Saguna in a 'dreamy unnatural state'—'the force of association' that brings to mind her dead brother.[47] The dead and the possibility of death once again press the question of faith with renewed urgency, even as it brings about the 'lesson [...] on selfishness'[48]—as much for chafing about her illness as for entertaining the idea of romantic love. This last, long sleepless night is a densely packed interior monologue with constant references to stars shining in the sky. The narrative's discomfort with human romance starts to strain through the writing of nature, and a light is said to 'break in on my soul'.[49] The suitor is now Christ and the romance is the test of the protagonist's faith in his teachings. As for the mortal lover, he becomes a kindred spirit who must then be tested, bonded and motivated by a shared Christian faith. The true nature of this coupling is clarified in a final image: Saguna holding her suitor's hands as they stand at the edge of a precipice, looking down a valley.

Both emotional fruition and the spiritual camaraderie are experienced by the protagonist as a glow of light and as mists rolling over the great mountains beyond. The physical body of the protagonist, as expressive of the scale of her multiple contentions with finitude and wavering health, finds comfort in the care of a sentient natural environment. The conclusion does not seek to offer resolution to the main struggles of the protagonist—neither with regard to her weakened constitution nor her interrupted drive for education—but pauses in ambiguities with striking authorial confidence. Suffering and crisis, it seems to suggest, do not always have resolutions, but rather open up new, assertive, expressions of personhood. The novel thus must be seen as defiant of the more conventional teleology of 'early Indian novel' or 'pioneering women's novel'—rather, such modulated poise in the manipulation of the elegiac form marks Krupabai Satthianadhan as a precocious novelist.

Journaling for an audience of sisters: Atiya Fyzee's *Zamana-i-Tahsil* (1921)

> *In 1906 I went to London on a government scholarship. The purpose of the trip was that I would become a teacher and come back to serve my compatriot sisters, but I became sick there, and after spending thirteen months abroad in hardship, I returned without obtaining my goal.*[50]

The forthright presentation of select biographical details—sponsorship to study abroad, intent to serve, hardship and illness, premature return—scaffolds a cross-genre literary self-presentation stipulated by a Muslim woman's unconventional life choices in early twentieth-century India. Atiya Fyzee (1877–1967) set out on a prestigious mission to be trained as a teacher in London, and similar to Krupabai Satthianadhan, whose sickness thwarted her quest for a medical degree, Atiya returned home before completing her studies. Such unplanned life detours and a philanthropic persona become hallmarks of Atiya's long career of several decades. She vocalized a desire to serve the women of her community and country—a crucial sisterhood that was continuously evoked in epistolary writing—and this overlapped with the need to preserve that serving self through illness, longing for home, and personal sorrows that could be revealed to a (mostly) faceless public readership. At the same time, while the degree in education may have been the explicit goal, the parallel intent of recording and communicating this process or experience of travelling to and living in the hub of the colonial enterprise was being fulfilled, even if it had to remain a tacit accomplishment. The writing on the page that speaks of failure is in itself a success of considerable magnitude at a time when few single Muslim women travelled abroad for an education and even fewer committed their experiences to print.

Sprinkled with periodic references to 'sisters' or at times specifically to *tahzibi bahinon* or 'newspaper sisters', Atiya Fyzee's *Zamana-i-tahsil* (A Time of Education, 1921) was first composed in instalments between 1906 and 1907 in the mode of a travel diary or *roznamchah*, and sent as periodic letters to her biological sisters, Zehra and Nazli. These were then published in serial form in the weekly Urdu journal *Tahzib un-Niswan* (translated by scholars as 'Women's Culture'[51] or 'The Women's Reformer'[52]). For the educated middle-class (Hindu and Muslim) in many northern parts of India during this period, Urdu as 'the language of public discourse and literary expression' had become a significant 'source of ideas concerning religious identity, educational curricula and social reform'.[53] This was sustained by regular access to and consumption of shorter narratives curated and collated by editors of journals. In her study of periodicals in Bengali at the turn of the twentieth century, Samarpita Mitra argues that 'the fulfillment of political modernity in the form of a nation was essentially a literary project that entailed the making of a vernacular reading public' wherein the publications played a crucial role in debating the aesthetical and social worth of authors.[54] Such a nation-making modernist literary project, in the context of a journal like *Tahzib* can be said to facilitate an accessible, inclusive, intimate loci to the participation and contribution of women. Composed in a conversational style that factored the reading level of women educated at home, its weekly format also facilitated dialogues between the publication, reader, and between readers.[55] Established in Lahore in 1898 by Sayyid Mumtaz Ali and his wife Muhammadi Begam,[56] the journal was also unique for the editorship of a woman—many of Atiya's despatches referred to Muhammadi Begam (who was around the same age as Atiya) as *bahan aiditar sahiba* with the triple address of sister-editor-madam.[57] Atiya thus participated in a public, gendered discourse of Urdu (across northern India, including the Punjab), one that thus added a necessary dimension to the public discussions about personal autonomy, community obligations and nationalist pride. Analogously, she was also a partaker of an established tradition of students who were actively engaged in the political and intellectual ferment of London[58] even as they worked towards qualifications that could open up new professional avenues, often with the colonial government back in India.

Born in Istanbul to a merchant family, and raised in Bombay as part of the prominent Tyabji clan that was at the forefront of promoting education, Atiya along with two older sisters became active participants in reformist activities for Indian Muslim women.[59] At a time when early marriage and observing the purdah was common practice among the readers of *Tahzib*, a nineteen-year-old unmarried woman travelling through Europe and sharing her impressions and opinions in print was unusual. Her instinctive frankness is unmistakable and is thus seen as requiring intervention by her first readers, her sisters. Siobhan Lambert-Hurley and Sunil Sharma, who are also recent editors and translators of her writings, note likely edits and elisions in the text by Zehra, Atiya's eldest sister, a 'sisterly censorship [...] that was intended to protect her reputation in the eyes of her Tahzibi sisters'.[60] However, any notions of privacy and propriety turn ambiguous for a text that takes on the personal diary format only to expressly address a public audience—the 'private life' featuring diaristic mullings or fastidious chronicling of what the author believes is of interest to her audience of Muslim women. This invites a scrutiny of the author's supposition of audience taste and interests as well as how these get represented in mutual textual engagements. How might the diary's prosaic monologue echo into sisterly *mahfils* or literary dialogues?

The *Mahfil*, or the traditional literary gathering, was evoked in the journal's regular section, *Mahfil-i-Tahzib*, which included letters/replies between editor and readers as well as letters from readers addressed to other readers, collectively referred to as the '*tahzibi bahin*, the sisterly network of Tahzib's subscribers'.[61] The ubiquitous presence of 'sisters' in such gender-segregated *mahfils* meant that any direct addresses to them were likely perfunctory or habitual, and part of the flourish of delivery. Yet, one also needs to account for Atiya Fyzee's writings occurring at a time of considerable personal distress and tribulations. The evocation of 'sisters' in Atiya's diaries is a charged space—it signals a reaching for the familiar, of bonding, coping, disclosing, strategizing, but it also includes strong distancing affects like avoidance, which will be discussed later.

The present study examines sections of the text that contain such direct addresses ('sisters') as both a conscious knitting and an unravelling of audiencehood when finally, at the end of the text, the audience is informed that Atiya had withheld many crucial developments (such as the fundamental decision to abandon her studies). The great majority of the text is preoccupied with buoyant minutia: somatic and sensory experiences of foreign vistas; kitchens, culinary processes and delicacies; social obligations and excursions; fashion and clothing; luxurious service and comforts. Additionally, this format of 'informal ethnography'[62] created a travelogue that is heavily peopled—mention is made of over one hundred and fifty individuals encountered by her during the thirteen months of travel, including British gentry and famed Muslim reformers and later nationalist leaders.[63] Nearly all of these are delivered with Atiya's discerning, deeply internalized class-consciousness, one that is particularly evident when she wishes to impress on the audience of sisters her encounters with hierarchies of privileges, some of which she is privy to, and others that clearly exclude her. Being a colonial subject who is received in social circles in London as representing her Indian Muslim community and as an unmarried woman building a career, it is perhaps unsurprising that many of her own class anxieties are displaced onto the working and service classes as will be discussed in this section.

The diary entries begin on 1 September 1906, with the launch of the steamboat that Atiya takes to London, and end on 27 September 1907, the day that she returns to the shores of Bombay. In their introductory commentaries to *Atiya's Journeys: A Muslim Woman from Colonial Bombay in Edwardian Britain*, Lambert-Hurley and Sharma describe the *roznamchah* to be a 'sub-genre of autobiographical writing [...] best translated as a "little day book"'[64] that was a long-standing tradition in Atiya Fyzee's family. Daily activities (such as picnics and visits to the dentist) as well as larger events (relocations or deaths) were recorded in family notebooks known as *Akbar ki Kitab*.[65] The specific channelling of Atiya's diary through letters to her sisters rather than directly to the *Tahzib* is notable. The three Fyzee sisters were know to be close confidants, and had become 'a clique unto themselves', even choosing to set up house together for nearly all their lives—none of them had children; two of them were separated from their husbands, and the third's husband lived with them.[66] Understandably, such strong anchoring in sisterhood then organically becomes the seamless leitmotif of Atiya's writings about her voyage and encounters in foreign climes. The fragmented quality of her text displays several spurts of information or family updates on specific relatives and quick asides—these contain subtexts that would likely baffle or escape all readers except the author's sisters. And yet, there is no mistaking the final destination for her compositions—the curiosity of her 'newspaper sisters' via a careful construction of her own identity as an attentive, composed, intrepid, informed chronicler of cosmopolitan adventures.

The first despatch, dated 1 September 1906, mentions its location—the S.S. Moldavia on its first day of voyage—and demonstrates the author's central formulations for her readers, both in content and presentation. The germinal affective note is of parting and the disorientation that comes from relinquishing the stability of land for the heaving of the waves:

> I did not know I was so weak as to be affected in this way by the separation of loved ones. When the launch [boat] started moving, I completely lost control over myself. The sea was also rough and at times the water would come into the launch. Anyway, I was not worried about this. I watched my loved ones at the shore until the

> end. As long as my vision enabled me. I kept looking there, but in the end they disappeared from sight. Ah! It is not easy going to Europe. I immediately realized how challenging my ambition was.[67]

The image evoked of the travelling self, standing alone on the deck of a steamboat, watching family on the shore vanish from sight and feeling overwhelmed by the enormity of the undertaking, is nevertheless accompanied with a seeming impudence of ambition. The authorial persona as also the narrative tonality here is one of isolation and troubled individualism with a hint of quiet pride in her quest. The passages that follow, however, reveal that Atiya is far from alone or isolated. In fact, she is travelling with two family members (brother and nephew) as well as two female passengers who are constantly with her—one of these women has also been awarded the same government scholarship as Atiya (Mrs Mitter, who Atiya claims is overwhelmed by her maiden voyage) and the second is the more enterprising Miss Das who has the wherewithal to pay her way for the same course. Atiya estimates that there must be around 100 to 125 other passengers on the boat. The reader feels included, enlisted to be a sympathetic fellow traveller, when she opens the second paragraph of the first entry of her diary with a direct address to the reader: 'Now let me tell you who my fellow travellers are.'[68] The second-person voice recedes into the background as the descriptive passages build tempo, but having been established so early in the text, the voice re-surfaces in later entries when Atiya needs her readers, women who likely have not travelled beyond familial spaces, to participate and empathize in her own unsteady location. While the unsteadiness mentioned in this entry is attributed to the viscerality of a sea voyage, the unsteadiness elsewhere in the text is equally from other exigencies, such as harsh weather, tiresome company or unpredictable health.

Apart from the initial experience of being sea-bound and following the introduction to her immediate companions, the first composition of Atiya's diary includes a description of the steamboat. The three levels or decks of the steamboat that align with the financial means of the passengers establish an orientation to class privilege or deprivation that repeats throughout the text—Atiya herself located in the middle, the deck that is preferred by first-class passengers as well as 'the ones from below'.[69] Atiya keeps her readers informed about the cost of things and experiences, about the comforts that can or cannot be afforded by people around her and the human resources required to maintain status. Early observations include the interior décor of the steamboat, such as its music room, and of the author being 'seized with laughter' by the condition of silver objects around her, which because of 'careless cleaning' bears imprints that look like 'footprints of tiny birds'.[70] Atiya's comments on the polishing of the silver not being on par with the work of her staff back at her house is an early establishment of her class positioning and credibility vis-à-vis the 'Tahzibi sisters'. The government scholarship therefore reinforces her sense of merit, rather than her financial straits, and more importantly, the serving class is approached as requiring continued scrutiny. She notes: 'The bearers (men and women) who are appointed to serve the passengers do their work well. They are not visible, but always keep doing their work with energy and skill. Although I tried to see them working—while cleaning the cabin, et cetera—I could never see when they do their service.'[71] The purported invisible efficiency of the serving class corresponds to a visible outcome whose assessment Fyzee keenly conducts.

In their study, *Cultures of Servitude: Modernity, Domesticity and Class in India*, Raka Ray and Seemin Qayum treat 'the nexus of labor relations that is domestic servitude as an institution rather than as an occupational category'.[72] In the process, they argue, is a normalization that needs to be understood in two ways: 'social relations are legitimized ideologically such that domination, dependency, and inequality are not only tolerated but accepted; and second, […] they are reproduced through everyday interaction and practice.'[73] We see an illustration of such naturalization via the everydayness of servitude in the much shorter second entry (dated September 2) in Atiya Fyzee's diary that comprises three compact paragraphs—the first given to a description of looking out of her window to see phosphorescence that had turned the night sea into 'molten lead [...] all white and shining'; the second paragraph reports on the health of her companions who are struggling with the sea's tumult; and the third returns to observing the steamboat service staff. This time, it is to not comment on their work but to deliver a homogenizing admiration that closely identifies the staff as being robust and attuned to the sea: 'It is obvious from their stature, appearance, and fit bodies that they are used to hard work. But from their weathered faces it seemed as if centuries have passed by them. It appeared from their expressions that they knew well what kind of waves would come next.'[74] The fascination and primacy that Atiya accords to the steamboat's service staff at the start of her journey continues through frequent mentions through the length of her text, when she comments on the nature and output of domestic help in the houses she is invited to visit in London.

In this textual representation of an international adventure to an audience reading from the comforts of their homes in India, the travel writer has to consider how to hold the attention of her readers beyond perfunctory word-sketches of sea and travel companions. Atiya Fyzee takes care to keep personal feelings on par with a matter-of-fact crisp reportage of what is encountered or experienced. The text includes narrative detailing of the materiality of social spaces (decor and cutlery), the calibre of the service staff and varied gastronomic experiences. Such itemizing of consumption of food and drink has been studied as reflecting and contributing to an emergent post-Enlightenment modernity in the long nineteenth century.[75] Far from being a novice sea voyager, Atiya's writing exudes the air of a consummate traveller and ethnographer. She requests the steamboat's chief officer for a tour of the kitchen, which she admires for the assembly-line efficiency in the cutting and prepping of meat as well as for washing dishes, wherein 'everything has reached the level of a skill'.[76] Six or seven women accompany her on this tour, the reader is told, and their interest in the professional kitchen has the quality of admiring but measured field notes.

As the steamboat moves through the Suez Canal, and enters the Mediterranean Sea, Atiya's notes start to include her observations on the diversity of people and ethnicities that she is encountering. She takes care to repeat her keen interest in fashion and clothing, and her own aesthetics and ability to notice or admire such 'harmonious and tasteful things'.[77] One of the longer despatches from the journey is after disembarking at Marseilles where Atiya is full of admiration for the city, the clothes and shoes of the women, the grandeur of a parade and the luxury of sightseeing on a fast train. 'I will describe the train for interested sisters [...] In these countries there is no light other than from electricity, that is why it seems very nice. [...] When our train set off the entire city was shimmering with light.'[78] As the author and her company return to the boat, they encounter a very cold wind and the gaiety of the city roads and speeding trains is replaced by this note of hardship, leading to a conclusion that is entirely leaning on the goodwill of her audience. 'I am sending this letter, and entreat Tahzibi sisters to remember in their prayers.'[79] A template is being set vis-à-vis the author's sisterly audience, and the rest of her travel notes slowly begin to construct an ambience that seems to invite more support.

Following eighteen days of travel time, Atiya Fyzee finally finds herself in her new living quarters and starts on her training program at Maria Grey Training College, London.[80] This entry dated 18 September is packed with a debutant's enthusiasm to all things big and small—from the furniture and living arrangements ('I am very happy with my fortune'[81]), the deportment and conversational skills of her fellow-students ('If only the men of our country were like these women'[82]), the finances involved in offering tea or lunch to an acquaintance, to the open windows in all the cold passageways. The final note of the entry gravitates once again to jottings on status, as well as minute everyday pleasures: 'How these people take care and how tasteful they are. Upper-class English people are of a different kind. Truly I have landed in a different world. [...] We had tea and went for a walk. Walking is a pleasurable activity in this country.'[83] This initial walk soon leads to several excursions around London and a few to the countryside, although three months later, in her entry dated 22 December, Atiya seems to indicate that her travelogue has not included as much travel as she might have anticipated when she began her despatches.[84] Nonetheless, the first few entries after reaching London and starting on her education are full of anticipation: she writes about her daily routine in classrooms and periodic after-school social engagements that included meeting family. 'To see relatives in exile is another kind of pleasure.'[85] After a few sentences naming the relatives who invite her to their house, Fyzee's travel notes turn back to a familiar subject—describing interior décor of the house and its lone 'energetic' domestic staff: 'Really, the servants here are a different breed of humans. They are so sensible and hard-working. If they don't do a task properly, they themselves feel so sorrowful that the mistress's sorrow is nothing compared to it.'[86] Fyzee's scrutiny and commentary on the domestic staff are the same irrespective of the wealth of the household or the number of people hired to service it. During her year in London, Fyzee is a frequent guest to the house of her friend, Navajbai Tata, who is married into one of India's most recognized and wealthy family of industrialists. During a visit in June 1907 to the mansion and stately estates of York House in Twickenham, a recent acquisition of the Tatas, Fyzee writes of her meeting with her 'sincere, nice and true friend' who she claims to be a blessing in 'this artificial world'.[87] This is followed by a long paragraph that says less about the friend and instead begins to profile the staff at hand:

> Right now they have twenty-one servants. A haughty and cunning doorman of long service—how many revolutions he must have seen—opened the door; the well-built and tall gardeners; the boys serving at the table with such well-bred manners, dressed in dark blue and gold uniforms; the cook's manner is unique; and there are four maids. [...] The sensibility, politeness, and propriety of the servants are perfect. None of them is visible, but whenever one is needed they are present. Their system of appearing is beyond my

> comprehension. [...] I had decided that I must see how these people serve so energetically, but it was not possible to see any maid. Indeed, it seems that they work like clockwork.[88]

Not only does such careful appraisal of the household showcase the affluence of Atiya's hosts and reiterate the author's need to comment on attending staff wherever she goes—whether it is their physical appearance or the quality of their work—but it equally reveals her admiration for efficiency and immediate, invisible service.

Indeed, there are several instances when Atiya wants to impress on her audience of sisters the need to fully appreciate and imbibe the organizing systems and ethics of work that she encounters during her European sojourn.[89] At times, this admiration for adeptness combines with the travelogue's fixation with food, and the service required in producing and presenting it. The writer is reflexive enough to recognize these patterns in her reportage: 'Perhaps I have written before regarding cooking, but I feel like writing about it again in greater detail. I hope my sisters will not be weary of it.'[90] Atiya proceeds to describe culinary processes she has observed in London:

> Food is prepared at such great speed, cleanliness and low cost. Cleanliness is to the highest degree—the hand hardly touches anything. Vegetables are cut by a machine. There are special kinds of tools for mixing and stirring them. [...] There is no trouble for them [the English] to observe the cleaning rules of us Muslims. To accept English ways in a Muslim manner is a simple, easy and effortless task. Then an excellent state of affairs can be achieved.[91]

Cleanliness is attributed to Muslims and also assumed to be a cardinal quality of English cooking, hence proposing the easy amenability of one culture to another. Such admiration of and quest for excellence, whether in the domestic and personal arena or in the professional and academic, requires Atiya to both represent personal experiences and place them in the context of an ostensible colonial fissure and cultural transnavigation. Another fixation for this diaryist, apart from the multiple notations about diet and food, is with clothes, wherein the reader is made aware of Atiya's own pride in her styling (and told of other people's praises for the same). This is in contrast is her disdain for the popular European fashion as seen on Regent Street or Bond Street.[92] Such juxtapositions and ideals in representation likely limit her ability to be entirely transparent with her audience with regard to the personal struggles that lead to her surrender of the government scholarship.

An early indication of the strain on the author can be discerned in her writing within a week of enrolling in her new program, and following a flurry of closely packed updates on her college, family visits, daily routine, extracurricular activities and several other demands on her time. Atiya has to decline an invitation from a friend and is barely able to keep up with the social niceties of replying to letters. The dialogue with the sisters that need to be sent out by weekly mail starts to feel like one more demand: 'I hope to God that I will be able to continue with this travelogue and that the sisters enjoy this new experience.'[93] A few months later, another line slips in the entry that does not give any explanations but states a fear: 'Sometimes I become very nervous. I had no idea of the effect of separation from dear ones. My plea to God is that we be fated to meet in happiness and I be worthy of this heavy responsibility.'[94] To travel and to write a diary of observations for the benefit of those who likely do not have the means or the freedom to travel is the freighted responsibility of having to constantly grasp and communicate an elusive, burgeoning wonderment as honestly as one can. This seems to be how Fyzee understood her commitment to her Tahzibi sisters. The narrative fragments showcase an accomplished and attentive narrator who is moving into the heart of the metropolis—whether it is tea and discussions with royalty (such as the Maharaja and Maharani of Baroda, as also the Maharani of Cooch Behar), evenings at the concert halls or watching dramatic productions, visits to the Royal Academy and British Museum, the lights and sounds of a bustling city, hedonistic pleasures in clothes and jewellery, flowers and flower arrangements, food and banquets. All these gratifications are dutifully relayed. After watching a production of *Sindbad* (from the *Arabian Nights*), Atiya writes about it in great detail, concluding with an address: 'Dear sister, I hope you find this account interesting. I saw it with excitement and wrote about it for you.'[95] To experience anything with such immediacy is grist for the travel writer's diary, and its almost immediate publication in India was a source of pride. In an undated entry, Atiya attends a meeting of the Indian section of the Royal Society of Arts where the speaker, Yusuf Ali, delivered a lecture on the accomplishments of Muslim women, naming several figures from past and present, including 'a needless cry for Miss Fyzee! [...] He described the family she belongs to and for what purpose she has come, and showed a picture.'[96] That Atiya, barely out of her teenage years, continues to refer to herself in the third person, after the speaker names her as a model Muslim woman, is a curious situation and makes room for enormous self-congratulatory emotions and assurance. At the same meeting, she reports another speaker calling the Muslims of India as 'a slothful community' that stays in the past, and Atiya is quick to follow up on this comment by addressing any affront her readers might feel: 'Dear sister, he spoke the truth, if we feel bad that's our choice.' This instance of her expressing an opinion that would side with the bias of someone who is not from the community may be seen as her acceptance of a public profile that does not shy from controversy or provocation. Atiya reports another such experience of encountering her 'writerly fame' unexpectedly.

In January 1907, she received three letters from friends in India, each including a reference to Atiya Khanum's travelogue and crediting it with opening up the world for them. 'I was happy that my Tahzibi sisters have honored me by enthusiastically reading about my experiences.'[97] It is not just this trickling in of reports about her popularity but Atiya also indicates that she closely monitors and enjoys the appearance of her writing in print, reminding her sister, Zehra, when the issues occasionally don't arrive in London on time.[98] The pride in her public persona, however, precludes much disclosure—such as of romantic entanglements,[99] or of breakdowns in health.

Atiya Fyzee's travel notes are reticent on the matter of physical or mental health,[100] apart from stray references to fever or indisposition, and a few references to strain or homesickness. A longer entry about intense bodily grieving on receiving news of her grandmother's death is an exception and perhaps stands in for a more cumulative exhaustion—'In six months how the world has turned upside down! [...] For eight days I lay there, listless with a fever and headache. I didn't feel like walking, talking or sitting.'[101] But this sentiment is quickly papered over by subsequent entries and the reason for selective disclosures about her health is presented in one of her final despatches: 'I did not want to mention my health problems in this travelogue because I knew that my kind sisters who had expressed their good wishes and joy before I left Bombay would be disappointed.'[102] The need to protect her readers from her discomforts or perhaps to shield her from their opinion draws attention to the challenges faced by women travellers in challenging norms and expectations, and the worry that all accomplishments will collapse in the face of any one single failure. Thus, any small unhappiness diminishes the whole, while always the larger, looming threat of utter failure—the premature abandonment of the studies undertaken—unfortunately does come true and thus casts a retrospective pall on all the sunny adventures she had taken such pains to construct.

The letter of 5th August 1907 would have come as a jolt to her readers. Atiya makes the announcement that instead of continuing on the second year of her scholarship, she would be leaving on a homebound ship later that month. Having taken this decision, she wants to share her plight—the high fever, weakness and headaches because of which the doctors have explicitly said that she would waste away if she were to stay longer. The desire of her heart, however, remains unchanged: 'I hope that I will be able to help my sisters with whatever I have learned.' Her duty to her audience is repeated the following week:

> Before I leave I consider it my duty to write that the way of life here is completely different. Sister sahiba, editor of the Tahzib, had

> especially asked me to inform the sisters about this, but for this more leisure is needed, which I didn't have here. Anyway, right now I will end my travelogue in this way, but when it is published in book form, I will certainly include it.[103]

As the travels end, so must the travelogue, but its merit is clear to the writer who seems quite certain that a fuller book version is due. Exactly a year following her sea voyage to London, Atiya Fyzee returns home via Harwich and Hook of Holland to visit Heidelberg and Munich in Germany and Paris in France. In September 1907, she boards a mailboat named *Arabia* that is headed to Bombay. Barely two sentences describe this voyage of several days—'Many days have passed in comfort and ease. The sea was more or less good.'[104] With this, Fyzee reports that 'the sea has reached its end' and she is reunited with loved ones. The parting note is unsurprisingly addressed to the empathetic listening of a sisterly audience that had kept her company on her brave odyssey: 'Now I take leave of the Tahzibi sisters and say goodbye. The mind is gladdened and the weak body energized.'[105] The journey of this courageous, sensitive teenager from the early twentieth century who resolutely travelled to another continent for her studies stands out for its perceptive, varied portrayal of the everyday life, whether the underground rail, streets, concert halls, classrooms or kitchens. The feat in itself was rare—thus, to have the awareness to observe minutely and in good humour, keeping in mind what was of interest to the audience in India, is a further accomplishment. It is only at the end that one realizes how strenuously Atiya Fyzee had to work to keep up that cheerful front—the elusive injuries of homesickness in an alien land cannot so quickly be glossed over. But Atiya would not return to print to dwell on what those deeper injuries may have been—even though she lived till ninety, and was a personal friend of public figures such as Muhammad Iqbal and Muhammad Ali Jinnah. Hence all one has is this tantalizing text—still distinctive a century later—of a youthful self bravely facing the many obscurities and shadows of the colonial enterprise.

All roads and words lead to the King: Dosebai Cowasjee Jessawalla's *The Story of My Life* (1911)

> *As we proceeded along the Lawn, His Majesty the King was seen coming towards us. As soon as he came near, I and my son were duly presented to His Majesty, who graciously shook hands with us. He looked in splendid health, and put on a smiling face all the time he conversed with us. We remained talking for about a quarter of an hour, during which I remarked that I had had the privilege of meeting him in Bombay in 1875 when he visited India. He looked pleased, and observed that it was many years ago, when he was quite a young man. I further assured him that we Parsees were happy under his benign rule, at which he expressed satisfaction. He also gave me great credit for courage and energy in undertaking a voyage around the world at my time of life.*[106]

Dosebai Cowasjee Jessawalla (1832–1911) was seventy-six years old when she managed to wrangle an invitation to Windsor to shake hands with the King and Queen of England. This singular event would come to represent for her the highest manifestation of her own astounding abilities and ambitions as a transcontinental traveller and global citizen. She would have been an unlikely contender—a married woman with children—to chronicle first-hand engagements with memorable events, places and people of her times. Dosebai was nearly a decade older than King Edward VII, and died a few months after him just as her autobiography *The Story of My Life* (1911) was being set to type—the first words of her book name the King, and their meeting in 1908 becomes the concluding event of note. This narrative arrangement around no less than the British Crown, as much synecdoche as the corporeal presence of the King, may be argued to reveal the potential and challenges of the travelogue in the mode of autobiography—one that is humbly and intensely personal even as it also turns resolutely outward-facing in its quest for social prestige and power. This is especially the case when the traveller explicitly takes a gendered position with complex motives for her travels. The scholar Shefali Chandra points to the many ways in which Dosebai 'crafts cultural capital from her performance of upper-class cosmopolitan femininity'.[107] Dosebai was not only seeking/getting legitimacy from the highest political authority (as might have been the case with famous travellers in preceding centuries) but the authorial voice itself becomes, by association, the new legitimate centre for narrative trespasses. 'I never hesitate to speak out my mind, even though my friends may not like to hear it'[108] is the authorial assertion, and the autobiography-travelogue has the same defiant approach with the traveller's body and presence—the claim to space and mobility is innate in the drive to be heard, seen and acknowledged. Despite being one of the earliest full-length travelogues written in English by a woman from India, teeming with social observations and buoyed by a distinct storytelling voice, the scholarship on this text and author is surprisingly sparse. This might suggest a lacuna either about the genre (travelogue as literary output) or about her location and position—an Indian woman travelling to and indeed seeming to uncritically celebrate the imperial centre. One notes this in comparison to the extended scholarship on travel narratives of British women in the colonies, as both agents and subjects of imperialist ideologies that they could strategically attend to or distance themselves from.[109] Such strategies required participation while retaining the distinction and safety of being outliers in the geopolitical enterprise, and there are fewer studies of Indian women who travelled and wrote about their experiences through the late nineteenth and early twentieth centuries.[110]

Unlike some of her compatriots included in this present study, Dosebai is neither among women motivated by an education abroad nor accompanying a male relative on their foreign sojourns, but indeed is someone who sees merit in putting her resources to work for the pleasures, knowledge and friendships that only travel might offer. Not only does Dosebai find her way to Paris to see an international exhibition that she reads about in the newspapers, she does not hesitate to get into a hot-air balloon that will hover above the great metropolis all day. It is chiefly a sense of pleasure, wonder and a sense of humour that drives her, and not the more moral or utilitarian ideals of education, or family obligation. Dosebai is also likely the only Asian woman of her generation to record meetings with both the most powerful monarch, the King of England, and the most influential religious head, Pope Leo XIII. The former is gifted a cap (embroidered by herself) bearing the portraits of all his immediate family members, and the latter is persuaded to accept photographs of herself in her best traditional attire. In all her encounters, her identity as a woman with early exposure to the ruler's culture[111] and her adherence to her Parsi identity, especially in clothing and creative expression (needlework), are intertwined and gleefully proclaimed.

Having acquired her first taste of travel at the age of twenty-eight when she makes a trip with thirty members of her extended family to the nearby city of Pune (about 150 km/93 miles from Bombay), Dosebai hankers for the freedom to experience more—within the country, and over her lifetime, she visits places such as Surat, Nashik, Matheran, Mahabaleshwar, Delhi, Agra, Lucknow, Benaras, Calcutta, Jabalpur, Pondicherry, Ooty, Madras, Bangalore, Kolar, Mysore, Gulbarga, Shrinagar, Rawalpindi and Lahore. Her journeys outside of the Indian subcontinent take her to London, Paris, Marseille, Bonn, Mainz, Geneva, Rome, Colombo, Penang, Singapore, Hong Kong, Shanghai, Yokohama, Tokyo, Atami, Honolulu, San Francisco, Chicago, New York and Washington. She is able to organize three voyages to England over her lifetime, this being the destination that she valorized the most, and in her seventies she launches on her final adventure for a 'tour around the world'.[112] The hyperbolic image and notion of circumlocuting an entire planet or human civilization was part of a larger rhetoric—as popularly emblematized by Jules Verne's novel *Around the World in Eighty Days* (1872)—not just of scientific achievement but also of human endurance, enterprise, survival and ingenuity.

Such constant and distant travels were unprecedented, even strongly dissuaded for Indian women, and made more stringent when attended by 'duties' of wifedom and motherhood. Dosebai writes of eleven pregnancies in a relatively short span of time, and of her 'husband's exceedingly retiring disposition'[113] because of which most of her travels were without him. Since some kind of suitable travel companion or 'chaperone' was the social expectation, she had to depend on her brothers (with whom she often had contentious, litigious, dealings, especially in financial matters) or her young sons. At one time, the bewildered companion is 'an old aunt with the comic disposition'[114]—the suggestion in scenes involving this aunt is of partial senility, but Dosebai seems determined to cobble together any entourage possible. Several of Dosebai's journeys were possible only through elaborate ruses, fibs and manoeuvrings, in addition to impeccable ingenuity and a strong sense of adventure and exploration. In the process, this study argues, Dosebai was essentially composing an elaborately detailed travel narrative that spoke the language of female emancipation, equating it with the freedom to travel openly in public spaces, to be acknowledged as a social equal in the upmost echelons, to expand her social circles to other nationalities, and to further personal interests without apologia.

One may draw from the scholar Yael Rachel Schlick's argument about the coincidence of feminist vindication and female travelogues from the eighteenth century onwards, 'given the Enlightenment understanding of travel as a means of gaining knowledge, of becoming a cosmopolitan individual, and as a prerequisite to political participation'.[115] Considering that travelling (especially between continents) took inordinate time and resources, and were often motivated by the quest for professional or social advancement, Dosebai did not travel in order to make social contacts but she relentlessly connected with multiple social circles just so that she could travel (get introductions, be hosted, have logistical support etc.), even as she gained access to spaces and experiences that satiated her curiosity and wanderlust. At the same time, she cannot be considered a conventional 'sight seer' although she travelled across multiple countries and participated in well-reported extravagances such as the Delhi Durbar of 1877 and the Paris Exhibition of 1878. Rather, her travels manifested her astute sense of a world that was rapidly on the move and her recognition of a compelling need to move with it. The sentiment that Oscar Wilde is said to have expressed to Walt Whitman in 1882 of his generation seeking to 'move in the very heart of today'[116] would be just as apt for their contemporary writer Dosebai Cowasjee Jessawalla, who sought to be unsurpassed in her peripatetic escapades.

In some distinction from Wilde and Whitman, Dosebai draws from a strong sense of female lineage. If the King is the celebrity to meet, it is her mother who gives her the capacities and tools to even wish for something so lofty and uncommon. Thus, Mother and King form the two constellations of affiliations and attributions, both composed in the idiom of belonging and filial pride—these two figures may be said to frame and orient Dosebai's autobiography. Despite the dutiful opening notes of praising British rule in India as 'perfectly equal distribution of justice',[117] the author's foremost preoccupation is towards instating her mother, Bai Meheribai, as 'the first to sow the seeds of education and emancipation among Indian women'[118] and towards placing 'historical facts publically on record'.[119] The historical fact was the decision to send Dosebai to study at Mrs. Ward's school in Bombay in 1842, an unprecedented act at a time when few girls in India were educated, and not always in a formal setting. Even among her wealthy, educationally progressive Parsi community of Bombay, the convention was to hire an English governess to teach the girls at home, rather than send them out to school to sit with students from other families or communities. Bai Meheribai, by all accounts, including her daughter's doting recollections, was unconventional in many ways, such as her decision to separate from her husband and set up her own household with her five children, as well as filing a property lawsuit against her maternal family. Bai Meheribai seems to have arranged for and bequeathed the nonconformism to her only daughter.

In a social milieu when it was unacceptable for girls to be unmarried beyond the age of twelve, Dosebai was married at the age of twenty, following a long engagement to a fellow-Parsee businessman, a widower with six children. Dosebai would have several children of her own with him, losing many of them to early deaths. She writes of her personal and social habits being perceived as too progressive or outlandish by the larger family, and which she attributes to an early exposure to colonial culture and education. Some of these habits were taking open carriage rides, wearing stockings, going for walks, maintaining separate cutlery and eating habits from the rest of the family, and receiving her husband's colleagues when they visit. Sitting on the same sofa as these visitors and conversing openly was especially considered to be a 'monstrous impropriety' by her in-laws.[120] Such everyday lifestyle choices that are perceived as serious effronteries merely form the prelude to the great aspiration of Dosebai's life: to meet the King of England. This trope (and Dosebai's agential hope)—of being in close proximity to the most powerful person in the British Empire—will be the focal point of analysis, not as much the actual physical encounter but more as to what it represents for an Indian woman of that period, especially as it helps to foreground a sense of independence and ambition spanning over three decades. The three episodes that link these are: the first time Dosebai sees the King from a distance (in 1875), her clandestine efforts to go on her first long-distance trip so as to attend the highly publicized Delhi Durbar (in 1877), where the dominion of the British Crown over India was to be heralded, and finally the cherished in-person introductions to the royal couple in Windsor (in 1908). For Dosebai, during the thirty-three years between first glimpses of British royalty to a direct conversation with the King, the collusions of travel and society unveil new senses of self, social participation and pleasure, as well as moral claims to forbidden spheres of authority and grandeur.

Irrespective of Dosebai's fixation with stature and royalty, it is important to recognize that Dosebai and her family were already taking much pride in engaging in many European conventions. Just as Dosebai's mother had invested in her daughter's English education, Dosebai is proud of her daughter, Goolbai Cama, for the six years that she lived in England (in the 1860s) and for being part of an even more cosmopolitan social circle. Mrs. D.D. Cama, as Goolbai was known, would make journeys to and from England unaccompanied, which Dosebai notes 'gave rise to scurvy remarks, but only she who moves in good society can venture on such untrodden paths.'[121] Dosebai also records her pride in her daughter for riding in an English habit and for being the first Parsi woman to openly dance at a ball in 1870. However, Dosebai would not concede better aesthetics or craftsmanship to her daughter: 'Although she lived for a considerable period in such an enlightened city as London, she had no refined taste like mine.'[122] Dosebai's penchant for beautiful and luxurious objects as well as her lifelong astuteness with financial matters becomes crucial trimmings of her life as the intrepid traveller. This sense of half-serious competition with her daughter is what partly fuels her desire for travel. But she has to husband resources carefully for this—before she ventures on her international travels, she starts to source clothes and jewellery from England to sell to her contacts in Bombay for considerable profit. She also creates objects with intricate embroidery (such as her own inventive design for a cap that is embellished with portraits of dear ones) that she can present as personal gifts to dignitaries she meets. Similarly, Dosebai's financial acumen led her to repeatedly rescue her husband and brothers from their multiple and often dire pecuniary difficulties, and such in-house clout in turn seems to have helped her fund her own travels.

When Dosebai first heard the news of the visit of the Prince of Wales (later Edward VII, King of England), she was preoccupied with 'domestic anarchy reigning in [her] own house'[123] owing to property disputes in the family after the death of her father-in-law. Even as she counselled her husband through the crisis, she also prepared for being a part of the public celebrations being planned in Bombay in 1875 to honour the arrival of the heir to the British crown.

> Laying aside my mourning for the occasion, I put on my handsomest dress and ornaments, and took my seat on one of the stands erected on the Esplanade, whence I had a good view of the Prince as he passed along amid the deafening cheers of his exultant subjects. [...] This Prince, coming amongst us, was considered an auspicious omen by the natives, and his advent afforded the Parsee ladies an amount of happiness and freedom unknown before; several salutary reforms arose then amongst the native females and have been preserved every since.[124]

Having mentioned 'reforms'—the dominant theme for women's rights in colonial India throughout the nineteenth century—Dosebai further elaborates how this royal visit had given 'great impetus' to the movement for 'greater emancipation for native females'.[125] The positive developments listed by Dosebai are the participation of widows in public events from which they were previously excluded; more women travelling in open carriages, not 'caged up'[126] by blinds and shutters, while others set foot on the streets for the first time; women out in the city till late hours to enjoy the ceremonial illuminations; the free mixing of conventional, orthodox people in large assemblies of women, which Dosebai notes as bringing for Parsee women in particular 'an amount of happiness and freedom unknown before'.[127] During this time, Dosebai manages to be present at a few more venues where she can see the Prince, but her gaze is always from a distance, and is unidirectional, for her existence is unknown to him.

Dosebai is soon pulled back into the domestic troubles that always seem to need her intervention, this time with regard to her husband's job and finances. But the advancement of freedom for women that Dosebai attributes to the visit of the Prince seems to have unsettled something in her as well—perhaps the desire to not just be a spectator to the moving gears of the Empire but to participate more actively. This desire turned more pressing a year later, with the arrival of Lord Lytton as Governor-General to India. A public announcement was issued for a grand Durbar in Delhi to pronounce Queen Victoria as the Empress of India. The Queen or her family were not scheduled to attend the Durbar, but all the royal houses of India that wished to reinforce their alignment to the British Crown were expected to gather alongside the full pageantry of the colonial government. Dosebai notes, 'It was said that something like half the population of India would be drawn towards Delhi [...] The subject was daily brought prominently forward in the leading native and English journals.'[128] It was unthinkable, the undertone suggests, for Dosebai to not be a part of such gravitation, and thus she must set forth no matter what the adventure might entail.

This sense of flouting norms is an oft-repeated theme through Dosebai's text, a text that may be considered as a 'traveling autobiography'—a term suggested by the scholar Javed Majeed, who studies the autobiographical writings of Nehru, Gandhi and Iqbal and proposes that influential agents of Indian modernity enact 'imaginary geographies' decentring the colonial experience through new concepts of selfhood.[129] The embodying of geographies in the process of travel and a subsequent scribal response to mark such embodiment as exclusive and worthy of dissemination are continuous with publications by women in the cusp of the nineteenth and twentieth centuries. For instance, Krishnabhabini Das wrote of her travels to England with her husband, *Englandey Bangamahila* (A Bengali Lady in England) in 1885, and her fellow-Bengali writer, Hariprabha Takeda, wrote of her travels to Japan to meet her Japanese in-laws in *Bangamohilar Japan Jatra* (The Journey of a Bengali Woman to Japan) in 1915.[130] Although at first glance such texts presented themselves within the idiom of wifehood (one who dutifully accompanies her husband through distant journeys across oceans), these women subtly undermine the genre via their own independent observations of the many international social worlds. Dosebai stands apart from the male writers studied by Javed Majeed as well as the women traveloguers preceding her by virtue of her primary identification as a self-anointed traveller, whose articulated mode and goal become the risk, adventure and social cache of travel itself.

The Delhi Durbar thus marks the turning point in Dosebai's career as a traveller—for the very desire to travel (when travel is still in the future, and thus imagined) is to prise open the traditional axes of what an Indian female subject could hope to materialize and embody. Till the Durbar, she had only ventured to nearby locations with the participation and approval of her large family, and her initial proposals to her husband, daughter and 'social coterie' were met with apprehensions about 'the great difficulties of the journey as well as of the expenses'.[131] Refusing to be discouraged, Dosebai sets about preparing for the journey by keeping it 'scrupulously secret to ward off the storm of ridicule and scandal which a rumour of this new departure from old custom would have called down on my devoted head. I fancied I could hear the jeering queries. Is it a Parsee female's business to mix in such demonstrations? How can she be so unwomanly as to venture on such a journey?'[132] The traditional notions of what constituted as 'womanly' or not was particularly irksome to Dosebai, who does not mince her words in pointing out that this rhetoric only enabled the men of her community to claim pleasures and indulgences (values that she aligned with travel) while relegating women entirely to domestic toils. Dosebai is clear about having no qualms of her secret arrangements.

> I have ever taken the lead in matters of female reform and have tried to stimulate the dormant energies of my sisters and to open up to them paths hitherto debarred, leading to innocent pleasures or enlarged interests. [...] Ever new act of female emancipation at first meets with disapprobation and sarcasm and that frightens many a one from gratifying her inclinations, and on this occasion no other Parsee lady, incited by a keen desire to witness so grand a spectacle, had the courage either to face the ridicule of her people or to undertake the long journey.[133]

To travel where and how one wants, when one has the wherewithal, irrespective of one's gender or community, remains the original premise for Dosebai's wanderlust. And yet, she also presents herself as the much-vilified *female traveller* flouting social norms. For

Dosebai, the journey to the seat of power, at this point of her life represented by the Delhi Durbar, is besieged by logistic challenges, which not only fail to deter her but also enable further travel. She begins to simultaneously make plans to continue her journey onwards to the capital (Calcutta) and writes to a friend who offers to host her. The living arrangements in Delhi are made through letters that claim they are for a European couple, but the news of her departure finds its way to the local papers and results in both congratulatory letters and disapproval. 'However, I would not allow their envy and folly to deprive me of one iota of the enjoyment placed within my reach.'[134] Thus Dosebai sets out with her two sons, the old aunt mentioned earlier, her brother and a trusted domestic help. Dosebai includes select observations through this long train journey and writes about being overwhelmed on their arrival at the crowded train platforms of Delhi. But any misgivings are fleeting with this traveller, and once Dosebai settles into her living quarters, she wastes no time in arranging for an open mail phaeton for sight-seeing and planning social visits to British women she has met through her social circles in Bombay.

All the ingenuities that Dosebai had to summon to make this trip to attend the Delhi Durbar inform the modus operandi for her future international travel. Through her socializing with the wives of European officials, she manages to get introductions and admissions to the venues of her choice. In one telling instance, her brother, who does not seem averse to sponging off her initiatives to further his circle of influence, is peeved at being refused a card of admission, insists that she not attend the Durbar either. Dosebai is not unaware of his selfish and shallow intentions, for she comments on her brothers abandoning her—'not caring what befell me now that their purpose was served'.[135] She therefore ignores his unreasonable tantrum, and instead approaches her contact, a certain Mrs. Burne, who is able to connect them to the Military Secretary to get them fresh cards of admission. This is just one illustration, an early one among many, of the dogged cultivation of relationships that expedite

Dosebai's travel plans. There are varying ruses—whether through the wives of British officials, through evoking clan loyalties with wealthy Parsi businessmen across the world or by striking and nurturing deep friendships with strangers. The latter is the most admirable, especially considering how Dosebai is able to plan an entire trip to the United States of America in her seventies, and only through reviving contacts she made with friendly American travellers she had met at a Paris hotel three decades prior.

After all the effort and uncertainty, finally on the first day of January 1877, Dosebai finds herself seated at the Delhi Durbar. Her card of admission ensures that she had 'a very conspicuous place in the front row amongst leading officials and their ladies; on the one hand sat the Governor-General of Goa and on the other Lady Staveley, wife of the Commander-in-Chief of Bombay [...] Oh, for the pen to describe the scene spread out before me! On entering this stately arena all eyes were turned towards me [...].'[136] In this highly self-congratulatory moment, Dosebai is fully aware of being seated in the heart of imperial grandeur, and among the most wealthy and powerful individuals in India. She lists the Indian princes against her seat, bejewelled and dressed in full regalia, with their banners waving over them, 'a princely gathering [such as] had never been known in the annals of India.'[137] And even though the evening would result in her returning home with the expensive dress and jewels encrusted in the volumes of dust raised by the crowd, exhausted, hoarse and running a high fever, Dosebai is triumphant at her own place in the scheme of things. Despite not belonging to a royal family, she had been a feted invitee to what she confidently calls 'one of the most brilliant and unique spectacles that the nineteenth century has ever witnessed'. In fact, she surmises that the pomp and pageantry would certainly be superior to anything similar in England (with its predominance of black clothing) because of the colourful dress and jewels in India.[138] To her, partaking in such grand success must ensure more travels, and even in her indisposed state, she begins to plan her trip onwards from Delhi, adding new locations to the itinerary as it pleases her.

Although Dosebai does not state it explicitly, it is evident that the experience of being the only one of her kind on a grand ceremonial stage gives her a precocious sense of a rapidly advancing social and epistemological world being within her reach. Not too long after the Durbar, her attention is caught by an announcement in the newspapers of an international exhibition to be held in Paris, the biggest of its kind, and she resolves to execute an impending visit to Europe, which would also fulfil her 'lifelong, dearly-cherished hope of seeing England'.[139] No sooner does Dosebai return to her home in Bombay before she once again sets about putting the wheels in motion for her overseas travel. Within a few months, at the age of forty-six, she sets sail in the company of her elder son, and the feeling she captures in her autobiography, upon finally arriving at the Waterloo Bridge station in London, is of the great aim of her life being realized.

The Story of My Life lovingly details the author's impressions of the 'greatness' of London, and it is also during this trip that she meets two sisters (the Halls) who claim to be working on a biography of their father. This spurs her to announce to them, 'I also was engaged in writing my autobiography.'[140] Unlike some of the other writers studied in this book, such as Rashsundari Debi or Binodini Dasi, Dosebai does not dwell too much on the act or the craft of writing, almost implying that the writing is in service of the talent for travel, or rather a duty to represent the many experiences that come her way. The vicissitudes of her personal life—the financial machinations of brothers, the bankruptcy of her husband and his brief disappearance, the death of her children, unhealed emotional ruptures with her mother as well as her daughter—are sprinkled narrative fragments in between the exultations of being in new places and being appreciated for her mobility and creativity. Her resourcefulness is not undermined by the constant bother of familial intrigue: 'I feel it uncouth to introduce such dark, uninteresting episodes in my smooth and happy career, and nothing but a desire to paint me as I am, induces me to do so.'[141] The career that is presented as smooth and happy cannot be explained away as posturing or façade for the undercurrents of the writing reiterate wonderment and pride in being a explorer constantly charting new experiences.

In the decades following her return from that first celebrated trip to Europe, Dosebai continued to travel frequently to different locations within India, even as her family situations prevented her from planning another trip abroad. She was engaged in clearing her husband's debts and finally completed a second, but much briefer, voyage to England in 1906—this was a few years after the death of her husband. A further two years later, at the age of seventy-six, Dosebai began to plan what she hoped would be the pinnacle of her life as a 'globe trotter'—a visit to North America, via south-east Asia and Japan, and then travelling from America to Europe. She noted that all this travel received wide publicity in the newspapers.[142] When she reached England, she was determined to be introduced to the King himself, and with her usual grit began to seek out officials she had known in India. Lord Ripon, who had been the viceroy of India, and was in his eighties, promised to use his influence on her behalf to secure a presentation in person to the King and the Queen. Due to various reasons, Dosebai's wait in London extended to eight long months to get the promised opportunity, but she was far from deterred: 'To be presented to our Sovereign and the Queen has been the most ardent wish of my life, and in the evening of my career it was about to be fulfilled.'[143] And as she waited for this appointment to materialize, she led an active life in the great metropolis—being present on the opening day of Parliament, attending gatherings and exhibitions, going to concerts and continuing to mingle with her many friends.

The much-anticipated encounter of Dosebai with the King finally took place at a garden party on the lawns of Windsor on 20 June 1908. Dosebai had opted for this locale over a presentation at Buckingham Palace on account of the garden party having many more people—to see, and be seen by. Being one of several people present at the party, it is unlikely that Dosebai's encounter with the King and Queen took anything more than the routine few minutes of courteous introductions, but Dosebai writes about it with paced care, including ancillary information such as the motor car breaking down and delaying their arrival, the personalized handcrafted gifts she sends ahead for the royal couple, the thoughtful hospitality extended to make sure she is enjoying herself, and one of her proudest moments—being dropped home in an official car bearing the royal crest.

Having met the King, and her presence there duly reported by the London press, Dosebai returned to India. Following this, the autobiography seems to fade out into a sprinkling of more minor facts and life events. Those events include the death of the King a few months after their encounter; the autobiography reproduces the letter she received from London in response to her telegram of condolence. Dosebai herself would pass away six months following that. The closing reflections of her autobiography are about the many prejudices around women's education that prevented her mother, Bai Meheribai, from being duly acknowledged as having 'the courage and foresight' in 'championing the cause of women's education'.[144] The link between her mother's spirit of enterprise and her own reputation as a traveller is perhaps the strongest narrative thread running through the length of Dosebai's travelogue. What forbidden education was for one generation (such as her mother's) had expanded into an education of not only the mind in the classroom but the entirety of the voyage of the body and all its senses, an expansion of the full range of one's personality.

> Thus it will easily be understood that the bold step which I had taken created some ill-feeling amongst my people, but I did not forego one iota of pleasure on that account nor swerve a hair's breadth from the course I had chalked out for myself. As long as females are ignorant and uneducated their thoughts cannot soar above the narrow limit of their domestic concerns, but, God be praised, the time has come for my sisters to demand with unmistakable voice their rights and privileges of which their selfish husbands have so long deprived them.[145]

It remains unfathomable to Dosebai as to why any woman with means would not swap their 'dull, inactive monotonous life' for 'culture and foreign travel' especially when the technology of steamship, and the freedom of education, had redefined mobility, whether of geographical space or of social interaction.[146] There is a cost in defying convention but it fades in the face of the cultural adventures, the cultivation of sympathy and sensibility, and the sheer beauty of varied geographies—all attesting to a traveller's life being measured not in the years lived but in the exuberant totality of experience. Towards this, Dosebai quotes a familiar adage that is delivered with a conviction and panache that is her own voice, demonstrating an intense sense of the reality of her hard-won experiences: 'better to travel and see much than to live long'.[147]

Conclusion

The Poet and the Chorus

In presenting the case for diversely stylized incantations of literary personhood staked by women writers in modern genres, this study has selected authors and texts across linguistic lines, genres and chronological progressions. Nonetheless, in closing the argument, one has to contend with 'beginnings' in a more literal and historical manner, both with genre (verse or lyric as cardinal to the premodern literary tradition in India) and with the self-consciously modern authorial debut. In 1854, twenty-three-year-old Savitribai Phule (1831–97) published a collection of poems in Marathi—*Kavya Phule* has been acclaimed for being the first book-length publication in verse by an Indian woman in the nineteenth century, and among the first books of modern poetry by an Indian in British India.[1] Published a year prior to the canonized 'Song of Myself' by Walt Whitman,[2] Savitribai writes of the singing self:

> This sermon that entices .... I sing
> This leisure that envelops the mind ... I sing
> This intelligible ethical education ... I sing
> This attainment of a sense of knowledge ... I sing[3]

The mnemonic and tonal qualities of singing and self that is foregrounded—other compositions of the collection are even more explicit about the resolve to entertain, educate and agitate—are determined to stand apart as well as move ahead with a multitude. The writer in speaking of a distinct self is equally speaking of a collective marked by gender and caste. In other words, this is a solo rendition that invites and joins a chorus—for what educates/liberates the singular is wont to do the same for many. This study will thus conclude its argument by examining how this timbre of poetic reflexivity and the future writings it anticipates may be read as a choric, collective manifestation of social non-conformism and inscriptional virtuosity.

Savitribai Phule had already been active in the public realm as an education and social activist when she entered the publishing sphere in her early twenties with the forty-one poems that comprise *Kavya Phule*. Along with her husband, Jotirao Phule, she had set up the first educational institution for girls in India, and become the first woman to teach and head a school—Phule was around twenty-one-year-old at the time, and Savitribai was sixteen.[4] The initiative was fiercely opposed.[5] The Phules, who belonged to the Mali caste, had enrolled nine girls in their school from communities that were oppressively othered in the Hindu ritual caste hierarchy.[6] The school itself was already a controversial idea—it involved an access to education for two groups (disenfranchised by caste or gender or both) that were strictly deprived of literacy by upper-caste traditionalists. Such a 'distinct brand of socio-cultural radicalism' aimed to unite overlapping categories of the oppressed or *stree-shudra-atishudra* (women-backward class-dalits) while also including other marginalized groups such as *adivasis* and Muslims.[7] Jotirao Phule's reputation as a pioneering reformer would continue to grow despite oppositions and setbacks, even as Savitribai developed the writing voice required for a strategic resistance that could accomplish extended mobilization.[8] Writing in both prose and verse was the preferred modality to consolidate these efforts, and Savitribai published four books over her lifetime, including two volumes of poetry of which the first, *Kavya Phule*, represents a truly modern beginning, both in content and presentation. While *Kavya Phule* falls outside the historical period in the ambit of the present study—Savitribai presaging the visibility of women in Indian print culture by a couple of decades—the lineage of literary trespassing as argued in preceding chapters would be an incomplete and partial view without reflecting on the text's canonical originality. The thematic spectrum of Savitribai's debut collection is wide, ranging from rallying calls for freedom or equality to admiration of the bounties of nature—the preeminent note, however, being the poet's commitment to justice. While being indebted to the scholarship on Savitribai Phule's contributions to caste equity and education, the concern of this study is to bring to light a less appreciated feature of her achievement. This is in the realm of literary stylistics—here too it must be granted that Phule's acute sense of a new social world interpenetrates and gives body and depth to her artistry in verse.

Nearly all the compositions in *Kavya Phule* are accompanied by a mention of a poetic sub-genre for performance or oral rendition, such as *abhang*, *ovi*, *anushtubh*, *dindi*, *padhya*, located primarily in the devotional idiom, often the Warkari.[9] The flourishes of familiar and customary lyric, as well as music and dance, are then combined with the crisp line-breaks of modern poetry that speaks of individual rights and social change. For instance, in the poem 'Rise to Learn and Act' the individual (woman/self) and the community (caste) interweave with the craving (for knowledge) and the rebellion (due to knowledge):

> An upsurge of knowledge is in my soul
> Crying out for knowledge to be whole
> This festering wound, mark of caste
> I'll blot out from my life at last.[10]

The crying out (for unbridled access to knowledge) and the blotting out (of the wound of casteism) are the performative action of the poem itself, as well as its desired goal. In this felicitous and hybrid germination of literary form, Savitribai manifests a central contention of this book—shared literary beginnings are not only about ruptures and new sutures but that they are also self-consciously stylized for an optimum creative and semantic amplification. The poet stands alone, but also speaks of society, thereby anticipating the writing chorus that is sympathetic of her vision, one that will eventually challenge a publication milieu hierarchical in terms of access and authorial reputation.

The literary contravention, which is playful, defiant and buoyant, opens with a clever word-play in the title of the collection: *Kavya Phule* could directly translate to 'Poetry's Blossoms' or 'Poetry Blossoms' (blossoms to be read in its verb form), while Phule is also the author's surname by marriage, which would then read as 'Poetry Phule' (poet identified by her craft, caste and wifehood in two words). The literary utterance was truly a blossoming by virtue of being one of its kind, which could be studied for its historical impact, its merging of vernacular poetic traditions with poetry of world literatures, or be read as spoken-word, a performative speech with internal rhyme schemes. This section will focus on two poems—'Visionary Poet' (numbered 22) and 'Crazy Poem and Crazed Poet' (numbered 23)—as illustrative of the synergies between the familiar binaries of artist and art, as well as art/artist and society. While poem 23 mocks traditional ideas of poetry, poem 22 enacts both as performance and explicit content the transformations that poetry can accomplish in the modern age.

It is important to first clarify the connotations and allusions in 'Crazy Poem and Crazed Poet'.[11] Savitribai modulates the cadence of the composition (presented in the sub-genre of *padhya* or song) around the colloquial term *khula* (translated here as crazy/crazed) to connote an out-of-kilter person who has turned delirious from indulging in their own emotions. No other criticism of poet or poetry is required—the terming of such a poet and their resultant poetry as *khula* suffices to make the case: such willing blindness and self-indulgence are untenable. Similarly, the alternation between the stanzas with longer lines and the more pithy, rhythm-infused shorter stanzas keeps the tone playful and gently aligned with the aesthetic position being questioned.

The poet composes his imagination
When he encounters grand joys and sorrows
He experiences heaven
He experiences hell
In an instant he cries
Crying, he dances
Invoking God

As was the literary convention, the figure of the poet is written in the masculine gender, and their desire or 'muse' as female (here, *pari* or 'fairy-like'). However, the appraisal of such 'crazed' fantasies is distinctly not conforming to a stable, gendered desire. The poet is fairly convinced about the futility of a certain strain of poetry, one that is shaped by 'inspiration' and presents itself entirely in contiguous hedonistic terms. Poet and poetry appear to be lost in each other, disconnected from any larger social world, lost in illusory communion:

He composes strange crazed poems
And sings a divine tune
Before the poet's eyes emerges a *pari*
Who showers love on him
Smiling and laughing
Sweetly talking
She beseeches him
Drawing him closer in a kiss
This is the image in the poet's mind

This kiss between the poet and the *pari* that embodies inspiration may be read as a critique of a tradition where 'aesthetic enjoyment is the ultimate purpose of art'.[12] The Sanskritic tradition of *shringar*[13] has prioritized aesthetics as that which invites an appreciation of an immediate, unquestioned and yet high-minded charm. In contrast, Savitribai's take on aesthetics is different—it is less about sensory pleasures and more concerned with a slower, more deliberative appreciation of self and the social. Savitribai avers that modern poetry should be sceptical of the idealized metre and its fairy/muse that may flatter to deceive, and trust the more everyday world of direct colloquial language.

This contrast is better understood through a close analysis of 'Visionary Poet',[14] where the poet and poem are transposed and assigned a dignified status from the start:

> Poetry is a great devotee of knowledge
> The bastion of the nine rasas
> The smooth flow of poetry from him
> Creates a formidable 'visionary' poetry like the Nava-Chandi[15]

The adjective 'drashta' (translated here as visionary[16]) is ascribed to both poet and poetry—it maintains the vital sematic link to eyesight and connects to the equally sensory rendition of speech. The vision that leads to speech and the speech that will ensue as the written poem will thus encapsulate its visionary qualities. Savitribai presents such flow as divine (the metaphor is of the river Ganga flowing through Shiva's locks). The narrative role of the *pari* in 'Crazy Poem and Crazed Poet' is taken up by a *devi* (goddess) in 'Visionary Poet': 'Goddess sings poetry through him'. Whereas tradition prized the more visceral pleasure of the seduction of the poet by the muse, Savitribai instead prioritizes a more aspirational and serene sense of a social self in consilience with the world. Literature presents a counter world where this utopia may unfold and be embodied in. The poet signifies a new beginning not only in terms of her ideas—the prioritization of a co-operative social world—but also in the very this-worldly sense of orality, rhythm, as well as the familiar, mundane and unabashedly colloquial diction that she deploys. Savitribai is prescient in actively seeking the intersection of the three axes of literary voice, gendered first-person perspective and genre-creation. Beyond this, one needs to further deliberate on the instantiation of such a tradition as it finds resonances in the work of the many writers that follow in her wake throughout the nineteenth and early twentieth centuries.

A polyphonic arrangement

While the present study has primarily focused on texts published between 1880 and 1920, one needs to take into account the wealth of insights offered by life narratives published at a later date (say, the second quarter of the twentieth century onwards), but recording the writers' experiences of the last quarter of the nineteenth century. Hence, as an extension of Savitribai's literary legacy, this section of the Conclusion will include three inimitable autobiographies: Sunity Devee's *The Autobiography of an Indian Princess* (1921) in English,[17] Parvatibai Athavale's *Majhi Kahani* (My Story, 1928) in Marathi[18] and Haimabati Sen's notebooks (published as late as 2000)[19] in Bengali. All three texts demonstrate an archive that greatly expands ideas of method, validation and scope. Sunity's life as the daughter of a prominent reformer and wife of the ruler of a princely state, while being privileged in an obvious sense, equally speaks to the truth of an unbearable entanglement with bereavement as it surfaces in new and potent narratological terms. Parvatibai's autobiography, apart from being one of the few to describe the experience of disfigurements imposed upon widowhood,[20] is a unique document about an Indian woman's struggles at eking a livelihood as a chambermaid in the United States and thus merits being read as a key component of global labour histories. Finally, Haimabati's hard-fought journey as a professional woman in medicine may also be better appreciated in the light of her devastating critique of the Indian family, which includes its exploitation of an earning member through the idealized (but dissimulative) rhetoric of motherhood. Each of these contrapuntal readings is deserving of greater engagements in the future, and in the context of the present text will gesture to such expansions even as they form the larger literary chorus of writers of the period.

The Autobiography of an Indian Princess (1921) by Sunity Devee attests to its author's accent on a public role, perhaps even an exotic one, as much for readers in England as in India. And yet, the more substantial and moving part of the book lies in the domestic and intimate, particularly when the princess speaks in the voice of a mother. This maps an entirely parallel affective topography wherein the textual 'dethronement' of the poised successful princess is to be found in chapters about death—first of her husband, and then of her adult son. Grief performs not only as the leveller (between royalty and 'commoner') but in causing the steep fall from what is publically considered good fortune, rendering the princess wretched and isolated in her pain.

Born as the daughter of a leading public intellectual of Bengal, Keshab Chandra Sen,[21] and married to the King of Cooch Behar, Sunity Devee is an educated and observant participant of an elite social echelon. The autobiography speaks of a halcyon childhood, a celebrated and controversial marriage to 'the fairy prince of my romance',[22] international travels and a cosmopolitan network that introduces her to the heads of various royal families in Europe. But the text soon gravitates to a central vein of suffering and endurance. The death of her thirty-one-year-old first-born son Raj Rajendra devastates her, and even her identification with her contemporary, Queen Alexandra of England, is through patterns of grief: 'Fate has dealt heavily with us both. We have each lost our idolized first-born. We have each lost the best of husbands. We have equally sorrowed.'[23] The sorrowing that dominates the second half of the autobiography eclipses the glittering social triumphs she presents with pride in the first half. All the wealth, influence and treatments with the best doctors in the world cannot extend the life of Sunity's son. Her sentences spiral into a visceral mourning.

> Thirty-one years ago this boy had brought me every possible happiness. Now the world is dark and gloomy, and I do not know how I shall travel the last part of my journey, so heavy-laden am I with my grief. [...] what remained for me? I had to suffer the long days and the misery of the hours when sleep forsook me and grief kept a watch by my pillow. I had to live and think that to live is sometimes the worst torture that can be inflicted upon mankind.[24]

The rest of the autobiography persists with more records of the author's social responsibilities, but is never able to re-trace the initial narrative orientation of being a chosen one, a princess. The intensity of grief becomes the sustained closing note of the autobiography. Sunity has to endure the death of another son. Grieving is now the only companion to the ageing princess, and she resolves that its company must be counterbalanced only through love and public service.

The emphasis on public service, which was often the outcome of loss or melancholia or led to severe personal consequences, equally marks the autobiography of Parvatibai Athavale (1870–1955). Widowed when her child was still young, Parvatibai came to be associated with an institution for widows in Poona set up by her brother-in-law, Dharmanand Karve, who had built a reputation as a social reformer. She gained an education in Marathi in her twenties and took on the position of a volunteer-participant at the institution to support the education of other young widows. The autobiography that she wrote in her fifties, *My Story*, may be seen to belong to a thematic cluster of women's life narratives that chronicled the 'tragedy of widowhood' (as was the collective consensus then) for the upper-caste woman in pre-independence India. In this, however, the text both supports and subverts its own genre. The narrative of widowhood is buttressed by the author's ingenuity in eking out an independent livelihood during circumstances that are unexpected and unprecedented.[25] Hence, it is more productively read as a narrative of resourcefulness—which included menial labour in public spaces—entirely taboo for the upper-caste woman. Unlike those who sought degrees in high-status disciplines such as medicine (Anandibai Joshee and Rukhmabai), or law (Cornelia Sorabji), or education (Atiya Fyzee), or those who travelled to raise funds for their social causes (Pandita Ramabai), Parvatibai had to support herself by working as a domestic help during a visit to the United States that extended for three years. One might contrast this necessity of janitorial labour for daily existence with the rather grander rhetoric of Mohandas Gandhi, who wrote and spoke extensively about cleaning latrines.[26] Yet, Gandhi went on a cleaning drive purely voluntarily—his basic survival did not depend on such labour. In fact, the precarity and centrality of class privileges and discriminations among and for women during this period—whether in the travel notes of the reasonably affluent Atiya Fyzee (see Chapter 3) or the livelihood struggles by a destitute Parvatibai—would require a more detailed interrogation in future scholarship. Likewise, Parvatibai's narrative of widowhood may also be contrasted with the stereotyping of widows in her time—either as hapless (needing chronic legislative support) or as sexually dangerous within the Indian family (as depicted in Bankimchandra Chattopadhyay's *Bishabriksha* in 1873 and Rabindranath Tagore's *Choker Bali* in 1903). Unlike these fictional counterparts or the disembodied figure of legal debates, not only did Parvatibai have to continually survive by drawing from her 'innate resourcefulness and talent for public speaking',[27] she also managed to raise substantial funds[28] and later made a laudable career as an educator in India.

The dual identities of a professionally qualified woman with a full-time career and the writer who is outspoken regarding their rare accomplishments can at times lead to near-obliteration as in the case of Haimabati Sen (1866–1933). Trained as a health professional in Bengal during the closing decades of the nineteenth century, Haimabati Sen wrote her recollections of her immensely challenging experiences decades later, likely beginning in 1923/4 till just before her death in 1933.[29] It was, however, only published in 2000. Presented as 'the most detailed personal narrative, so far uncovered, which has a bearing on the lives of Indian women born in the nineteenth century',[30] the autobiography showcases the vagaries of publication for reflective life narratives. The hardships endured and recorded by Haimabati are tremendous—an early marriage and widowhood (before the age of ten), a second marriage of great discord including physical abuse, raising children as a single mother, sexual harassment and marginalization in professional roles, persistent financial woes even as she takes philanthropic responsibilities (for orphans and widows) and several illnesses leading to blindness. The text's 'intimacy and directness of tone and the attention to detail'[31] are noted as exemplary by Geraldine Forbes, a historian specializing in women's movements in India who chanced upon Haimabati's notebooks towards the end of the twentieth century.

Although not cast in the rhetoric of rights and citizenship, Haimabati's life narrative becomes an active participant in the construction of what can only be considered a feminist archive by virtue of its exposing narrative affects typically disdained and suppressed by the image of the 'good reformer woman'. Such an archive permits itself to catalogue unbridled emotions and experiences that women were discouraged from expressing against family—for instance, jealousy, outrage, abandonment, resentment, libidinal cravings, disinterest, disgust and disagreement. Even in sections where the woman (author) chooses to cast her life in the language of gratitude, the archive invites the reader to tilt against the grain. The distinguishing feature of Haimabati's writing is unrelenting bluntness—what she experiences and how she feels about it is closely fused with candour, particularly the ingratitude of her children. The closing pages voice an inventory of grievances against her children, a rare moment (in literature) of dissecting motherhood as often unrelenting, thankless and exploitative. The writer's dilemma is about what can be shared: public, legal matters demand delicacy, and yet familial betrayals need exposure.

> I avoid both close relationships and quarrels with people. […] Meanwhile, a number of things happened which lowered me in the esteem of people. […] The harassment I suffered at the hands of my intelligent sons and daughter on this account was in no way insignificant. […] No matter how much I looked after my family with care, the world did not fail to persecute me. My children oppressed me to an extraordinary degree even though I had done nothing wrong.[32]

The textual trace of persecution by the world and harassment by one's kin is likely to have further implications for the text's appearance and longevity in the public eye—its fate is more likely invisibility, rather than celebration as soon as it gets written. There was a real danger of the notebook staying unread but for a descendant of Haimabati who showed the notebooks to a historian (Forbes) who finally introduced it to a readership.

The intention of writing (artistry, sharing, community) and the material reality of writing (print, market, readership) are inseparable from the affective language of suffering, love, service or triumph, and can be said to be the hallmark of the feminist beginnings that founded a modern literary tradition in India. The wielding of the first-person voice in fact and fiction took the shape of genres as distinct as their lives. The present study argues for the irrefutable and ground-breaking nature of their contribution: an unparalleled language of wit, sarcasm, anger and debate in the service of social protest and pamphleteering by Tarabai Shinde; the voice of intelligence, resourcefulness and resistance in Anandibai Joshee's letters to a demanding martial partner; shades of legalese across conjugal and institutional debates about autonomy in marriage by Rukhmabai; Rashsundari Debi's strategically delivered dream narratives that mark and conserve desires and fears at risk of being rendered invisible by social conventions and expectations; Binodini Dasi's life narrative of operatic interiority that registered the tension of being simultaneously celebrated and derided even as she participated in the creation of modern Indian theatre; a renewed rhetoric of romance by Swarnakumari Debi Ghosal located in tenuous, hypnotic borders between the plausible and the implausible in romantic dalliances by assuming a reader's exposure to a broader novelistic tradition; an elegiac vocabulary and metaphors drawn from the natural world to capture the mourning of illness and finitude in Krupabai Satthianadhan's autobiographical novel; Atiya Fyzee's fastidious notes to her 'newspaper sisters' on domestic help, clothing and aesthetics (and other such seemingly innocuous observations) presented on the same plane as the intellectual gatherings and public events in London; and Dosebai Cowasjee Jessawalla's tremendous *joie de vivre* that is expressed through tenacious curiosity and the dexterity of locomotion, be it experiential, geographical or social.

Far from being silent actors trapped in a house and invisible to the outside world, these women have explicitly reflected and articulated on the entirety of their variegated experience—from the most internal anguish (as with the death of one's children) to the most determined sense of citizenship (educating the most disenfranchised). They have rendered forever indeterminate the boundaries of the public and the private, by insisting on the public dimensions of private hells (marriage, domestic drudgery)—and they have done this at a level of literary and conceptual articulation that often seem far more incisive and far-reaching than anything their male counterparts had envisaged. For instance, the author-actor at the heart of memoirs as different as Rashsundari Debi (who barely stepped out of her domestic sphere during her long quest for literacy in Bengali) or Dosebai Cowasjee Jessawalla (the traveller who revelled in public spaces and wrote for English readers) can be easily seen as powerful critiques of the female personhood that were being imagined by the nationalist or reformist projects, especially those formulated by male agents for the male citizen-subject. The intertwined literary and political, affective and deliberative registers thus give a new Archimedean point from which to revisit a feminist project of authorship and citizen-making that was inaugurated in the last quarter of the nineteenth century—an episteme which still holds up, arguably, to the very present.

Notes

Introduction

1 The year of the first edition is claimed by Rashsundari to be 1868, but scholars suggest 1875 as the first publication, and that remains the earliest edition to be located. See Tanika Sarkar, *Words to Win: The Making of a Modern Autobiography* (New Delhi: Zubaan, 2013), 14.

2 Tanika Sarkar describes *Chaitanya Bhagabat* as 'the first Bengali biography of Chaitanya, the Krishna-maddened saint of mediaeval Bengal, who promised salvation to the wretched, the low caste, the women – categories excluded by brahmanical orthodoxy from higher spiritual aspirations and learning'. In Sarkar, 3.

3 Sarkar, *Words to Win*, 196.

4 Sarkar, *Words to Win*, 2.

5 Jyotirindranath Tagore (1849–1925) was a writer, playwright, composer, actor, translator and painter who belonged to the famed Jorasanko Tagore family of Calcutta. Apart from editing two monthly magazines, he also founded organizations for the promotion of Bengali language and literature. His younger sister Swarnakumari Debi Ghosal is studied in Chapter 2 of this book.

6 Sarkar, *Words to Win*, 159.

7 Bidik Bhattacharya and Sambudha Sen, *Novel Formations: The Indian Beginnings of a European Genre* (Ranikhet: Permanent Black, 2019); Sascha Ebeling, *Colonizing the Realm of Words: The Transformation of Tamil Literature in Nineteenth-Century South India* (Ranikhet: Permanent Black, 2011); Meenakshi Mukherjee, *Early Novels in India* (New Delhi: Sahitya Akademi, 2002); Vasudha Dalmia, *The Nationalization of Hindu Traditions: Bharatendu Harishchandra and Nineteenth-Century Benaras* (Delhi: Oxford University Press, 1997).

8 Sudhir Chandra notes that Rukhmabai presented herself without a surname in her lifetime and hence 'there can be no justification for meddling with the name she used for herself'. In Sudhir Chandra, *Rukhmabai: The Life and Times of a Child Bride Turned Rebel-Doctor* (New Delhi: Macmillan, 2024), x.

9 Meenakshi Mukherjee, *Realism and Reality: The Novel and Society in India* (New Delhi: Oxford University Press, 1994), 6.

10 Sudipta Kaviraj considers the '*Invention of Private Life* (also the title of his book) as located in the introduction of new literary forms (such as the novel and the autobiography) to Indian literature that served as a 'great field of reflection on the nature of modernity'. See Sudipta Kaviraj, *The Invention of Private Life: Literature and Ideas* (New York: Columbia University Press, 2015), 4.

11 Kedar Arun Kulkarni, *World Literature and the Question of Genre in Colonial India: Poetry, Drama, and Print Culture 1790–1890* (New Delhi: Bloomsbury India, 2022), 3.

12 J. Devika, *En-Gendering Individuals: The Language of Reforming in Early Twentieth Century Keralam* (Hyderabad: Orient Longman, 2006), 17.

13 Meera Kosambi, *Feminist Vision or Treason against Men?: Kashibai Kanitkar and the Engendering of Marathi Literature* (Ranikhet: Permanent Black, 2011b), 84.

14 Kosambi, *Feminist Vision or Treason against Men?*, 84.

15 Kosambi, 84.

16 Kanitkar's representation of the life and work of Anandibai Joshee, the first Indian woman to receive a medical degree, is arguably the first biography of an Indian woman by another in modern prose, and is titled *Kai Sou. Dr. Anandibai Joshee Yanche Charitra* (Pune: Kulkarni ani Mandali 1889). Anandibai Joshee's letters to her husband are studied in the first chapter of the present study.

17 Recent decades have witnessed a growing body of scholarship on the print culture in nineteenth-century India, and the resultant developments discussed here. See, Ashokan Nambiar C., *Print and the Novel in 19th-Century Kerala: Reconsidering Colonial Modernity* (New Delhi: Bloomsbury Academic, 2025); Rosinka Chaudhuri, *The Literary Thing: History, Poetry and the Making of a Modern Cultural Sphere* (Lausanne: Peter Lang, 2014); Francesca Orsini, ed. *The History of the Book in South Asia* (New York: Ashgate Publishing, 2013); Meera Kosambi, *Crossing Thresholds: Feminist Essays in Social History* (Ranikhet: Permanent Black, 2011a); Francesca Orsini, *Print and Pleasure: Popular Literature and Entertaining Fictions in Colonial North India* (Ranikhet: Permanent Black, 2009b); Ulrike Stark, *An Empire of Books: The Naval Kishore Press and the Diffusion of the Printed Word in Colonial India* (New Delhi: Orient Blackswan, 2008); Stuart

Blackburn and Vasudha Dalmia, eds. *India's Literary History: Essays on the Nineteenth Century* (Delhi: Permanent Black, 2004).

18 Ranjana Saha, *Modern Maternities: Medical Advice about Breastfeeding in Colonial Calcutta* (Oxon: Routledge, 2024), 9.

19 Tanika Sarkar asserts that a distinctive tradition of women's writings in print had been around in Bengal for at least twenty years before Rashsundari Debi's autobiography. In Sarkar, *Words to Win*, 131.

20 Meera Kosambi studies the writings of women in nineteenth-century Maharashtra and observes that her primary sources (seven autobiographies) all come from a homogeneous caste group (Chitpavan Brahmin) who spanned a wide economic spectrum but were all born in the 1860s, except for Pandita Ramabai, who was born two years earlier. Most of the debut texts by these women thus appeared in the 1880s. In Kosambi, *Crossing Thresholds*, 34.

21 Susie Tharu and K. Lalita, *Women Writing in India: Vol 1* (New Delhi: Oxford University Press, 1993), 37.

22 Edward Said, *Beginnings: Intention and Method* (London: Granta Publication, 2012), xviii–xix.

23 Said, *Beginnings*, 34–5.

24 Charu Gupta, *Sexuality, Obscenity, Community: Women, Muslims, and the Hindi Public in Colonial India* (New York: Palgrave Macmillan, 2002); Shobna Nijhawan, *Women and Girls in the Hindi Public Sphere* (New Delhi: Oxford University Press, 2012); Sujata S. Mody, *The Making of Modern Hindi* (New Delhi: Oxford University Press, 2018); David Arnold and Stuart Blackburn, eds. *Telling Lives in India: Biography, Autobiography and Life History* (Delhi: Permanent Black, 2004); Francesa Orsini, *The Hindi Public Sphere, 1920–1940: Language and Literature in the Age of Nationalism* (New Delhi: Oxford University Press, 2009a); Udaya Kumar, *Writing the First Person: Literature, History and Autobiography in Modern Kerala* (Ranikhet: Permanent Black, 2016).

25 Stuart Blackburn, *Print, Folklore and Nationalism in Colonial South India* (Delhi: Permanent Black, 2003); V. Rajesh, Manuscripts, *Memory and History: Classical Tamil Literature* (New Delhi: Cambridge University Press, 2013).

26 Gauri Viswanathan, *Outside the Fold: Conversion, Modernity, and Belief* (Princeton, NJ: Princeton University Press, 1998).

27 Tanika Sarkar, *Hindu Wife, Hindu Nation: Community, Religion and Cultural Nationalism* (Delhi: Permanent Black, 2001); Uma Chakravarti, *Rewriting History: The Life and Times of Pandita Ramabai* (New Delhi: Kali for Women, 1998).

28 Kathryn Hansen, *Stage of Life: Indian Theatre Autobiographies* (Delhi: Permanent Black, 2011); Anshu Malhotra and Siobhan Lambert-Hurley, eds. *Speaking of the Self: Gender, Performance, and Autobiography in South Asia* (Durham, NC: Duke University Press, 2015); Rimli Bhattacharya, *Public Women in British India: Icons and the Urban Stage* (Oxon: Routledge, 2018).

29 Toral Jatin Gajarawala, *Untouchable Fictions: Literary Realism and the Crisis of Caste* (New York: Fordham University Press, 2013); Ulka Anjaria, *Realism in the Twentieth-Century Indian Novel: Colonial Difference and Literary Form* (New York: Cambridge University Press, 2012).

30 Rosalind O'Hanlon, *Caste, Conflict and Ideology: Mahatma Jotirao Phule and Low Caste Protest in Nineteenth-Century Western India* (Cambridge: Cambridge University Press, 1985); Geraldine Forbes, *Women in Colonial India: Essays on Politics, Medicine, and Historiography* (New Delhi: Chronicle Books, 2005); Tanika Sarkar, *Rebels, Wives, Saints: Designing Selves and Nations in Colonial Times* (Calcutta: Seagull Books, 2009).

31 Edward Said, *Out of Place: A Memoir* (New York: Alfred A. Knopf, 1999), 3.

32 Krupabai Satthianadhan, *Saguna: A Story of Native Christian Life* (Oxford: Oxford University Press, 1998), 19.

33 In her 'Note on the Text' to the novel *Saguna*, the scholar and editor Chandani Lokuge writes that Queen Victoria expressed an interest in reading other works by the author of *Saguna*. See, Satthianadhan, *Saguna*, ix.

34 Ellen Brinks, *Anglophone Indian Women Writers, 1870–1920* (Oxon: Routledge, 2016), 59.

35 The opening page makes explicit the protagonist's preoccupation with Christian faith, but one may argue that this 'newness' is just as much about the hunger for formal education in a woman, her family's rebellions against normative social expectations and the constant striving for an individualistic voice and identity. Women of the late

nineteenth century who were thus 'educated, articulate, mobile, and increasingly involved in public activities' were called 'new women' according to the historian Geraldine Forbes. See Geraldine Forbes, *Women in Modern India* (Delhi: Cambridge University Press, 2015), 28. Drawing from Forbes's research on the term 'new woman' which was in vogue in the late nineteenth century, Chandani Lokuge refers to any writing that promotes or exemplifies this ideal of education, self-reliance and active participation as 'New-Woman writing' in her Introduction to Saguna (see Satthianadhan, *Saguna*, 1). Further, in her Introduction to Krupabai's second novel, *Kamala*, Lokuge applies this term of 'new woman' specifically to the writer Krupabai herself. See, Chandani Lokuge, 'Introduction' in Krupabai Satthianadhan, *Kamala: The Story of a Hindu Child-Wife* (New Delhi: Oxford University Press, 1998), 1.

36 'My greatest trials come through my tongue. I had got into the habit of thinking loudly'. This disclosure by the narrator leads to an authority figure correcting her assumption that free speech cannot be directed at superiors. Satthianadhan, *Saguna,* 154–5.

37 Kumar, *Writing the First Person,* 2.

38 Satthianadhan, *Saguna,* 230–1.

39 Satthianadhan, 231.

40 Mrinalini Sinha argues that by relegating women to a metaphorical or symbolic presence and men as metonymic or agential, the discourse of Indian nationalism produced 'the figure of the "modern Indian woman" as the unique signifier of Indianness and of the national culture's absolute difference from the West'. See, Mrinalini Sinha, 'Gender and Nation' in *Women's History in Global Perspective. Vol 1* ed. Bonnie G. Smith (Chicago, IL: University of Illinois Press, 2004), 239.

41 Lata Mani, *Contentious Traditions: The Debate on Sati in Colonial India* (Berkeley, CA: University of California Press), 2.

42 Sumathi Ramaswamy, *The Goddess and the Nation: Mapping Mother India* (Durham, NC: Duke University Press, 2010), 1.

43 Sudhir Chandra, *Enslaved Daughters: Colonialism, Law, and Women's Rights* (New Delhi: Oxford University Press, 2008).

44 Kumkum Sangari and Suresh Vaid, 'Recasting Women: An Introduction' in *Recasting Women: Essays in Colonial History* eds.

Kumkum Sangari and Suresh Vaid (New Brunswick, NJ: Rutgers University Press, 1999), 5.

45 J. Devika, *Her-Self: Early Writings on Gender by Malayalee Women, 1898–1938* (New Delhi: Sage, 2021), xx–xxi.

46 Geraldine Forbes, *Women in Modern India*, 28.

47 Rosalind O'Hanlon, *A Comparison between Women and Men: Tarabai Shinde and the Critique of Gender Relations in Colonial India* (Madras: Oxford University Press, 1994), 13.

48 Kosambi, *Crossing Thresholds*, 9.

49 Kosambi, *Crossing Thresholds*, 33.

50 Meera Kosambi, *Women Writing Gender: Marathi Fiction before Independence* (Ranikhet: Permanent Black, 2012), 66–67.

51 Padma Anagol, *The Emergence of Feminism in India, 1850–1920* (Oxon: Routledge, 2016), 10. Geraldine Forbes draws parallel between Western feminism and Indian feminism (between 1880s and 1940s) over reform efforts in suffrage, education and legal and civil rights. See Forbes, *Women in Colonial India,* 11.

52 Priyamvada Gopal, *Literary Radicalism in India: Gender, Nation and the Transition to Independence* (Oxon: Routledge, 2005).

53 Gyanendra Pandey, *The Construction of Communalism in Colonial North India* (New Delhi: Oxford University Press, 2012); Neeti Nair, *Changing Homelands: Hindu Politics and the Partition of India* (Boston, MA: Harvard University Press, 2011); Shahid Amin, *Event, Metaphor, Memory: Chauri Chaura* (New Delhi: Oxford University Press, 1995).

54 David Hardiman, *Gandhi in His Times and Ours* (London: Hurst & Company, 2003).

55 Dilip M. Menon, *Caste, Nationalism and Communism in South India: Malabar 1900–1948* (Cambridge: Cambridge University Press, 2007).

56 K. Srilata, *The Other Half of the Coconut: Women Writing Self-Respect History* (New Delhi: Kali for Women, 2003).

57 For instance, Women's Indian Association in 1917, National Council for Women in 1925, and the All India Women's Conference in 1927.

58 Tharu and Lalita, *Women Writing in India: Vol 1,* 36.

59 Cornelia Sorabji, *Between the Twilights: Being Studies of Indian Women by One of Themselves* (London: Harper and Brothers, 1908), vii–viii.

60 Richard Sorabji, *Opening Doors: The Untold Story of Cornelia Sorabji* (Gurgaon: Penguin, 2010), xii.
61 Antoinette Burton, *Dwelling in the Archive: Women Writing House, Home, and History in Late Colonial India* (New York: Oxford University Press, 2003), 70.
62 Sorabji, *Opening Doors*, xii.
63 Carolyn Steedman, *Past Tenses: Essays on Writing, Autobiography and History* (London: Rivers Oram Press, 1992), 48. The narrative at the start is emphatic about not being history but ends with the affirmation and recognition 'that what I have produced *is* [italics in original] history' (45).
64 Carolyn Kay Steedman, *Landscape for a Good Woman: A Story of Two Lives* (New Brunswick, NY: Rutgers University Press, 1987).
65 Steedman, *Landscape*, 5.
66 Kumar, *Writing the First Person*, 13.
67 Kumar, *Writing the First Person*, 14.
68 Barnita Bagchi, 'Introduction' to Rokeya Sakhawat Hossain, in *Sultana's Dream and Padmarag: Two Feminist Utopias* (New Delhi: Penguin, 2005); Bharati Ray, *Early Feminists of Colonial India: Sarala Devi Choudhrani and Rokeya Sakhawat Hossain* (New Delhi: Oxford University Press, 2002).
69 Rokeya Sakhawat Hossain, *Motichur: Sultana's Dreams and Other Writings of Rokeya Sakhawat Hossain*, trans. Ratri Ray and Prantosh Bandopadhyay (New Delhi: Oxford Univesity Press, 2015b), xi–xii.
70 Hossain, *Motichur*, xi.
71 Frieda Ekotto and Abigail E. Celis, 'Introduction to World Literature 1771 to 1919' in *A Companion to World Literature. Volume 4: 1771 to 1919* (Chichester, West Sussex: Wiley Blackwell, 2020), 1939–54.
72 Swarnakumari Debi Ghosal, *An Unfinished Song* (New Delhi: Oxford University Press, 2008), 55–6.
73 Gauri Viswanathan, *Masks of Conquest: Literary Study and British Rule in India* (New York: Columbia University Press, 2015).
74 Ghosal, *An Unfinished Song*, 58.
75 Ghosal, *An Unfinished Song*, 58.
76 John Rignall, 'George Eliot's Impact as Novelist and Critic on World Literature' in *A Companion to World Literature. Volume 4: 1771 to 1919* eds. Frieda Ekotto and Abigail E. Celis (Chichester, West Sussex: Wiley Blackwell, 2020), 2405–16.

77 Rosinka Chaudhuri, 'Modernity at Home: The Nationalization of the Indian Drawing Room, 1830–1930' in *Interpreting Homes in South Asian Literature* eds. Malashri Lal and Sukrita Paul Kumar (Noida: Pearson Longman, 2007), 222.

78 Nancy Armstrong, *Desire and Domestic Fiction: A Political History of the Novel* (New York: Oxford University Press, 2006), 31.

79 Armstrong, *Desire and Domestic Fiction*, 15.

80 Novels that have been claimants to being the first in India appear around the middle of the century, such as Baba Padamji's *Yamuna Paryatan* (1857) in Marathi and Bankimchandra's *Rajmohum's Wife* (1862) in Bengali.

81 Dosebai Cowasjee Jessawalla, in Dedication to *The Story of My Life* (New Delhi: Speaking Tiger, 2023).

82 Jessawalla, *The Story of My Life*, 1.

83 Binodini Dasi, *My Story and My Life as an Actress*, trans. Rimli Bhattacharya (New Delhi: Kali for Woman), 49.

84 Meenakshi Mukherjee, 'Epic and Novel in India' in *The Novel: Vol 1* ed. Franco Moretti (Princeton, NJ: Princeton University Press, 2006), 596–631.

85 Leigh Gilmore, *Autobiographics: A Feminist Theory of Women's Self-Representation* (Ithaca, NY: Cornell University Press, 1994), 5.

86 David Duff, 'Introduction' in *Modern Genre Theory* ed. David Duff (Oxon: Routledge, 2000), 2.

Chapter 1

1 Meera Kosambi, *Feminist Vision or Treason against Men?: Kashibai Kanitkar and the Engendering of Marathi Literature* (Ranikhet: Permanent Black, 2011b), 70.

2 Kashibai Kanitkar writes this in her book review of Pandita Ramabai's *The Peoples of the United States* that was first published in *Manoranjan ani Nibandha-chandrika* in 1889. See Kosambi, *Feminist Vision or Treason against Men?*, 69–70.

3 Meera Kosambi, *Crossing Thresholds: Feminist Essays in Social History* (Ranikhet: Permanent Black, 2011), 6.

4 Veena Naregal, *Language, Politics, Elites, and the Public Sphere: Western India under Colonialism* (Ranikhet: Permanent Black, 2014), 54.

5 Padma Anagol, *The Emergence of Feminism in India, 1850–1920* (Oxon: Routledge, 2016), 6.
6 Prachi Deshpande, *Creative Pasts: Historical Memory and Identity in Western India 1700–1960* (Ranikhet: Permanent Black, 2007), 7.
7 *Kavya Phule* in 1854 and *Bavan Kashi Subodh Ratnakar* in 1881.
8 Pandita Ramabai, *A Testimony of Our Inexhaustible Treasure* (Kedgaon: Ramabai Mukti Mission, 1907).
9 Ramabai Ranade, *Himself: The Autobiography of a Hindu Lady*, trans. Katherine Van Akin Gates (New York: Longmans, Green and Co., 1938).
10 Parvati Athavale, *My Story: The Autobiography of a Young Widow*, trans. Justin E. Abbott (New York: G. P. Putnam's Sons, 1939).
11 Lakshmibai Tilak, *Smritichitre*, trans. Shanta Gokhale (New Delhi: Speaking Tiger, 2017). For a study of the discursive engagements between medicine and environment as understood through an analysis of the literary genre of this autobiography, see Gayathri Prabhu, 'Tropics, Medicine, and Pandemic: The Bubonic Plague in Lakshmibai Tilak's *Smritichitre*' *Interdisciplinary Studies in Literature and Environment*, Vol 27, no. 4 (2020), 823–35.
12 Anandibai Karve, *Maze Puran*, ed. Kaveri Karve (Mumbai: Keshav Bhikaji Dhawale, 1944).
13 Yashodabai Joshi, *A Marathi Saga: The Story of Sir Moropant and Lady Yashodabai Joshi*, trans. V. V. Bhide (New Delhi: Roli Books, 2003).
14 The first instalment of *Rangarao* was published in 1886 and completed in book form in 1903. See the section 'Writerliness and the First-Person Stance' in the Introduction of this book.
15 Krupabai's *Saguna: A Story of Native Christian Life* was serialized in 1887–8 in Madras Christian College magazine. See also Shevantibai Nikambe, *Ratanbai: A High-Caste Child-Wife* (New Delhi: Oxford University Press, 2004).
16 Padma Anagol, 'Rebellious Wives and Dysfunctional Marriages: Indian Women's Discourses and Participation in Debates over Restitution of Conjugal Rights and the Child Marriage Controversy in the 1880s and 1890s' in *Women and Social Reform in Modern India, Vol 1 & 2* eds. Sumit Sarkar and Tanika Sarkar (Ranikhet: Permanent Black, 2012), 426.
17 In her critique of Partha Chatterjee's dichotomy of home and the outside in the late nineteenth century, Meera Kosambi insists that

the home was not a private sphere and the boundaries between them were porous. See Kosambi, *Crossing Thresholds*, 9–11.

18 Rosalind O'Hanlon, *A Comparison between Women and Men: Tarabai Shinde and the Critique of Gender Relations in Colonial India* (Madras: Oxford University Press, 1994), 85.

19 Henceforth referred to as *A Comparison.*

20 O'Hanlon explains her decision to add a long Introductory essay to the text as part of her efforts to address themes and wider significance to the text and she appears to bring this flexibility or fluidity to translating specific words as well. See O'Hanlon, *A Comparison,* 2.

21 O'Hanlon claims it to be the first text in India that to her knowledge 'a woman addresses herself so squarely and polemically at the question of women's relationships with men'. See O'Hanlon, *A Comparison*, 8.

22 Kosambi, *Crossing Thresholds*, 34.

23 Tanika Sarkar and Sumit Sarkar, 'Introduction' to *Women and Social Reform in Modern India, Vol 1 & 2* eds. Sumit Sarkar and Tanika Sarkar (Ranikhet: Permanent Black, 2012), 1–12.

24 O'Hanlon, *A Comparison*, 75.

25 O' Hanlon, *A Comparison*, 5. Tarabai Shinde's father held a clerical job with the colonial government and was a member of the Satyashodhak Samaj or 'Truth Seeking Society' set up by Jotirao Phule.

26 O'Hanlon, *A Comparison*, 6.

27 O'Hanlon, *A Comparison*, 7.

28 O'Hanlon, *A Comparison*, 13.

29 Meera Kosambi, *Pandita Ramabai: Life and Landmark Writings* (Oxon: Routledge, 2016), 30.

30 Kosambi, *Pandita Ramabai*, 30.

31 Kosambi, *Crossing Thresholds*, 39. Padma Anagol discusses Tarabai Shinde's insights as representing 'a common set of social and political problems that faced women at that time'. See Anagol, *The Emergence*, 13.

32 Gilbert and Gubar overturn Harold Blooms' proposition of the 'anxiety of influence' experienced by (male) authors, to argue that the relationship of women artists to their professional output is more likely to be a 'profoundly debilitating' anxiety of authorship. Gilbert and Gubar see this anxiety as caused by a woman writer's 'socially determined sense of her own biology' that becomes 'a disaffection, a

disturbance, a distrust, that spreads like a stain throughout the style and structure of much literature by women […] before the twentieth century'. Sandra M. Gilbert and Susan Gubar, *Madwoman in the Attic* (New Delhi: Worldview Publications, 2007), 51.

33 O'Hanlon, *A Comparison*, 77.

34 O'Hanlon, 77.

35 O'Hanlon, 79.

36 O'Hanlon, 79.

37 Malini Bhattacharya, 'Introduction' to *Talking of Power: Early Writings of Bengali Women*, eds. Malini Bhattacharya and Abhiji Sen (New Delhi: Sage, 2021), 4.

38 Sumit Sarkar and Tanika Sarkar, eds. *Women and Social Reform in Modern India, Vol 1 & 2* (Ranikhet: Permanent Black, 2012).

39 Eunice de Souza and Lindsay Pereira, ed. *Women's Voice: Selections from Nineteenth and Early-Twentieth Century Indian Writing in English* (New Delhi: Oxford University Press, 2004), xi.

40 Mary Wollstonecraft, *A Vindication of the Rights of Women with Strictures on Political and Moral Subjects* (London: T. Fisher Unwin, 1891), vii.

41 Writers who are aware of their audience being male or the privileged other tend to self-consciously avoid references to man or manhood. This target has been referred to here as other-than-women to encompass writers who avoided naming their offending other as man.

42 Kailashbasini Devi, 'The Woeful Plight of Hindu Women' in *Talking of Power: Early Writings of Bengali Women* eds. Malini Bhattacharya and Abhiji Sen (New Delhi: Sage, 2021), 27.

43 Pandita Ramabai, 'Stri Dharma Niti' in *Pandita Ramabai: Life and Landmark Writings* ed. and trans. by Meera Kosambi (New Delhi: Routledge, 2021a), 42.

44 Radhabai Inamdar, 'Position of Widows: Experiences of Widows and Other Girls' *Shadow Lives: Writings on Widowhood* eds. Uma Chakravarti and Preeti Gill (New Delhi: Zubaan, 2007), 92.

45 Uma Chakravarti, *Rewriting History: The Life and Times of Pandita Ramabai* (New Delhi: Kali for Women, 1998), 260.

46 O'Hanlon, *A Comparison*, 87.

47 There are many instances of this across the text between pages 87 and 120. See O'Hanlon, *A Comparison.*
48 O'Hanlon, 84.
49 O'Hanlon, 94.
50 O'Hanlon, 90.
51 O'Hanlon, 92.
52 O'Hanlon, 111, 113.
53 O'Hanlon, 89.
54 O'Hanlon, 116.
55 O'Hanlon, 117.
56 Pandita Ramabai, 'Englandcha Pravas (Voyage to England, 1883, Abridged Translation)' in Meera Kosambi ed. *Pandita Ramabai: Life and Landmark Writings* (Oxon: Routledge, 2016), 102.
57 The addressee is Mr. S. P. Kelkar of the Prarthana Samaj. See Kosambi, *Pandita Ramabai*, 120.
58 Chakravarti, *Rewriting History*, vii.
59 Gauri Viswanathan, *Outside the Fold: Conversion, Modernity and Belief* (Princeton, NJ: Princeton University Press, 1998), 125.
60 The letter was published three months later in 1883 in Subodh Patrika. See Kosambi, *Pandita Ramabai*, 82. Ramabai was likely wanting to directly address public apprehensions: She was a high-caste widow travelling abroad without a male escort, staying with Christian nuns and seeking an English education. It was speculated that her loss of high-caste purity/status be made worse if she were to convert to Christianity.
61 Antoinette Burton posits, 'In an era when travel for high-caste Hindu women was considered unsexing and heretical, those who left India seeking support and education in the West were roundly condemned for defiling themselves, their families, and indeed the very category of "Indian womanhood" itself.' See Antoinette Burton, *At the Heart of the Empire: Indians and the Colonial Encounter in Late-Victorian Britain* (Delhi: Munshiram Manoharlal, 1998a), 73.
62 Andrew O. Winckles and Angela Rehbein, 'Afterword' in ed. *Women's Literary Networks and Romanticism: A Tribe of Authoress* (Liverpool: Liverpool University Press, 2017), 300. Lindsay O'Neill writes of letters as 'networking practices' that local, familiar, international and

professional. See, Lindsay O' Neill, *The Opened Letter: Networking in the Early Modern British World* (Philadelphia, PA: University of Pennsylvania Press, 2015), 2.

63 Maire Cross and Caroline Bland, ed. *Gender and Politics in the Age of Letter Writing, 1750–2000* (United Kingdom: Taylor & Francis, 2017).

64 Sabyasachi Bhattacharya, ed. *The Mahatma and the Poet: Letters and Debates between Gandhi and Tagore 1915–1941* (New Delhi: National Book Trust, 2015).

65 Nikhil Govind reads the correspondence between Premchand and Jainendra as 'a continuity of the literary to the political, as also the relative access and privilege these writers had to political leadership'. See Nikhil Govind, *Between Love and Freedom: The Revolutionary in the Hindi Novel* (New Delhi: Routledge, 2014), 85.

66 Sonja Boon writes that while letters are 'shaped by conventions of epistolary practices, they are still highly personal and individual documents that do not easily confirm to external dictates'. See Sonja Boon, *Telling the Flesh: Life Writing, Citizenship, and the Body in the Letters to Samuel Auguste Tissot* (Qubec: McGill-Queen's University Press, 2015), 37.

67 Meera Kosambi, *A Fragmented Feminism: The Life and Letters of Anandibai Joshee*, ed. Ram Ramaswamy, Madhavi Kolhatkar and Aban Mukherji (New Delhi: Routledge, 2020), 4.

68 Anandibai referred to Mrs Carpenter as 'aunt' and developed a close bond with the Carpenter family. Upon her subsequent return to India and untimely death, her ashes were sent to Pennsylvania to be interred in the Carpenter family cemetery.

69 The letter is dated 17 February 1887. See Sudhir Chandra, *Enslaved Daughters: Colonialism, Law and Women's Rights* (New Delhi: Oxford University Press, 2008), 213.

70 Pandita Ramabai, 'About Government Provisions during Plague Epidemic, 1897' in *Pandita Ramabai: Life and Landmark Writings* ed. Meera Kosambi (New Delhi: Routledge, 2021b), 231.

71 The letters were published in the *Tahzib un-niswan* in 1907 and under the title of *Zamana – i-tahsil* (A Time of Education) in 1921. See Siobhan Lambert-Hurley and Sunil Sharma, *Atiya's Journeys: A Muslim*

Woman from Colonial Bombay to Edwardian Britain (New Delhi: Oxford University Press, 2010), 1.

72 Aban Mukherji writes of the contradictions between the popular imagination of Gopalrao Joshee as an ardent social reformer and his often 'inhuman treatment' of his wife. An alternate view of Gopalrao is proposed as being 'vain, shallow, publicity hungry, frustrated, and ungrateful'. See Aban Mukherji, 'Introduction' in Meera Kosambi *A Fragmented Feminism: The Life and Letters of Anandibai Joshee* ed. Ram Ramaswamy, Madhavi Kolhatkar and Aban Mukherji (New Delhi: Routledge, 2020), xxvii–xxviii.

73 Kosambi, *A Fragmented,* 3.

74 Kosambi, 19.

75 Mukherji, 'Introduction', xxv.

76 Kosambi, *A Fragmented,* 18.

77 Anandibai writes of the harassment she faced while walking on the streets during her school years. People would mock and laugh, make vulgar gestures, spit at her and even throw pebbles at her. Kosambi, 25.

78 Kosambi, 89.

79 Narim Hassan, *Diagnosing Empire: Women, Medical Knowledge, and Colonial Mobility* (Surrey: Ashgate Publishing, 2011), 10.

80 Mukherji, 'Introduction' xxv.

81 Kashibai Kanitkar, *Kai. Sou. Dr. Anandibai Joshee Yanche Charitra* (Pune: Kulkarni ani Mandali, 1889).

82 Kosambi, *A Fragmented,* 100–4.

83 Kosambi, 6.

84 Kosambi, 102.

85 Kosambi, 101–3.

86 Kosambi, 101.

87 Kosambi, 110.

88 Kosambi, 112.

89 Kosambi, 112–13.

90 Kosambi, 140.

91 In a letter to Theodocia Carpenter in February 1886, Anandibai writes, 'Love and duty are sacred and my own [underlined in original]. I can always love, although I cannot always expect to be loved.' Kosambi, 186.

92 Kosambi, 140.

93 These excerpts from her letter were often prefaced or contextualized by the newspapers as a favourable contrast to the choices made by Pandita Ramabai. See Kosambi, 117, 130–1.

94 Kosambi, 153.

95 Kosambi, 153.

96 Caroline Healey Dall, *The Life of Dr. Anandabai Joshee, A Kinswoman of the Pundita Ramabai* (Boston, MA: Roberts Brothers, 1888), 185.

97 For more on the Age of Consent debates, see Ishita Pande, *Sex, Law and Politics of Age: Child Marriage in India, 1891–1937* (Ontario: Cambridge University Press, 2020); Rochona Majumdar, *Marriage and Modernity: Family Values in Colonial Bengal* (Durham, NC: Duke University Press, 2009).

98 Rukhmabai, 'Reply' in Appendix D of Sudhir Chandra, *Enslaved Daughters: Colonialism, Law and Women's Rights* (New Delhi: Oxford University Press, 2008), 234–42.

99 Sudhir Chandra, *Enslaved Daughters: Colonialism, Law, and Women's Rights* (New Delhi: Oxford University Press, 2008); Sudhir Chandra, *Rukhmabai: The Life and Times of a Child Bride Turned Rebel-Doctor* (New Delhi: Macmillan, 2024), x.

100 Rukhmabai, 'Reply', 234.

101 Rukhmabai, 235.

102 Some of her reasons for this denouncement are provided: he used abusive language towards her mother, defied the efforts at education provided to him and was morally dissolute.

103 Chandra, *Enslaved Daughters*, 15.

104 A sub-caste of Brahmins from the Konkan region, the same caste as the Peshwas who ruled from Poona and were defeated by the British in 1818. See Naregal, 273.

105 Suthar or Pachkalshi, typically a caste of carpenters. See Chandra, *Enslaved Daughters,* 15; Kosambi, *Crossing Thresholds*, 244.

106 Chandra, *Enslaved Daughters*, 17. Rukhmabai reiterated in her letter of 1887, 'I had a great liking for study while a great disgust for married life'. See Chandra, 215.

107 Chandra, 1.

108 Chandra, 7.

109 The letters were dated 26 June 1885 and 19 September 1885.

110 Rukhmabai, 'Reply', 216.

111 Justice Pinhey said, ' I am not obliged to grant the plaintiff the relief which he seeks, and to compel this young lady of twenty-two to go to the house of the plaintiff in order that he may consummate the marriage arranged for her during her helpless infancy.' See Sudhir Chandra, *Enslaved Daughters,* 39.

112 Chandra, 50.

113 Kanika Sharma, Laura Lammasniemi and Tanika Sarkar, 'Dadaji Bhikaji v Rukhmabai (1886) ILR 10 Bom 301: Rewriting Consent and Conjugal Relations in Colonial India' *Indian Law Review*, Vol 5, no. 3 (2021), 265. The article imagines an alternate legal history that could completely overturn patriarchal assumptions on marriage and the Hindu law in late colonial India.

114 Antoinette Burton, 'From Child Bride to "Hindoo Lady": Rukhmabai and the Debate on Sexual Respectability in Imperial Britain' *The American Historical Review*, Vol 103, no. 4 (1998b), 1123.

115 Antoinette Burton, 'Conjugality on Trial: The Rukhmabai Case and the Debate on Indian Child-Marriage in Late-Victorian Britian' *Disorder in the Court: Trials and Sexual Conflict at the Turn of the Century* ed. George Robb and Nancy Erber (London: Palgrave Macmillan, 1999), 33.

116 Burton, 'Conjugality on Trial', 34.

117 Kanika Sharma, Laura Lammasniemi and Tanika Sarkar, 'Dadaji Bhikaji v Rukhmabai', 273.

118 Chandra, *Enslaved Daughters*, 103.

119 Chandra, 164.

120 Rukhmabai, 'Reply', 234.

121 Rukhmabai, 234.

122 Rukhmabai, 235. All the excerpts that follow in this paragraph are from this same page.

123 Rukhmabai, 241.

124 Chandra further adds that 'the person believed to have "revised" Dadajee's "notes" was Dr. Kirtikar, the England-returned self-styled reformist who had lived as a dependent in Sakharam Arjun's house before Rukhmabai's marriage [...] Rukhmabai insinuated in unmistakable terms that Kirtikar had authored the "Exposition"'. See Chandra, *Enslaved Daughters*, 246.

125 Chandra, 246.

126 Rukhmabai, 'Reply', 240.
127 Rukhmabai, 252.
128 Rukhmabai, 252.
129 Rukhmabai, 255.
130 Chandra, *Enslaved Daughters*, 163.
131 Shreya Roy, *State, Law and Gender: Debating the Age of Marriage in India, 1872–1978* (New Delhi: Manohar Publishers, 2024), 180.
132 Tanikar Sarkar, 'Rhetoric against Age of Consent: Resisting Colonial Reason and the Death of a Child-Wife' *Economic and Political Weekly*, Vol 28, no. 36, (1993), 1869–78.

Chapter 2

1 Rokeya Sakhawat Hossain, 'The Better Half' in *Motichur: Sultana's Dreams and Other Writings of Rokeya Sakhawat Hossain* trans. Ratri Ray and Prantosh Bandopadhyay (New Delhi: Oxford University Press, 2015a).
2 Hossain, 'The Better Half', 46.
3 Gregory Claeys, 'Preface' in *The Cambridge Companion to Utopian Literature* ed. Gregory Claeys (Cambridge: Cambridge University Press, 2010), xi.
4 Meredith Borthwick, *The Changing Role of Women in Bengal, 1849–1905* (Princeton, NJ: Princeton University Press, 1984), 29.
5 Tanika Sarkar, 'Foreword' in *Talking of Power: Early Writings of Bengali Women* eds. Malini Bhattacharya and Abhiji Sen (New Delhi: Sage, 2021), ix.
6 In her book, *High Caste Hindu Woman*, Pandita Ramabai writes of the daily realities of the widow who is addressed in abusive language, guarded like a prisoner, disfigured by shaving her head and depriving her of ornaments, food intake is curtailed, confined to the house. 'Her life then, destitute as it is of the least literary knowledge, void of all hope, empty of every pleasure and social advantage, becomes intolerable, a curse to herself and to society at large.' See Kosambi, *Pandita Ramabai*, 165.
7 Sekhar Bandyopadhyay, 'Caste, Widow-Remarriage, and the Reform of Popular Culture in Colonial Bengal' in *Women and Social Reform in*

Modern India Vol 1 eds. Sumit Sarkar and Tanika Sarkar (Ranikhet, Permanent Black, 2011), 147.

8 See Geraldine Forbes, *Women in Modern India* (Delhi: Cambridge University Press, 2015), 33.

9 Malini Bhattacharya, 'Introduction' in *Talking of Power: Early Writings of Bengali Women* eds. Malini Bhattacharya and Abhiji Sen (New Delhi: Sage, 2021), ix.

10 Maroona Murmu, *Words of Her Own: Women Authors in Nineteenth-Century Bengal* (New Delhi: Oxford University Press, 2020), 14–15.

11 Tanika Sarkar, *Words to Win: The Making of a Modern Autobiography* (New Delhi: Zubaan, 2013), 204.

12 'I am Born' is the title of the first chapter of Charles Dickens' *David Copperfield* (1849–1850) and the first-person narrative voice dwells at length on the circumstances of their own birth.

13 Sarkar, *Words to Win*, 218.

14 Sarkar, 1.

15 The philosopher and social reformer Debendranath Tagore published his autobiography *Atmajibani* in 1898. This is noted by Susie and Lalita, who consider 1876 as the first publication date of Rashsundari's autobiography. See Susie Tharu and K. Lalita, *Women Writing in India: Vol 1* (New Delhi: Oxford University Press, 1993), 190.

16 Sarkar, *Words to Win*, 1. For more on this edition, refer to the opening section of the Introduction to the present study.

17 Sarkar writes that the second part is enormously repetitive. Sarkar, *Words to Win*,12.

18 Sarkar, 13.

19 Margery Kempe, *The Book of Margery Kempe* trans. B.A. Windeatt (London: Penguin Books, 2004).

20 Sarkar, *Words to Win*, 162.

21 Sumit Sarkar, 'Vidyasagar and Brahmanical Society' in *Women and Social Reform in Modern India, Vol 1* eds. Sumit Sarkar and Tanika Sarkar (Ranikhet: Permanent Black, 2012), 202.

22 Sarkar, *Words to Win*, 166.

23 Sarkar, 173–4.

24 Sarkar, 180.

25 Sarkar, 191.

26 Sarkar, 175.

27 Sarkar, 177, 180.
28 Sarkar, 177.
29 Sarkar, 182.
30 Sarkar, 191.
31 Sarkar, 190.
32 This sixteenth-century text is *Chaitanya Bhagabat*, 'the first Bengali biography of the Krishna-maddened saint of medieval Bengal, who promised salvation to the wretched, the low caste, the women – categories excluded by brahmanical orthodoxy from higher spiritual aspirations and learning'. Sarkar, 3.
33 Sarkar, 192.
34 Sarkar, 195–6.
35 Sarkar, 194.
36 Sarkar, 204.
37 Sarkar, 203.
38 Sarkar, 210.
39 Sarkar, 296.
40 Sarkar, 296.
41 Sarkar, 224.
42 Sarkar, 224.
43 Sarkar, 235.
44 Sarkar, 7.
45 Sarkar, 219.
46 Sarkar, 220.
47 Sarkar, 222.
48 Binodini Dasi, *My Story and My Life as an Actress*, ed. and trans. Rimli Bhattacharya (New Delhi: Kali for Woman, 1998), 57.
49 Tanika Sarkar observes, 'It is women from lesser-know circles – housewives fully engaged with domestic chores, professional women like prostitutes-turned-actresses who suffered from low social esteem for the nature of their work – who seem more preoccupied with a public self-disclosure, self-definition: either of an individual or of a collective self.' See Sarkar, *Words to Win*, 150.
50 Tharu and Lalita, *Women Writing in India: Vol 1*, 290.

51 Bishnupriya Dutt, 'Actress Stories: Binodini and Amal Allana' in *Staging International Feminisms* eds. Elaine Aston and Sue-Ellen Case (New York: Palgrave Macmillan, 2007), 69.

52 Rimli Bhattacharya, *Public Women in British India: Icons and the Urban Stage* (Oxon: Routledge, 2018), 78–9. See also Lata Singh, *Raising the Curtain: Recasting Women Performers in India* (Hyderabad: Orient BlackSwan, 2017), 49.

53 Lata Singh writes, 'effeminacy and home-eroticism was considered as greater threats to society than hiring prostitutes for female roles.' See Singh, *Raising the Curtain*, 52. Kathryn Hansen studies autobiographical texts by four men associated with Parsi theatre at the end of the nineteenth century and comments on 'woman' as a 'kind of spectacle' on stage, particularly in the parallel presence of female impersonators (male actors playing female parts) and professional actresses on stage. See Kathryn Hansen, *Stage of Life: Indian Theatre Autobiographies* (Delhi: Permanent Black, 2011), 14–15.

54 Bhattacharya, *Public Women*, 3.

55 Partha Chatterjee, *The Black Hole of Empire: History of a Global Practice of Power* (Ranikhet: Permanent Black, 2015), 232.

56 Bhattacharya, *Public Women*, 80.

57 Binodini Dasi, *My Story*, 82.

58 The first theatre companies in Bengal were started by middle-class young men of North Calcutta, dissolving the dominance of upper-class patrons and their private amateur shows. See Tanika Sarkar, *Hindu Wife, Hindu Nation: Community, Religion and Cultural Nationalism* (Delhi: Permanent Black, 2001), 64.

59 Chatterjee, *The Black Hole of Empire*, 232.

60 Tanika Sarkar, *Rebels, Wives, Saints: Designing Selves and Nations in Colonial Times* (Calcutta: Seagull Books, 2009), 172.

61 Rimli Bhattacharya, 'Binodini Dasi and the Public Theatre in Nineteenth-Century Bengal' in Binodini Dasi's *My Story and My Life as an Actress*, trans. Rimli Bhattacharya (New Delhi: Kali for Woman, 1998), 1.

62 Bhattacharya, 'Binodini Dasi and the Public Theatre in Nineteenth-Century Bengal', 18.

63 Bhattacharya, 30.

64 Ben Singer, *Melodrama and Modernity: Early Sensational Cinema and Its Contexts* (New York: Columbia University Press, 2001), 2.

65 Chatterjee, *The Black Hole of Empire*, 228.
66 Sarkar, *Rebels, Wives, Saints*, 162.
67 Nandi Bhatia, *Acts of Authority/Acts of Resistance: Theatre and Politics in Colonial and Postcolonial India* (Ann Arbor, MI: The University of Michigan Press, 2004), 18. See also Kathryn Hansen, *Grounds for Play: The Nautanki Theatre of North India* (Berkeley, CA: University of California Press, 1992); Sharmistha Saha, *Theatre and National Identity in Colonial India: Formation of a Community through Cultural Practice* (Singapore: Springer, 2018); Rashna Darius Nicholson, *The Colonial Public and the Parsi Stage: The Making of the Theatre of Empire (1853–1893)* (Switzerland: Springer, 2021); Meera Kosambi, *Gender, Culture and Performance: Marathi Theatre and Cinema before Independence* (Oxon: Routledge, 2015).
68 Chatterjee, *The Black Hole of Empire*, 231.
69 One surmises these to be Sarah Siddons (1755–1831), Alice Ellen Terry (1847–1928) and Daniel E. Bandmann (1837–1905).
70 Binodini Dasi, *My* Story, 78–80.
71 Carolyn Williams, 'Introduction' to *The Cambridge Companion to English Melodrama* (Cambridge: Cambridge University Press, 2018), 1.
72 James Chandler, 'Foreword' to *The Melodramatic Moment: Music and Theatrical Culture, 1790–1820* eds. Katherine G Hambridge and Jonathan Hicks (Chicago, IL: The University of Chicago Press, 2018), x–xii.
73 Bhattacharya, 'Binodini Dasi and the Public Theatre in Nineteenth-Century Bengal' 18.
74 Singer, *Melodrama and Modernity*, 6.
75 Singer, 44–9.
76 Bhattacharya notes, '*Byatha, bedona, jantrana, jatana, jale:* pain – physical hurt, emotional scar, anguish, torment. These are the words that recur most frequently in *My Story*'. See Binodini Dasi, *My Story*, 245.
77 The phrase is mentioned twice in Ghosh's preface, 'Srimati Binodini and the Bengali Stage'. See Binodini Dasi, 212, 219.
78 Binodini Dasi, 220.
79 For more on Rimli Bhattacharya's argument on 'the discourse of redemption' of the public theatre, see 'Afterword' to Binodini Dasi's *My Story*, 194–5.
80 Binodini Dasi, 59.
81 Binodini Dasi, 49.

82 Binodini Dasi, 54.

83 Rimli Bhattacharya calls Binodini's autobiography 'a dialogic text' similar to her mentor Ghosh's writings about her. See Binodini Dasi, 206.

84 Binodini Dasi, 108.

85 Binodini Dasi, 58.

86 Binodini Dasi, 59–60.

87 Binodini Dasi, 60.

88 Binodini Dasi, 87.

89 Binodini Dasi, 87.

90 Binodini Dasi, 84–5.

91 Rimli Bhattacharya, *Public Women in British India*, 91.

92 Binodini Dasi, *My Story*, 92.

93 Bhattacharya, 'Afterword', 233.

94 Binodini Dasi, *My Story*, 78–9.

95 Chatterjee, *The Black Hole of Empire*, 232.

96 Binodini Dasi, *My Story* 93.

97 Amiya P. Sen, *Ramakrishna Paramahamsa: Sadhaka of Dakshineswar* (New Delhi: Penguin, 2010).

98 Binodini Dasi, *My Story*, 95. Gayathri Prabhu and Nikhil Govind observe that the female performer's 'body [often] inaugurated a new set of postures' to exemplify resistance and defiance. See *Shadow Craft: Visual Aesthetics of Black and White Hindi Cinema* (New Delhi: Bloomsbury Academic, 2021).

99 Binodini Dasi, 96.

100 Sheetala Bhat, *Performing Self/Performing Gender: Reading the Lives of Women Performers in Colonial India* (Manipal: Manipal University Press, 2017), 76.

101 Binodini Dasi, 107.

102 Binodini Dasi, 107.

103 Bhattacharya, 'Introduction', 31.

104 Binodini Dasi, *My Story*, 113.

105 Binodini Dasi, 114.

106 Ghosal, *An Unfinished Song*, 9.

107 Katherine Sobba Green argues that courtship novels are distinguished from other contemporary novels by thematically offering a revisionist view of women as actors rather than victims. See Katherine Sobba Green, *The Courtship Novel 1740–1820: A Feminized Genre* (Lexington,

KY: University Press of Kentucky, 1991), 2. In this context, for a more recent book regarding the romance typology in colonial Bengal, see Sreemati Mukherjee, *Women and the Romance of the Word: 19th-Century Contexts in Bengal* (New Delhi: Bloomsbury Academic, 2025).

108 David Damrosch, *What Is World Literature?* (Princeton, NJ: Princeton University Press, 2003), 5–6.

109 C. Vijayasree, 'Introduction' in Swarnakumari Debi Ghosal's *An Unfinished Song* (New Delhi: Oxford University Press, 2008), xxvi.

110 Ghosal, *An Unfinished Song*, 79.

111 Ghosal, 10.

112 Ghosal, 78.

113 Anne K. Kaler, 'Conventions of the Romance Genre' in *Romantic Conventions* eds. Anne K. Kaler and Rosemary E. Johnson-Kurek (Bowling Green: Bowling Green State University Popular Press, 1999), 1.

114 Ghosal, *An Unfinished Song*, 22.

115 Ghosal, 42.

116 Ghosal, 29.

117 Ghosal, 21.

118 Ghosal, 21.

119 Ghosal, 48.

120 Ghosal, 32.

121 Priya Joshi, *In Another Country: Colonialism, Culture, and the English Novel in India* (New York: Columbia University Press, 2002), 4.

122 Meenakshi Mukherjee, 'Introduction' in *Early Novels in India* ed. Meenakshi Mukherjee (New Delhi: Sahitya Akademi, 2005), ix.

123 Bankimchandra Chatterjee's Bishabriksha (1873), Rabindranath Tagore's Choker Bali (1903), Govardhanram Tripathi's *Saraswatichandra* (four volumes between 1887 and 1902) and Premchand's *Ham Khurma Wa Ham Sawab* (1906) and Prema (1907) are some noteworthy examples.

124 Krupa Shandilya, *Intimate Relations: Social Reform and the Nineteenth-Century South Asian Novel* (Evanston, IL: Illinois, 2017), 10.

125 Ghosal, *An Unfinished Song*, 53.

126 Ghosal, 56.

127 Ghosal, 56.

128 Tharu and Lalita, *Women Writing in India: Vol 1*, 236.

129 Tharu and Lalita, 235–6.

130 Vijayasree, 'Introduction', viii.

131 The dates change in different sources. C. Vijayasree suggests 1856 based on accounts by Swarnakumari's daughters. See Vijayasree, vii.

132 Rabindranath Tagore, *Selected Letters of Rabindranath Tagore*, eds. Krishna Dutta and Andrew Robinson (Cambridge: Cambridge University Press, 1997), 141.

133 Nora E. H. Parr, 'Nation: The Mighty Idea and the Novel' in *A Companion to World Literature. Volume 4: 1771 to 1919* eds. Frieda Ekotto and Abigail E. Celis (Chichester, West Sussex: Wiley Blackwell, 2020), 2095–102.

134 Barnita Bagchi, '"Because Novels Are True, and Histories Are False": Indian Women Writing Fiction in English, 1860—1918' in *A History of the Indian Novel in English* ed. Ulka Anjaria (New York: Cambridge University Press, 2015), 68–70.

135 The editors write, 'The peep into a girl's heart is touching enough, but its psychology is a little too unsearching for an European audience.' See Tagore, *Selected Letters*, 142.

136 Susan Stanford Friedman, '"Shakespeare's Sister": Woolf in the World before *a Room of One's Own*' in *Virginia Woolf: Writing the World* eds. Pamela L. Caughie and Diana L. Swanson (Clemson, South Carolina: Clemson University Press, 2015), 124.

Chapter 3

1 The first Pan-Anglican Congress was held in London from June 15 to June 24 1908 and was initiated by Bishop Henry H Montgomery. It was attended by both clergy and laity.

2 Cornelia Sorabji, 'Social Relations – England and India' in *An Indian Portia: Selected Writings of Cornelia Sorabji 1866–1954* ed. Kusoom Vadgama (New Delhi: Zubaan, 2011), 361.

3 Sorabji, 'Social Relations', 361.

4 Richard Sorabji, *Opening Doors: The Untold Story of Cornelia Sorabji* (London: I. B. Tauris, 2010), 13.

5 The Bar was open to women in 1922. Cornelia wrote the exam and was awarded the degree in 1924.

6 Antoinette Burton, *Dwelling in the Archive: Women Writing House, Home, and History in Late Colonial India* (New York: Oxford University Press, 2003), 4.

7 Burton, *Dwelling in the Archive*, 14.
8 Sorabji, *Opening Doors*, xv.
9 Ellen Brinks, *Anglophone Indian Women Writers, 1870–1920* (Oxon: Routledge, 2016), 12–13.
10 Antoinette Burton, *At the Heart of the Empire: Indians and the Colonial Encounter in Late-Victorian Britain* (New Delhi: Munshiram Manoharlal, 1998a), 17.
11 Suparna Gooptu, *Cornelia Sorabji: India's Pioneer Woman Lawyer* (New Delhi: Oxford University Press, 2010).
12 Sorabji, 'Social Relations', 364.
13 Cornelia Sorabji, *Between the Twilights: Being Studies of Indian Women by One of Themselves* (London: Harper and Brothers, 1908), ix.
14 Burton, *At the Heart of the Empire*, 115.
15 Dosebai Cowasjee Jessawalla, in Dedication to *The Story of My Life* (New Delhi: Speaking Tiger, 2023), xvii.
16 Krupabai Satthianadhan, *Saguna* (New Delhi: Oxford University Press, 1998), unpaginated.
17 David Kennedy, *Elegy* (Oxon: Routledge, 2007), 13.
18 John B. Vickery, *The Modern Elegiac Temper* (Baton Rouge, LA: Louisiana State University Press, 2006), 7.
19 Chandani Lokuge, 'Introduction' to *Saguna* (New Delhi: Oxford University Press, 1998), 2.
20 Ardene Hegele, *Romantic Autopsy: Literary Form and Medical Reading* (Oxford: Oxford University Press, 2022), 3.
21 Satthianadhan, *Saguna*, 160.
22 Anne Hunasker Hawkins defines pathography as 'a form of autobiography or biography that describes personal experiences of illness, treatment, and sometimes death [...] In some sense, the pathography is our modern adventure story'. Anne Hunasker Hawkins, *Reconstructing Illness: Studies in Pathography* (West Lafayette, Indiana: Prudue University Press, 1999), 1.
23 Satthianadhan, *Saguna*, 21.
24 Satthianadhan, 23.
25 Satthianadhan, 22.
26 David Arnold, *The Tropics and the Traveling Gaze: India, Landscape, and Science, 1800–1856* (Seattle, WA: University of Washington Press, 2006), 7.

27 David Arnold, 'Introduction: Tropical Medicine before Mason' to *Warm Climates and Western Medicine: The Emergence of Tropical Medicine 1500–1900* (Atlanta, GA: Rodopi, 2003), 6.
28 Satthianadhan, *Saguna,* 23.
29 Satthianadhan, 71.
30 Satthianadhan, 73.
31 Satthianadhan, 88.
32 Satthianadhan, 88–9.
33 Satthianadhan, 93.
34 Satthianadhan, 109.
35 Satthianadhan, 109.
36 Satthianadhan, 111.
37 Satthianadhan, 112.
38 Satthianadhan, 112.
39 Satthianadhan, 119.
40 Satthianadhan, 111–2.
41 Satthianadhan, 124.
42 Satthianadhan, 157.
43 Satthianadhan, 140.
44 Satthianadhan, 155.
45 Satthianadhan, 158.
46 Satthianadhan, 158.
47 Satthianadhan, 159–60.
48 Satthianadhan, 160.
49 Satthianadhan, 161.
50 Siobhan Lambert-Hurley and Sunil Sharma, *Atiya's Journeys: A Muslim Woman from Colonial Bombay in Edwardian* Britain (New Delhi: Oxford University Press, 2010), 109.
51 Lambert-Hurley and Sharma, *Atiya's Journeys*, 1.
52 Gail Minault, 'Sayyid Mumtaz Ali and Tahzib un-Nizwan: Women's Rights in Islam and Women's Journalism in Urdu' in *Women and Social Reform in Modern India, Vol 2* eds. Sumit Sarkar and Tanika Sarkar (Ranikhet: Permanent Black, 2012), 71.
53 Gail Minault, *Secluded Scholars: Women's Education and Muslim Social Reform in Colonial India* (Oxford: Oxford University Press, 1998), 12.

54 Samarpita Mitra, *Periodicals, Readers and the Making of a Modern Literary Culture: Bengal at the Turn of the Twentieth Century* (Leiden: Brill, 2020), 11.

55 Minault, *Secluded Scholars*, 119. The sociologist Mahua Sarkar attests to Muslim women 'as intellectuals in their own right beginning in the early twentieth century, and as members of a class with considerable influence on the cultural life of that time'. See Mahua Sarkar, *Visible Histories, Disappearing Women: Producing Muslim Womanhood in Late Colonial Bengal* (New Delhi: Zubaan, 2008), 21.

56 Muhammadi Begum (1878?–1908) had been educated at home and 'wrote prolifically – articles, housekeeping manuals cookbooks, poetry and novels – in a down-to-earth style that appealed to a newly literate readership'. See Gail Minault, *Gender, Language and Learning: Essays in Indo-Muslim Cultural History* (Ranikhet: Permanent Black, 2009), 88.

57 Lambert-Hurley and Sharma, *Atiya's Journeys*, 8.

58 Starting with four students in 1845, there were more than 700 Indians studying in London in 1910. The Indian community in London as well as the British government extensively debated on the physical and moral well-being of these students, many of them struggling with racial prejudice. See Rozina Visram, *Ayahs, Lascars and Princes: The Story of Indians of Britain 1700–1947* (Oxon: Routledge, 2015), 348–59.

59 Siobhan Lambert-Hurley, Daniel Majchrowicz and Sunil Sharma, eds. *Three Centuries of Travel Writing by Muslim Women* (Bloomington, IN: Indian University Press, 2022), 293.

60 Lambert-Hurley and Sharma, *Atiya's Journeys*, 57.

61 Under Muhammadi Begam's editorship, the journal included articles on a range of subjects – 'education, housekeeping, and child care, gave recipes, advice to the daughter-in-law on how to get along with her mother-in-law and tips on etiquette'. See Gail Minault, 'Sayyid Mumtaz Ali and Tahzib un-Nizwan' in *Women and Social Reform in Modern India, Vol 2* eds. Sumit Sarkar and Tanika Sarkar (Ranikhet: Permanent Black, 2012), 86.

62 Lambert-Hurley and Sharma, *Atiya's Journeys*, 83.

63 Lambert-Hurley and Sharma, 65.

64 Lambert-Hurley and Sharma, 7.

65 Lambert-Hurley and Sharma, 28.

66 Lambert-Hurley and Sharma, 23–5.

67 Lambert-Hurley and Sharma, 110.

68 Lambert-Hurley and Sharma, 110.
69 Lambert-Hurley and Sharma, 111.
70 Lambert-Hurley and Sharma, 112.
71 Lambert-Hurley and Sharma, 112.
72 Raka Ray and Seemin Qayum, *Cultures of Servitude: Modernity, Domesticity and Class in India* (New Delhi: Oxford University Press, 2010), 4.
73 Ray and Qayum, *Cultures of Servitude*, 4.
74 Lambert-Hurley and Sharma, *Atiya's Journeys*, 113.
75 Tamara S. Wagner and Narin Hassan, 'Preface' to *Consuming Culture in the Long Nineteenth Century: Narratives of Consumption, 1700–1900* ed. Tamara S Wagner and Narin Hassan (Plymouth, MN: Rowman & Littlefield, 2007), ix.
76 Lambert-Hurley and Sharma, *Atiya's Journeys*, 121.
77 Lambert-Hurley and Sharma, 119.
78 Lambert-Hurley and Sharma, 123.
79 Lambert-Hurley and Sharma, 123.
80 The Maria Grey Training College was the first teacher training college in Great Britain and was founded in 1878.
81 Lambert-Hurley and Sharma, *Atiya's Journeys*,124.
82 Lambert-Hurley and Sharma, 125.
83 Lambert-Hurley and Sharma, 126.
84 Atiya address any doubts about the travelogue that does not constantly record seeing of sights thus: 'But you must have gathered from my travelogue that I have hardly seen a single new place. The reason is that there is a lot of studying; that is why I would like to postpone sightseeing for another time.' See Lambert-Hurley and Sharma, 166.
85 Lambert-Hurley and Sharma, 127.
86 Lambert-Hurley and Sharma, 129.
87 Lambert-Hurley and Sharma, 193.
88 Lambert-Hurley and Sharma, 194.
89 The myth and oft-repeated idea of 'the lazy native' that had become integral to justify the colonial enterprise seems echoed in the acceptance of the complementary figure of an enterprising European. See Syed Hussein Atalas, *The Myth of the Lazy Native: A Study of the Image of the Malays, Filipinos and Javanese from the 16th to the 20th Century and its Function in the Ideology of Colonial Capitalism* (London: Frank Cass, 1977).

90 Lambert-Hurley and Sharma, *Atiya's Journeys*, 149.
91 Lambert-Hurley and Sharma, 149.
92 Lambert-Hurley and Sharma, 139.
93 Lambert-Hurley and Sharma, 133.
94 Lambert-Hurley and Sharma, 160–1.
95 Lambert-Hurley and Sharma, 169.
96 Lambert-Hurley and Sharma, 162.
97 Lambert-Hurley and Sharma, 174.
98 Lambert-Hurley and Sharma, 175.
99 Much of the public interest in Atiya Fyzee's life came from her relationship with the poet and philosopher Iqbal, with whom she developed a close friendship during her stay in London. She also spent time with him in Germany on her way back to India and later wrote a book about their association and correspondence. Lambert-Hurley and Sharma surmise that 'her indifferent health at this time [the year spent in London] may have been the effect of a more romantic liaison: the proverbial lovesickness'. See Lambert-Hurley and Sharma, 57.
100 Lambert-Hurley and Sharma write that Atiya was likely inclined to depression and that her father had suffered severe depression throughout his life. See Lambert-Hurley and Sharma, 90.
101 Lambert-Hurley and Sharma, 179.
102 Lambert-Hurley and Sharma, 209.
103 Lambert-Hurley and Sharma, 209.
104 Lambert-Hurley and Sharma, 216.
105 Lambert-Hurley and Sharma, 216.
106 Jessawalla, *The Story of My Life*, 289.
107 Shefali Chandra, *The Sexual Life of English: Languages of Caste and Desire in Colonial India* (Durham: Duke University Press, 2012), 174.
108 Jessawalla, *The Story of My Life*, 105.
109 Sutapa Dutta, ed. *British Women Travellers: Empire and Beyond, 1770–1870* (New York: Routledge, 2020). See also Indrani Sen, *Gendered Transactions: The White Woman in Colonial India, c. 1820–1930* (Manchester: Manchester University Press, 2019); Sara Mills, *Discourses of Difference: An Analysis of Women's Travel Writing and Colonialism* (London: Routledge, 1991); Indira Ghose, *Women*

Travellers in Colonial India: The Power of the Female Gaze (New Delhi: Oxford University Press, 1998); Mary Louise Pratt, *Imperial Eyes: Travel Writing and Transculturation* (London: Routledge, 1992).

110 Jayati Gupta, *Travel Culture, Travel Writing and Bengali Women, 1870–1940* (Oxon: Routledge, 2021); Inderpal Grewal, *Home and Harem: Nation, Gender, Empire and the Cultures of Travel* (Durham, NC: Duke University Press, 1996).

111 In the dedication to her autobiography, Dosebai described herself as 'the first Indian girl to receive the benefits of English education'. See Jessawalla, *The Story of My Life*, unpaginated.

112 Jessawalla, 241.

113 Jessawalla, 78.

114 Jessawalla, 108.

115 Yael Schlick, *Feminism and the Politics of Travel after the Enlightenment* (Plymouth, MN: Bucknell University Press, 2012), 7.

116 Gary Schmidgall, *Containing Multitudes: Walt Whitman and the British Literary Tradition* (Oxford: Oxford University Press, 2014), 272.

117 Jessawalla, *The Story of My Life*, 1.

118 Jessawalla, 21.

119 Jessawalla, 304.

120 Jessawalla, 55.

121 Jessawalla, 75.

122 Jessawalla, 87.

123 Jessawalla, 98.

124 Jessawalla, 101–2.

125 Jessawalla, 102.

126 Jessawalla, 113.

127 Jessawalla, 102.

128 Jessawalla, 106.

129 Javed Majeed, *Autobiography, Travel and Postnational Identity: Gandhi, Nehru and Iqbal* (New York: Palgrave Macmillan, 2007), 6.

130 See Nabanita Sengupta, *A Bengali Lady in England: Annotated and Translation with a Critical Introduction to Krishnabhabini Das'* Englandey Bangamahila (Calcutta: Shambhavi, 2020); Hariprabha Takeda, *The Journey of a Bengali Woman to Japan*, trans. Somdatta Mandal (Kolkata: Jadavpur University Press, 2019).

131 Jessawalla, *The Story of My Life*, 107.
132 Jessawalla, 107.
133 Jessawalla, 107.
134 Jessawalla, 110.
135 Jessawalla, 122.
136 Jessawalla, 120.
137 Jessawalla, 121.
138 Jessawalla, 147–8.
139 Jessawalla, 159.
140 Jessawalla, 174.
141 Jessawalla, 71.
142 Jessawalla, 242.
143 Jessawalla, 283.
144 Jessawalla, 304.
145 Jessawalla, 141.
146 Jessawalla, 141.
147 Jessawalla, 141.

Conclusion

1 Sunil Sardar and Victor Paul, 'Pioneering Engaged Writing: Savitribai Phule's Poetry' in *A Forgotten Liberator* eds. Braj Ranjan Mani and Pamela Sardar (Delhi: Mountain Beak, 2008), 65.
2 The much-studied and acclaimed poem appeared in the first edition of *Leaves of Grass*, which was self-published by Walt Whitman in 1855.
3 M. G. Mali, *Savitribai Phule Samagra Wangmaya* (Mumbai: Maharastra Rajya Sahitya ani Sanskrit Mandal, 2011), unpaginated. Unless otherwise specified, all references to Savitribai's poems are from Mali's edited volume in Marathi and have been translated in consultation with the historian Dr Prabodhan Pol. The author is sincerely grateful to Dr Pol for his generous guidance at many stages of this study and particularly with the nuances of language and poetry.
4 Jotirao Phule (1827–90) had completed his secondary school education from a school in Pune run by the missionaries of the Free Church of Scotland and had read Thomas Paine's work in depth. He began educating his young wife at home. Following their setting up

of the school, and on his insistence that the drinking water tank of his house be made available to Dalit communities, the couple were asked to leave the family home. See G. P. Deshpande, ed. *Selected Writings of Jotirao Phule* (New Delhi: Left Word, 2022). Rosalind O'Hanlon, *Caste, Conflict and Ideology: Mahatma Jotirao Phule and Low Caste Protest in Nineteenth-Century Western India* (Cambridge: Cambridge University Press, 1985). Hari Narke, 'On Savitribai Phule: Dnyanjyoti Savitribai Phule' in NCERT Memorial Lecture Series, ed. T. Sundararaman. NCERT 2008.

5 Savitribai was at the receiving end of abuses and intense harassment as she would walk to school, and 'stones, mud and dirt were flung at her as she passed'. Cynthia Stephen, 'The Stuff Legends Are Made of' in *A Forgotten Liberator* eds. Braj Ranjan Mani and Pamela Sardar (Delhi: Mountain Beak, 2008), 17.

6 The Malis are considered to be gardeners by profession and relegated *Shudras* or a lowered status in the four-fold *varna* system. The students of the school came from Muslim families or from castes that were denigrated as 'untouchable'. The school was opened in Pune with Fatima Sheikh in the *wada* or residential premises of Fatima's brother, Usman Sheikh.

7 Braj Ranjan Mani, 'Introduction' in *A Forgotten Liberator* eds. Braj Ranjan Mani and Pamela Sardar (Delhi: Mountain Beak, 2008), 5.

8 The insight belongs to Dr Prabodhan Pol, who shared it during an in-person consultation.

9 The etymology of the word *wari* indicates time and travel and is associated with pilgrimage/pilgrim. Developing out of a religious movement attached to the Vithal temple in Pandharpur in Maharashtra, the Warkari tradition invited participation from men and women of different castes.

10 Savitribai Phule, 'Rise to Learn and Act' in *A Forgotten Liberator* trans. Sunil Sardar and Victor Paul (Delhi: Mountain Beak, 2008), 66–7.

11 Savitribai Phule, 'Khula Kavya va Khula Kavi' in *Savitribai Phule Samagra Wangmaya* ed. M. G. Mali (Mumbai: Maharastra Rajya Sahitya ani Sanskrit Mandal, 2011a), unpaginated.

12 Mini Chandran and Sreenath V. S., Preface to *An Introduction to Indian Aesthetics: History, Theory and Theoreticians* (New Delhi: Bloomsbury, 2021).

13 *Shringar* is one of the *rasas* in Indian aesthetic traditions. Sheldon Pollock translates *rasa* as taste or 'emotion tropes [that] represent expressions of heightened feeling'. See, Sheldon Pollock, 'Introduction' to *A Rasa Reader: Classical Indian Aesthetics* Edited and Translated by Sheldon Pollock (New York: Columbia University Press, 2016), 10. *Shringar* may be understood as beauty and the feeling of love that can arise in union or in separation from one's beloved.

14 Savitribai Phule, 'Drishta Kavi' in *Savitribai Phule Samagra Wangmaya*, ed. M. G. Mali (Mumbai: Maharastra Rajya Sahitya ani Sanskrit Mandal, 2011b), unpaginated.

15 Nava-Chandi translates as the nine aspects to the Goddess Chandi. The word can refer to a *homam* or ritual practice to the Goddess or the *mantras* or chants in her praise – in this instance, it is the latter.

16 Priyamvada Redican Chakne translates 'drashta' as prophet. See Priyamvada Redican Chakne, *Kaavya Phule* (self pub., 2022). However, the word 'visionary' has been preferred in the present study for its relevant sematic link to eyesight.

17 Sunity Devee, *The Autobiography of an Indian Princess* (Kolkata: Ababil Books, 2021).

18 Parvati Athavale, *My Story: The Autobiography of a Hindu Widow* (New York: G. P. Putnam, 1930).

19 Geraldine Forbes and Tapan Raychaudhuri, *The Memoirs of Dr Haimabati Sen: From Child Widow to Doctor*, trans. Tapan Raychaudhuri, ed. Geraldine Forbes and Tapan Raychaudhuri (New Delhi: Roli Books, 2019).

20 Kosambi, *Crossing Thresholds,* 345.

21 Keshab Chandra Sen (1838–84) was one of the most prominent Bengali social and religious reformers of the nineteenth century who sought to meld Hindu and Christian theological precepts.

22 Sunity Devee's father who had canvassed against the marriage of girls under the legal age arranged her marriage when she was underage, thereby inviting public criticism and controversy. The marriage that Sunity writes as perfect is also one that laid several strictures upon her. The king-husband was absolute in his diktats about the company she kept and the clothes she wore. She writes, 'He had the strictest ideas about my conforming to his ideals. He did not like loud laugher or loud

talking I was not allowed to ride, dance, or play tennis.' See Devee, *The Autobiography*, 58.

23 Devee, 85.

24 Devee, 145.

25 Her trip to the United States was undertaken with Karve and his children – she was to housekeep for them during Karve's tenure at Harvard University (as an instructor of Pali language). Parvatibai wanted to expand her education in English and had been told that she would learn the language more quickly by 'the direct method' or if she were to live in an English-speaking milieu. However, due to situations that include unexpected health problems, and continuous health problems, Parvatibai was left to fend for herself by taking up jobs that involved cleaning and cooking. See Athavale, *My Story*.

26 There are multiple references to clean and unclean latrines in Gandhi's autobiography, and he attributes high status to his act of cleaning. See M. K. Gandhi, *An Autobiography: The Story of My Experiments with Truth*, trans. Mahadev Desai (Ahmedabad

27 Meera Kosambi, *Crossing Thresholds: Feminist Essays in Social History* (Ranikhet: Permanent Black, 2007), 345.

28 She proudly records that even though it was a life of distress and hardships for her in California and upstate New York, she raised 3000 rupees for Karve's institution during her stay. See Athavale, *My Story*.

29 Geraldine Forbes, 'Introduction' to *The Memoirs of Dr Haimabati Sen: From Child Widow to Doctor*, trans. Tapan Raychaudhuri, ed. Geraldine Forbes and Tapan Raychaudhuri (New Delhi: Roli Books, 2019), 29.

30 Forbes, 'Introduction', 2.

31 Forbes, 31.

32 Forbes, 353.

Bibliography

Amin, Shahid. *Event, Metaphor, Memory: Chauri Chaura*. New Delhi: Oxford University Press, 1995.

Anagol, Padma. 'Rebellious Wives and Dysfunctional Marriages: Indian Women's Discourses and Participation in Debates over Restitution of Conjugal Rights and the Child Marriage Controversy in the 1880s and 1890s' in *Women and Social Reform in Modern India, Vol 1 & 2*. Edited by Sumit Sarkar and Tanika Sarkar, 420–57. Ranikhet: Permanent Black, 2012.

Anagol, Padma. *The Emergence of Feminism in India, 1850–1920*. Oxon: Routledge, 2016.

Anjaria, Ulka. *Realism in the Twentieth-Century Indian Novel: Colonial Difference and Literary Form*. New York: Cambridge University Press, 2012.

Armstrong, Nancy. *Desire and Domestic Fiction: A Political History of the Novel*. New York: Oxford University Press, 2006.

Arnold, David. 'Introduction: Tropical Medicine before Mason' in *Warm Climates and Western Medicine: The Emergence of Tropical Medicine 1500–1900*. Edited by David Arnold, 1–19. Atlanta, GA: Rodopi, 2003.

Arnold, David. *The Tropics and the Traveling Gaze: India, Landscape, and Science, 1800–1856*. Seattle, WA: University of Washington Press, 2006.

Arnold, David and Stuart Blackburn. Eds. *Telling Lives in India: Biography, Autobiography and Life History*. Delhi: Permanent Black, 2004.

Atalas, Syed Hussein. *The Myth of the Lazy Native: A Study of the Image of the Malays, Filipinos and Javanese from the 16th to the 20th Century and its Function in the Ideology of Colonial Capitalism*. London: Frank Cass, 1977.

Athavale, Parvati. *My Story: The Autobiography of a Young Widow*. Translated by Justin E. Abbott. New York, London: G. P. Putnam's Sons, 1939.

Bagchi, Barnita. 'Introduction' to Rokeya Sakhawat Hossain, in *Sultana's Dream and Padmarag: Two Feminist Utopias*, vii–xxvi. New Delhi: Penguin, 2005.

Bagchi, Barnita. '"Because Novels Are True, and Histories Are False": Indian Women Writing Fiction in English, 1860–1918' in *A History of the Indian Novel in English*. Edited by Ulka Anjaria. New York: Cambridge University Press, 2015.

Bandyopadhyay, Sekhar. 'Caste, Widow-Remarriage, and the Reform of Popular Culture in Colonial Bengal' in *Women and Social Reform in Modern India Vol 1*. Edited by Sumit Sarkar and Tanika Sarkar, 145–71. Ranikhet: Permanent Black, 2011.

Bhat, Sheetala. *Performing Self Performing Gender: Reading the Lives of Women Performers in Colonial India*. Manipal: Manipal University Press, 2017.

Bhatia, Nandi. *Acts of Authority/Acts of Resistance: Theatre and Politics in Colonial and Postcolonial India*. Ann Arbor, MI: The University of Michigan Press, 2004.

Bhattacharya, Bidik and Sambudha Sen. *Novel Formations: The Indian Beginnings of a European Genre*. Ranikhet: Permanent Black, 2019.

Bhattacharya, Malini. 'Introduction' in *Talking of Power: Early Writings of Bengali Women*. Edited by Malini Bhattacharya and Abhiji Sen, 1–17. New Delhi: Sage, 2021.

Bhattacharya, Rimli. 'Binodini Dasi and the Public Theatre in Nineteenth-Century Bengal' in Binodini Dasi's *My Story and My Life as an Actress*. Translated by Rimli Bhattacharya, 3–46. New Delhi: Kali for Woman, 1998.

Bhattacharya, Rimli. *Public Women in British India: Icons and the Urban Stage*. Oxon: Routledge, 2018.

Bhattacharya, Sabyasachi. Ed. *The Mahatma and the Poet: Letters and Debates between Gandhi and Tagore 1915–1941*. New Delhi: National Book Trust, 2015.

Blackburn, Stuart. *Print, Folklore and Nationalism in Colonial South India*. Delhi: Permanent Black, 2003.

Blackburn, Stuart and Vasudha Dalmia. Eds. *India's Literary History: Essays on the Nineteenth Century*. Delhi: Permanent Black, 2004.

Boon, Sonja. *Telling the Flesh: Life Writing, Citizenship, and the Body in the Letters to Samuel Auguste Tissot*. Qubec: McGill-Queen's University Press, 2015.

Borthwick, Meredith. *The Changing Role of Women in Bengal, 1849–1905*. Princeton, NJ: Princeton University Press, 1984.

Brinks, Ellen. *Anglophone Indian Women Writers, 1870–1920*. Oxon: Routledge, 2016.

Burton, Antoinette. *At the Heart of the Empire: Indians and the Colonial Encounter in Late-Victorian Britain*. Delhi: Munshiram Manoharlal, 1998a.

Burton, Antoinette. 'From Child Bride to "Hindoo Lady": Rukhmabai and the Debate on Sexual Respectability in Imperial Britain'. *The American Historical Review* Vol 103, no. 4, 1998b, 1119–46.

Burton, Antoinette. 'Conjugality on Trial: The Rukhmabai Case and the Debate on Indian Child-Marriage in Late-Victorian Britian' in *Disorder in the Court: Trials and Sexual Conflict at the Turn of the Century*. Edited by George Robb and Nancy Erber, 33–56. London: Palgrave Macmillan, 1999.

Burton, Antoinette. *Dwelling in the Archive: Women Writing House, Home, and History in Late Colonial India*. New York: Oxford University Press, 2003.

Chakne, Priyamvada Redican. *Kaavya Phule*. Self pub., 2022.

Chakravarti, Uma. *Rewriting History: The Life and Times of Pandita Ramabai*. New Delhi: Kali for Women, 1998.

Chandler, James. 'Foreword' in *The Melodramatic Moment: Music and Theatrical Culture, 1790–1820*. Edited by Katherine G Hambridge and Jonathan Hicks, x–xii. Chicago, IL: The University of Chicago Press, 2018.

Chandra, Shefali. *The Sexual Life of English: Languages of Caste and Desire in Colonial India*. Durham, NC: Duke University Press, 2012.

Chandra, Sudhir. *Enslaved Daughters: Colonialism, Law, and Women's Rights*. New Delhi: Oxford University Press, 2008.

Chandra, Sudhir. *Rukhmabai: The Life and Times of a Child Bride Turned Rebel-Doctor*. New Delhi: Macmillan, 2024.

Chandran, Mini and Sreenath V. S. Preface in *An Introduction to Indian Aesthetics: History, Theory and Theoreticians*, xi–xii. New Delhi: Bloomsbury, 2021.

Chatterjee, Partha. Ed. *Texts of Power: Emerging Disciplines in Colonial Bengal*. Minneapolis, MN: University of Minnesota Press, 1995.

Chatterjee, Partha. *The Black Hole of Empire: History of a Global Practice of Power*. Ranikhet: Permanent Black, 2015.

Chaudhuri, Rosinka. 'Modernity at Home: The Nationalization of the Indian Drawing Room, 1830–1930' in *Interpreting Homes in South Asian Literature*. Edited by Malashri Lal and Sukrita Paul Kumar, 221–39. Noida: Pearson Longman, 2007.

Chaudhuri, Rosinka. *The Literary Thing: History, Poetry and the Making of a Modern Cultural Sphere*. Lausanne: Peter Lang, 2014.

Claeys, Gregory. 'Preface' in *The Cambridge Companion to Utopian Literature*. Edited by Gregory Claeys, xi–xiii. Cambridge: Cambridge University Press, 2010.

Cross, Maire and Caroline Bland. Eds. *Gender and Politics in the Age of Letter Writing, 1750–2000*. United Kingdom: Taylor & Francis, 2017.

Dall, Caroline Healey. *The Life of Dr. Anandabai Joshee: A Kinswoman of the Pundita Ramabai*. Boston, MA: Roberts Brothers, 1888.

Dalmia, Vasudha. *The Nationalization of Hindu Traditions: Bharatendu Harishchandra and Nineteenth-Century Benaras*. Delhi: Oxford University Press, 1997.

Damrosch, David. *What Is World Literature?* Princeton, NJ: Princeton University Press, 2003.

Dasi, Binodini. *My Story and My Life as an Actress*. Translated by Rimli Bhattacharya. New Delhi: Kali for Woman, 1998.

Deshpande, G. P. Ed. *Selected Writings of Jotirao Phule*. New Delhi: Left Word, 2022.

Deshpande, Prachi. *Creative Pasts: Historical Memory and Identity in Western India 1700–1960*. Ranikhet: Permanent Black, 2007.

Devee, Sunity. *The Autobiography of an Indian Princess*. Kolkata: Ababil Books, 2021.

Devi, Kailashbasini. 'The Woeful Plight of Hindu Women' in *Talking of Power: Early Writings of Bengali Women*. Edited by Malini Bhattacharya and Abhijit Sen, 27–54. New Delhi: Sage, 2021.

Devika, J. *En-Gendering Individuals: The Language of Reforming in Early Twentieth Century Keralam*. Hyderabad: Orient Longman, 2006.

Devika, J. *Her-Self: Early Writings on Gender by Malayalee Women, 1898–1938*. New Delhi: Sage, 2021.

Duff, David. *Modern Genre Theory*. Oxon: Routledge, 2000.

Dutt, Bishnupriya. 'Actress Stories: Binodini and Amal Allana' in *Staging International Feminisms*. Edited by Elaine Aston and Sue-Ellen Case. New York: Palgrave Macmillan, 2007.

Dutta, Sutapa. Ed. *British Women Travellers: Empire and Beyond, 1770–1870*. New York: Routledge, 2020.

Ebeling, Sascha. *Colonizing the Realm of Words: The Transformation of Tamil Literature in Nineteenth-Century South India*. Ranikhet: Permanent Black, 2011.

Ekotto, Friedas and Abigail E. Celis. 'Introduction to World Literature 1771 to 1919' in *A Companion to World Literature. Volume 4: 1771 to 1919*. Edited by Friedas Ekotto and Abigail E. Celis, 1939–54. Chichester, West Sussex: Wiley Blackwell, 2020.

Forbes, Geraldine. *Women in Colonial India: Essays on Politics, Medicine, and Historiography*. New Delhi: Chronicle Books, 2005.

Forbes, Geraldine. *Women in Modern India*. Delhi: Cambridge University Press, 2015.

Forbes, Geraldine, 'Introduction' to *The Memoirs of Dr Haimabati Sen: From Child Widow to Doctor*. Translated by Tapan Raychaudhuri. Edited by Geraldine Forbes and Tapan Raychaudhuri. New Delhi: Roli Books, 2019.

Friedman, Susan Stanford. '"Shakespeare's Sister": Woolf in the World before a Room of One's Own' in *Virginia Woolf: Writing the World*. Edited by Pamela L. Caughie and Diana L. Swanson, 122–7. Clemson, South Carolina: Clemson University Press, 2015.

Gajarawala, Toral Jatin. *Untouchable Fictions: Literary Realism and the Crisis of Caste*. New York: Fordham University Press, 2013.

Gandhi, M. K. *An Autobiography: The Story of My Experiments with Truth*. Translated by Mahadev Desai. Ahmedabad: Navajivan Publishing House, 2015.

Ghosal, Swarnakumari Debi. *An Unfinished Song*. New Delhi: Oxford University Press, 2008.

Ghose, Indira. *Women Travellers in Colonial India: The Power of the Female Gaze*. New Delhi: Oxford University Press, 1998.

Gilbert Sandra, M. and Susan Gubar. *Madwoman in the Attic*. New Delhi: Worldview Publications, 2007.

Gilmore, Leigh. *Autobiographics: A Feminist Theory of Women's Self-Representation*. Ithaca, NY: Cornell University Press, 1994.

Gooptu, Suparna. *Cornelia Sorabji: India's Pioneer Woman Lawyer*. New Delhi: Oxford University Press, 2010.

Gopal, Priyamvada. *Literary Radicalism in India: Gender, Nation and the Transition to Independence*. Oxon: Routledge, 2005.

Govind, Nikhil. *Between Love and Freedom: The Revolutionary in the Hindi Novel*. New Delhi: Routledge, 2014.

Green, Katherine Sobba. *The Courtship Novel 1740–1820: A Feminized Genre*. Lexington, KY: University Press of Kentucky, 1991.

Grewal, Inderpal. *Home and Harem: Nation, Gender, Empire and the Cultures of Travel*. Durham, NC: Duke University Press, 1996.

Gupta, Charu. *Sexuality, Obscenity, Community: Women, Muslims, and the Hindi Public in Colonial India*. New York: Palgrave Macmillan, 2002.

Gupta, Jayati. *Travel Culture, Travel Writing and Bengali Women, 1870–1940*. Oxon: Routledge, 2021.

Hansen, Kathryn. *Grounds for Play: The Nautanki Theatre of North India*. Berkeley, CA: University of California Press, 1992.

Hansen, Kathryn. *Stage of Life: Indian Theatre Autobiographies*. Delhi: Permanent Black, 2011.

Hardiman, David. *Gandhi in His Times and Ours*. London: Hurst & Company, 2003.

Hassan, Narin. *Diagnosing Empire: Women, Medical Knowledge, and Colonial Mobility*. Surrey: Ashgate Publishing, 2011.

Hawkins, Anne Hunasker. *Reconstructing Illness: Studies in Pathography*. West Lafayette, Indiana, IN: Prudue University Press, 1999.

Hegele, Ardene. *Romantic Autopsy: Literary Form and Medical Reading*. Oxford: Oxford University Press, 2022.

Hossain, Rokeya Sakhawat. 'The Better Half' in *Motichur: Sultana's Dreams and Other Writings of Rokeya Sakhawat Hossain*. Translated by Ratri Ray and Prantosh Bandopadhyay, 43–54. New Delhi: Oxford Univesity Press, 2015a.

Hossain, Rokeya Sakhawat. *Motichur: Sultana's Dreams and Other Writings of Rokeya Sakhawat Hossain*. Translated by Ratri Ray and Prantosh Bandopadhyay. New Delhi: Oxford University Press, 2015b.

Inamdar, Radhabai. 'Position of Widows: Experiences of Widows and Other Girls' in *Shadow Lives: Writings on Widowhood*. Edited by Uma Chakravarti and Preeti Gill, 92–104. New Delhi: Zubaan, 2007.

Jessawalla, Dosebai Cowasjee. *The Story of My Life*. New Delhi: Speaking Tiger, 2023.

Joshi, Priya. *In Another Country: Colonialism, Culture, and the English Novel in India*. New York: Columbia University Press, 2002.

Joshi, Yashodabai. *A Marathi Saga: The Story of Sir Moropant and Lady Yashodabai Joshi*. Translated by V. V. Bhide. New Delhi: Roli Books, 2003.

Kaler, Anne K. 'Conventions of the Romance Genre' in *Romantic Conventions*. Edited by Anne K. Kaler and Rosemary E. Johnson-Kurek. Bowling Green: Bowling Green State University Popular Press, 1999.

Kanitkar, Kashibai. *Kai. Sou. Dr. Anandibai Joshee Yanche Charitra*. Pune: Kulkarni ani Mandali, 1889.

Karve, Anandibai. *Maze Pura*. Edited by Kaveri Karve. Mumbai: Keshav Bhikaji Dhawale, 1944.

Kaviraj, Sudipta. *The Invention of Private Life: Literature and Ideas*. New York: Columbia University Press, 2015.

Kempe, Margery. *The Book of Margery Kempe*. Translated by B. A. Windeatt. London: Penguin Books, 2004.

Kennedy, David. *Elegy*. Oxon: Routledge, 2007.

Kosambi, Meera. *Crossing Thresholds: Feminist Essays in Social History*. Ranikhet: Permanent Black, 2011a.

Kosambi, Meera. *Feminist Vision or Treason against Men?: Kashibai Kanitkar and the Engendering of Marathi Literature*. Ranikhet: Permanent Black, 2011b.

Kosambi, Meera. *Women Writing Gender: Marathi Fiction before Independence*. Ranikhet: Permanent Black, 2012.

Kosambi, Meera. *Gender, Culture and Performance: Marathi Theatre and Cinema before Independence*. Oxon: Routledge, 2015.

Kosambi, Meera. *Pandita Ramabai: Life and Landmark Writings*. Oxon: Routledge, 2016.

Kosambi, Meera. *A Fragmented Feminism: The Life and Letters of Anandibai Joshee*. Edited by Ram Ramaswamy, Madhavi Kolhatkar and Aban Mukherji. New Delhi: Routledge, 2020.

Kulkarni, Kedar Arun. *World Literature and the Question of Genre in Colonial India: Poetry, Drama, and Print Culture 1790–1890*. New Delhi: Bloomsbury India, 2022.

Kumar, Udaya. *Writing the First Person: Literature, History and Autobiography in Modern Kerala*. Ranikhet: Permanent Black, 2016.

Lambert-Hurley, Siobhan and Sunil Sharma. *Atiya's Journeys: A Muslim Woman from Colonial Bombay to Edwardian Britain*. New Delhi: Oxford University Press, 2010.

Lokuge, Chandani. 'Introduction' to Krupabai Satthianadhan, in *Kamala: The Story of a Hindu Child-Wife*, 1–18. New Delhi: Oxford University Press, 1998.

Majeed, Javed. *Autobiography, Travel and Postnational Identity: Gandhi, Nehru and Iqbal*. New York: Palgrave Macmillan, 2007.

Majumdar, Rochona. *Marriage and Modernity: Family Values in Colonial Bengal*. Durham, NC: Duke University Press, 2009.

Malhotra, Anshu and Siobhan Lambert-Hurley. Eds. *Speaking of the Self: Gender, Performance, and Autobiography in South Asia*. Durham, NC: Duke University Press, 2015.

Mali, M. G. *Savitribai Phule Samagra Wangmaya*. Mumbai: Maharastra Rajya Sahitya ani Sanskrit Mandal, 2011.

Mani, Braj Ranjan. 'Introduction' in *A Forgotten Liberator*. Edited by Braj Ranjan Mani and Pamela Sardar, 1–13. Delhi: Mountain Beak, 2008.

Mani, Lata. *Contentious Traditions: The Debate on Sati in Colonial India.* Berkeley, CA: University of California Press, 1998.

Menon, Dilip M. *Caste, Nationalism and Communism in South India: Malabar 1900–1948.* Cambridge: Cambridge University Press, 2007.

Mills, Sara. *Discourses of Difference: An Analysis of Women's Travel Writing and Colonialism.* London: Routledge, 1991.

Minault, Gail. *Secluded Scholars: Women's Education and Muslim Social Reform in Colonial India.* Oxford: Oxford University Press, 1998.

Minault, Gail. *Gender, Language and Learning: Essays in Indo-Muslim Cultural History.* Ranikhet: Permanent Black, 2009.

Minault, Gail. 'Sayyid Mumtaz Ali and Tahzib un-Nizwan: Women's Rights in Islam and Women's Journalism in Urdu' in *Women and Social Reform in Modern India, Vol 2.* Edited by Sumit Sarkar and Tanika Sarkar, 70–98. Ranikhet: Permanent Black, 2012.

Mitra, Samarpita. *Periodicals, Readers and the Making of a Modern Literary Culture: Bengal at the Turn of the Twentieth Century.* Leiden: Brill, 2020.

Mody, Sujata S. *The Making of Modern Hindi.* New Delhi: Oxford University Press, 2018.

Mukherjee, Meenakshi. *Realism and Reality: The Novel and Society in India.* New Delhi: Oxford University Press, 1994.

Mukherjee, Meenakshi. *Early Novels in India.* New Delhi: Sahitya Akademi, 2002.

Mukherjee, Meenakshi. 'Introduction' in *Early Novels in India.* Edited by Meenakshi Mukherjee, vii–xix. New Delhi: Sahitya Akademi, 2005.

Mukherjee, Meenakshi. 'Epic and Novel in India' in *The Novel: Vol 1.* Edited by Franco Moretti, 596–631. Princeton, NJ: Princeton University Press, 2006.

Mukherjee, Sreemati. *Women and the Romance of the Word: 19th-Century Contexts in* Bengal. New Delhi: Bloomsbury Academic, 2025.

Mukherji, Aban. 'Introduction' in Meera Kosambi, in *A Fragmented Feminism: The Life and Letters of Anandibai Joshee.* Edited by Ram Ramaswamy, Madhavi Kolhatkar and Aban Mukherji. New Delhi: Routledge, 2020.

Murmu, Maroona. *Words of Her Own: Women Authors in Nineteenth-Century Bengal.* New Delhi: Oxford University Press, 2020.

Nair, Neeti. *Changing Homelands: Hindu Politics and the Partition of India.* Boston, MA: Harvard University Press, 2011.

Nambiar C., Ashokan. *Print and the Novel in 19th-Century Kerala: Reconsidering Colonial Modernity.* New Delhi: Bloomsbury Academic, 2025.

Naregal, Veena. *Language, Politics, Elites, and the Public Sphere: Western India under Colonialism.* Ranikhet: Permanent Black, 2014.

Narke, Hari. 'On Savitribai Phule: Dnyanajyoti Savitribai Phule' in NCERT Memorial Lecture Series. Edited by T. Sundararaman, 7–27. NCERT, 2008.

Nicholson, Rashna Darius. *The Colonial Public and the Parsi Stage: The Making of the Theatre of Empire (1853–1893).* Switzerland: Springer, 2021.

Nijhawan, Shobna. *Women and Girls in the Hindi Public Sphere.* New Delhi: Oxford University Press, 2012.

Nikambe, Shevantibai. *Ratanbai: A High-Caste Child-Wife.* New Delhi: Oxford University Press, 2004.

O'Hanlon, Rosalind. *Caste, Conflict and Ideology: Mahatma Jotirao Phule and Low Caste Protest in Nineteenth-Century Western India.* Cambridge: Cambridge University Press, 1985.

O'Hanlon, Rosalind. *A Comparison between Women and Men: Tarabai Shinde and the Critique of Gender Relations in Colonial India.* Madras: Oxford University Press, 1994.

O'Neill, Lindsay. *The Opened Letter: Networking in the Early Modern British World.* Philadelphia, PA: University of Pennsylvania Press, 2015.

Orsini, Francesa. *The Hindi Public Sphere, 1920–1940: Language and Literature in the Age of Nationalism.* New Delhi: Oxford University Press, 2009a.

Orsini, Francesca. *Print and Pleasure: Popular Literature and Entertaining Fictions in Colonial North India.* Ranikhet: Permanent Black, 2009b.

Orsini, Francesca. Ed. *The History of the Book in South Asia.* New York: Ashgate Publishing, 2013.

Pande, Ishita. *Sex, Law and Politics of Age: Child Marriage in India, 1891–1937.* Ontario: Cambridge University Press, 2020.

Pandey, Gyanendra. *The Construction of Communalism in Colonial North India.* New Delhi: Oxford University Press, 2012.

Parr, Nora E. H. 'Nation: The Mighty Idea and the Novel' in *A Companion to World Literature. Volume 4: 1771 to 1919.* Edited by Frieda Ekotto and Abigail E. Celis, 2095–102. Chichester, West Sussex: Wiley Blackwell, 2020.

Phule, Savitribai. 'Rise to Learn and Act' in *A Forgotten Liberator.* Translated by Sunil Sardar and Victor Paul, 66–7. Delhi: Mountain Beak, 2008.

Phule, Savitribai. 'Khula Kavya va Khula Kavi' in *Savitribai Phule Samagra Wangmaya.* Edited by M. G. Mali. Mumbai: Maharastra Rajya Sahitya ani Sanskrit Mandal, 2011a.

Phule, Savitribai. 'Drishta Kavi' in *Savitribai Phule Samagra Wangmaya.* Edited by M. G. Mali. Mumbai: Maharastra Rajya Sahitya ani Sanskrit Mandal, 2011b.

Pol, Prabodhan. 'National Rhetoric and the Politics of Panic: The Political Aftermath of the Plague Epidemic of 1896 in Western India'. *Economic and Political Weekly* Vol 57, no. 18, 2022, 42–7.

Pollock, Sheldon. 'Introduction' in *A Rasa Reader: Classical Indian Aesthetics*. Translated and Edited by Sheldon Pollock, 1–45. New York: Columbia University Press, 2016.

Prabhu, Gayathri. 'Tropics, Medicine, and Pandemic: The Bubonic Plague in Lakshmibai Tilak's *Smritichitre*'. *Interdisciplinary Studies in Literature and Environment* Vol 27, no. 4, 2020, 823–35.

Prabhu, Gayathri and Nikhil Govind. *Shadow Craft: Visual Aesthetics of Black and White Hindi Cinema*. New Delhi: Bloomsbury Academic, 2021.

Pratt, Mary Louise. *Imperial Eyes: Travel Writing and Transculturation*. London: Routledge, 1992.

Rajesh, V. Manuscripts. *Memory and History: Classical Tamil Literature*. New Delhi: Cambridge University Press, 2013.

Ramabai, Pandita. *A Testimony of Our Inexhaustible Treasure*. Kedgaon: Ramabai Mukti Mission, 1907.

Ramabai, Pandita. 'Voyage to England' in *Pandita Ramabai: Life and Landmark Writings*. Edited and Translated by Meera Kosambi, 102–21. Oxon: Routledge, 2016.

Ramabai, Pandita. 'Stri Dharma Niti' in *Pandita Ramabai: Life and Landmark Writings*. Edited and translated by Meera Kosambi, 38–79. New Delhi: Routledge, 2021a.

Ramabai, Pandita. 'About Government Provisions during Plague Epidemic, 1897' in *Pandita Ramabai: Life and Landmark Writings*. Edited by Meera Kosambi, 231–3. New Delhi: Routledge, 2021b.

Ramaswamy, Sumathi. *The Goddess and the Nation: Mapping Mother India*. Durham, NC: Duke University Press, 2010.

Ranade, Ramabai. *Himself: The Autobiography of a Hindu Lady*. Translated by Katherine Van Akin Gates. New York: Longmans, Green and Co., 1938.

Ray, Bharati. *Early Feminists of Colonial India: Sarala Devi Choudhrani and Rokeya Sakhawat Hossain*. New Delhi: Oxford University Press, 2002.

Ray, Raka and Seemin Qayum. *Cultures of Servitude: Modernity, Domesticity and Class in India*. New Delhi: Oxford University Press, 2010.

Rignall, John. 'George Eliot's Impact as Novelist and Critic on World Literature' in *A Companion to World Literature. Volume 4: 1771 to 1919*. Edited by Frieda Ekotto and Abigail E. Celis, 2405–16. Chichester, West Sussex: Wiley Blackwell, 2020.

Rukhmabai. 'Reply' in Appendix D of Sudhir Chandra, *Enslaved Daughters: Colonialism, Law and Women's Rights*, 234–42. New Delhi: Oxford University Press, 2008.

Saha, Sharmistha. *Theatre and National Identity in Colonial India: Formation of a Community through Cultural Practice*. Singapore: Springer, 2018.

Saha, Ranjana. *Modern Maternities: Medical Advice about Breastfeeding in Colonial Calcutta*. Oxon: Routledge, 2024.

Said, Edward. *Out of Place: A Memoir*. New York: Alfred A. Knopf, 1999.

Said, Edward. *Beginnings: Intention and Method*. London: Granta Publication, 2012.

Sangari, Kumkum and Suresh Vaid. 'Recasting Women: An Introduction' in *Recasting Women: Essays in Colonial History*. Edited by Kumkum Sangari and Suresh Vaid, 1–26. New Brunswick, NJ: Rutgers University Press, 1999.

Sardar, Sunil and Victor Paul. 'Pioneering Engaged Writing: Savitribai Phule's Poetry' in *A Forgotten Liberator*. Edited by Braj Ranjan Mani and Pamela Sardar, 65–9. Delhi: Mountain Beak, 2008.

Sarkar, Mahua. *Visible Histories, Disappearing Women: Producing Muslim Womanhood in Late Colonial Bengal*. New Delhi: Zubaan, 2008.

Sarkar, Sumit. 'Vidyasagar and Brahmanical Society' in *Women and Social Reform in Modern India, Vol 1*. Edited by Sumit Sarkar and Tanika Sarkar, 172–214. Ranikhet: Permanent Black, 2012.

Sarkar, Tanika. *Hindu Wife, Hindu Nation: Community, Religion and Cultural Nationalism*. Delhi: Permanent Black, 2001.

Sarkar, Tanika. *Rebels, Wives, Saints: Designing Selves and Nations in Colonial Times*. Calcutta: Seagull Books, 2009.

Sarkar, Tanika and Sumit Sarkar. 'Introduction' in *Women and Social Reform in Modern India, Vol 1 & 2*. Edited by Sumit Sarkar and Tanika Sarkar, 1–18. Ranikhet: Permanent Black, 2012.

Sarkar, Tanika. *Words to Win: The Making of a Modern Autobiography*. New Delhi: Zubaan, 2013.

Sarkar, Tanika. 'Foreword' in *Talking of Power: Early Writings of Bengali Women*. Edited by Malini Bhattacharya and Abhiji Sen, ix–xiv. New Delhi: Sage, 2021.

Sarkar, Tanikar. 'Rhetoric against Age of Consent: Resisting Colonial Reason and the Death of a Child-Wife', *Economic and Political Weekly* Vol 28, no. 36, 1993, 1869–78.

Satthianadhan, Krupabai. *Saguna: A Story of Native Christian Life*. Oxford: Oxford University Press, 1998.

Schlick, Yael. *Feminism and the Politics of Travel after the Enlightenment*. Plymouth, MN: Bucknell University Press, 2012.

Schmidgall, Gary. *Containing Multitudes: Walt Whitman and the British Literary Tradition*. Oxford: Oxford University Press, 2014.

Sen, Amiya P. *Ramakrishna Paramahamsa: Sadhaka of Dakshineswar*. New Delhi: Penguin, 2010.

Sen, Indrani. *Gendered Transactions: The White Woman in Colonial India, c. 1820–1930*. Manchester: Manchester University Press, 2019.

Sengupta, Nabanita. *A Bengali Lady in England: Annotated and Translation with a Critical Introduction to Krishnabhabini Das'* Englandey Bangamahila. Calcutta: Shambhavi, 2020.

Shandilya, Krupa. *Intimate Relations: Social Reform and the Nineteenth-Century South Asian Novel*. Evanston, IL: Illinois, 2017.

Sharma, Kanika Laura Lammasniemi and Tanika Sarkar. 'Dadaji Bhikaji v Rukhmabai (1886) ILR 10 Bom 301: Rewriting Consent and Conjugal Relations in Colonial India'. *Indian Law Review* Vol 5, no. 3, 2021, 265–87.

Singer, Ben. *Melodrama and Modernity: Early Sensational Cinema and Its Contexts*. New York: Columbia University Press, 2001.

Singh, Lata. *Raising the Curtain: Recasting Women Performers in India*. Hyderabad: Orient Blackswan, 2017.

Sinha, Mrinalini. 'Gender and Nation'. in *Women's History in Global Perspective. Vol 1*. Edited by Bonnie G. Smith, 229–74. Chicago, IL: University of Illinois Press, 2004.

Srilata, K. *The Other Half of the Coconut: Women Writing Self-Respect History*. New Delhi: Kali for Women, 2003.

Sorabji, Cornelia. *Between the Twilights: Being Studies of Indian Women by One of Themselves*. London: Harper and Brothers, 1908.

Sorabji, Richard. *Opening Doors: The Untold Story of Cornelia Sorabji*. Gurgaon: Penguin, 2010.

Sorabji, Cornelia. 'Social Relations – England and India' in *An Indian Portia: Selected Writings of Cornelia Sorabji 1866–1954*. Edited by Kusoom Vadgama, 361–4. New Delhi: Zubaan, 2011.

Souza, Eunice de and Lindsay Pereira. Eds. *Women's Voice: Selections from Nineteenth and Early-Twentieth Century Indian Writing in English*. New Delhi: Oxford University Press, 2004.

Stark, Ulrike. *An Empire of Books: The Naval Kishore Press and the Diffusion of the Printed Word in Colonial India*. New Delhi: Orient Blackswan, 2008.

Steedman, Carolyn. *Past Tenses: Essays on Writing, Autobiography and History*. London: Rivers Oram Press, 1992.

Steedman, Carolyn Kay. *Landscape for a Good Woman: A Story of Two Lives*. New Brunswick, NJ: Rutgers University Press, 1987.

Stephen, Cynthia. 'The Stuff Legends Are Made Of' in *A Forgotten Liberator*. Edited by Braj Ranjan Mani and Pamela Sardar, 14–27. Delhi: Mountain Beak, 2008.

Tagore, Rabindranath. *Selected Letters of Rabindranath Tagore*. Edited by Krishna Dutta and Andrew Robinson. Cambridge: Cambridge University Press, 1997.

Takeda, Hariprabha. *The Journey of a Bengali Woman to Japan*. Translated by Somdatta Mandal. Kolkata: Jadavpur University Press, 2019.

Tilak, Lakshmibai. *Smritichitre*. Translated by Shanta Gokhale. New Delhi: Speaking Tiger, 2017.

Tharu, Susie and K. Lalita. *Women Writing in India: Vol 1*. New Delhi: Oxford University Press, 1993.

Vickery, John B. *The Modern Elegiac Temper*. Baton Rouge, LA: Louisiana State University Press, 2006.

Vijayasree, C. 'Introduction' in Swarnakumari Debi Ghosal's *An Unfinished* Song, xi–xxxvi. New Delhi: Oxford University Press, 2008.

Visram, Rozina. *Ayahs, Lascars and Princes: The Story of Indians of Britain 1700–1947*. Oxon: Routledge, 2015.

Viswanathan, Gauri. *Outside the Fold: Conversion, Modernity, and Belief*. Princeton, NJ: Princeton University Press, 1998.

Viswanathan, Gauri. *Masks of Conquest: Literary Study and British Rule in India*. New York: Columbia University Press, 2015.

Wagner, Tamara S. and Narin Hassan. 'Preface' in *Consuming Culture in the Long Nineteenth Century: Narratives of Consumption, 1700–1900*. Edited by Tamara S. Wagner and Narin Hassan, vii–xvii. Plymouth, MN: Rowman & Littlefield, 2007.

Williams, Carolyn. 'Introduction' in *The Cambridge Companion to English Melodrama*. Edited by Carolyn Williams, 1–9. Cambridge: Cambridge University Press, 2018.

Winckles Andrew, O. and Angela Rehbein. 'Afterword' in *Women's Literary Networks and Romanticism: A Tribe of Authoress*. Edited by Andrew O. Winckles and Angela Rehbein, 298–306. Liverpool: Liverpool University Press, 2017.

Wollstonecraft, Mary. *A Vindication of the Rights of Women with Strictures on Political and Moral Subjects*. London: T. Fisher Unwin, 1891.

Index

About the Author

Gayathri Prabhu is a Professor of Literary Studies at the Manipal Academy of Higher Education (MAHE), Manipal, India. Alongside articles in leading international journals and edited volumes, she has also authored the following books: *Love in Seven Easy Steps* (Magic Mongrel, 2021); *Shadow Craft: Visual Aesthetics of Black and White Hindi Cinema* (with Nikhil Govind, Bloomsbury Academic, 2021); *Vetaal and Vikram* (HarperCollins, 2019); *If I Had to Tell It Again* (HarperCollins, 2017); *The Untitled* (HarperCollins, 2016); *Birdswim Fishfly* (Rupa, 2006); and *Maya* (Indialog, 2003). She is the recipient of the R.K. Narayan Award for 2019.